Baby Ninth Amendments

Baby Ninth Amendments

How Americans Embraced Unenumerated Rights
and Why It Matters

ANTHONY B. SANDERS

University of Michigan Press
Ann Arbor

For questions or permissions, please contact um.press.perms@umich.edu

Published in the United States of America by the
University of Michigan Press
Manufactured in the United States of America
Printed on acid-free paper
First published May 2023

A CIP catalog record for this book is available from the British Library.

Library of Congress Cataloging-in-Publication data has been applied for.

ISBN 978-0-472-07615-4 (hardcover : alk. paper)
ISBN 978-0-472-05615-6 (paper : alk. paper)
ISBN 978-0-472-90349-8 (open access ebook)

DOI: https://doi.org/10.3998/mpub.12676756

Funding for Open Access publication generously provided by
the Institute for Justice.

The University of Michigan Press's open access publishing program is made possible thanks to additional funding from the University of Michigan Office of the Provost and the generous support of contributing libraries.

Cover design by Laura Maurice-Apel. Cover photo © iStock.com/Sean Pavone

To my father, Jeremy Sanders, who wrote many books.
Now his son can place one next to them.

ANNA: Oh, yes, I'm sure we could see many things . . . such as iron bars, guards at the doors, et cetera, et cetera.

THE KING: What is this "et cetera"?

ANNA: Well, it means "and all the rest and so forth," Your Majesty.

—The King & I

Contents

ACKNOWLEDGMENTS   xi

Introduction   1

1 The Path to Judicially Enforceable Unenumerated Rights   15

2 The Growth of Baby Ninths Before the Civil War   41

3 Baby Ninths from the Civil War to Today   61

4 Judges (Mostly) Haven't Agreed   75

5 What Do Baby Ninths Mean?   93

6 What Individual Rights Do Baby Ninths Protect?   113

Afterword: What Do Baby Ninths Tell Us?   139

APPENDIX   149

NOTES   161

INDEX   191

Acknowledgments

My idea of writing about Ninth Amendment equivalents in state constitutions goes back almost an entire Jeffersonian cycle. During law school at the University of Minnesota I nearly took a seminar on state constitutional law, but, probably in deference to "more important" classes, chose not to. I later kicked myself for that as my roommate David Asp told me of the interesting ideas he was picking up from Professor David Schultz. Thank you to both of them, even if indirectly, for launching my fascination with state constitutions.

At some point I linked in my head state constitutions with the over-two-century injustice of the Ninth Amendment getting no respect. It may have been when I was clerking at the Montana Supreme Court and noticed a "Baby Ninth" in the Montana Constitution. But after many months of my co-clerk Jared Pettinato and I gabbing about state constitutions, unenumerated rights, life, the Universe, and everything (when we weren't drafting opinions), I put the practicalities of state constitutionalism to one side and headed off to a firm job in Chicago. There, when the boss wasn't barking orders (one of our former clients had connections to the Mob, and the firm was run similarly), I slowly compiled the various Ninth Amendment analogues on a Word document and tucked it away for later. It was only after I arrived in 2010 at my present employer, the Institute for Justice, that I made further inroads.

Those inroads were primarily enabled through the wonderful clerks and interns we have at the Institute for Justice. They've gone on to various careers, and I have already thanked them in my previous articles, but they very much deserve it again. Maxwell Czerniawski, Rebecca Furdek, Jonathan Gammon, Cameron Gower, Chris Hanson, Bryan Huntington, and Dan Loeser learned a lot about state constitutional records and constitutional convention transcripts, all of it helpful to me and hopefully, in some esoteric way, to them. After some writing and a number of others reading a few drafts—including my fabulous colleagues Ari Bargil, Michael Bindas, Margaret Daggs, Sheldon Gilbert, Clark Neily, and Justin Pearson (of those I can remember)—I submitted and published two articles, one on "Baby Ninths" before the Civil War and, later, one for subsequent history.

This book draws heavily from both articles and then expands on their research and analysis. The articles are *Baby Ninth Amendments and Unenumerated Individual Rights in State Constitutions Before the Civil War*, published in the *Mercer Law Review* in 2017 (vol. 68, p. 389) and *Baby Ninth Amendments Since 1860: The Unenumerated Rights Americans Repeatedly Want (and Judges Often Don't)* published in the *Rutgers University Law Review* in 2018 (vol. 70, p. 859). I have nothing except extreme appreciation for the many student editors—some of whom are unknown to me—who shepherded these pieces from raw submissions to final articles. Those whose names I know are then-students Joanna Gardner, Blair Gerold, Christina Lidondici, Savanna Roughen, Stephanie Terzano, and Alexis Way. Thank you. In addition, Professor Robert Williams, the dean of state constitutional law, kindly invited me to submit to Rutgers and has also provided repeated encouragement over the years. If you want to write about state constitutional law you're best off talking to Bob.

Writing scholarship is one thing. Writing a *book* is a whole different matter. This project could not have made it to the book stage without many fantastic colleagues. Two who warrant special mention are Scott Bullock, president of the Institute for Justice, and John Kramer, our vice president for communications. Scott somehow believed that a book about "babies" could grow into so much more. And Kramer (as the world calls him) moved the text along from jargon-heavy law-speak to something resembling prose. He also put all he has learned from more than three decades in the media business (and being an author himself) into finding a home for this codex. Further, Bob McNamara gave special insight when Kramer and I did not agree on edits (Bob, rightly, said Kramer was correct). Dana Berliner brilliantly gave me the idea for the introduction to demonstrate all the liberties inherent in someone going about their daily life. Our CFO Dan Knepper lent his unlawyerly (in such a good way) business touch and good nature. Evan Lisull applied his unrivaled editing skills. Adam Shelton provided loads of helpful thoughts and politely listened to me even when I wasn't making sense. Kim Norberg, without solicitation, continually affirmed the worth of this project from a non-lawyer perspective. Dick Carpenter rendered the kindest of publishing advice. Bert Gall gave constant support, especially during the long, uncertain pauses inherent in publishing. Don Wilson and Laura Maurice-Apel lifted me up with their artistic touch. And so many others not mentioned here assisted me through countless discussions on unenumerated rights, state constitutions, and the difficulties of reading the compilations of Francis Newton Thorpe. Speaking of which, this project would be impossible without the amazing resources projects such as the Internet Archive, Google Books, and HathiTrust have given to low-level researchers and scholars like me. Their work is an incalculable gift to humanity.

In finding a publisher, special thanks goes to Andrew Davison for getting Elizabeth Demers at University of Michigan Press interested in my manuscript. Thank you Andrew, as Elizabeth and the Press could not be more delightful to work with. She, Haley Winkle, Kevin Rennells, and the rest of its staff and board have been encouraging, receptive, and extremely constructive in taking what I gave them and turning it into a work so much better. That includes the outside, blind reviews I received. Thank you whoever you are. Elizabeth has also helped explain to this book novice many confusing aspects of modern publishing and answered innumerable anxious questions. To her and her colleagues I owe an immense debt of gratitude.

Many others who had a part to play, and to whom I give my sincere thanks for various readings, conversations, and email exchanges over the years, are Randy Barnett, David Bernstein, Keith Blackwell, Stephen Calabresi, Dale Carpenter, Judge Stephen Dillard, Mitchell Gordon, Jonathan Den Hartog, Louis Seidman, and Michael Stokes-Paulsen. Also special mention to John Yoo for first using the wonderful term "Baby Ninths" in print, and to Akhil Amar, who told me that Yoo, his student, heard Amar say "Baby Ninths" in class and adopted it. Finally, thank you to my parents for always encouraging me to ask questions (and tirelessly answering them), and my wife Amy and our children Geneva and Everett for making every day of writing an unenumerated joy once I leave the keyboard. Dad loves you all. Etcetera, etcetera.

Anthony Sanders
West Lakeland Township, Minnesota
May 28, 2022

Introduction

Take an average American. We will call her "Jane." Think about what she may have done yesterday.

Jane rose at a time best suited to her schedule for the day so she could walk her dog, get the kids breakfast and off to school, or get to work. Or maybe she was lucky enough to sleep in.

She ate a breakfast that conformed to her cravings, or health needs, or budget.

She got ready, choosing clothes best suited for her plans for that day.

Then Jane went to an office, or went in search of work, or went to school. Perhaps she took her child to school, which might be a school she chose for the child over other options.

When she returned home she pored over her stamp collection or tended to her garden, or attended to some DIY home repairs, or played with the dog in the yard. Perhaps that was followed by poker with some friends, having someone over to dinner, or playing a late-night basketball game at the local gym. Just before bed she might have meditated, in an effort to seek inner peace or control chronic pain.

Whatever Jane did yesterday, she chose to do it because she believed it was best for her and those in her life. She did these actions—and chose not to perform others—because she believed they would further her goals, give her pleasure, expand her income, help her children, or improve the world around her.

If someone forced her to make different choices, however, things might not have gone as well.

What if her state legislature passed a law that limited or even banned her choices? For example, what if the law mandated she wake up at six o'clock in the morning? Or required her to send her child to a certain school? Or forbade her from working her job unless she earned a degree she did not have and could not obtain anytime soon? Or forced her to sell her stamp collection? Or threatened her with punishment if she meditated? Or banned home gardens or residential poker games? Or required her to hire a government-licensed contractor for any home renovations? Or set a curfew?

Sound farfetched?

Many such restrictions are all too real.

Miami Shores, Florida, for example, prosecuted Hermine Ricketts and Tom Carroll for growing vegetables in their front yard. A city ordinance arbitrarily banned vegetable gardens in the front of one's home, which happened to be the only part of their property where vegetables could grow.

The Utah Board of Cosmetology told Jestina Clayton she could not braid hair for a living because state law required her to have a cosmetology license. This was true even though the state's cosmetology schools taught virtually no hair braiding and the state's licensing exam contained no questions about hair braiding. (Nationwide, many other occupational licensing laws require entrepreneurs to acquire qualifications with little relationship to the occupation they wish to pursue.)

Oregon's Society of Sisters, a nonprofit that ran a private school, saw the state legislature outright forbid their school and other private schools from operating, under a law that required children to attend public schools. And laws restricting diet, from restrictions on purchasing home-baked bread to bans on margarine, are unfortunately commonplace in modern times.

Furthermore, the experience of the recent COVID-19 pandemic has introduced everyone to the possibility of all kinds of restrictions, including on something as simple as leaving one's home, that Americans had not experienced (or perhaps even imagined) in modern times. Whether those restrictions are justified at certain moments under certain conditions is another story, but whether they might be imposed is now plain to see.

What recourse would Jane have if a law restricted a liberty she exercised yesterday and wanted to exercise again today? Well, she could go to her state capital and ask the legislature—which just passed the law—to repeal it. She would be faced with all the forces of the legislative process, such as busy and indifferent legislators who are inclined to justify and defend their earlier actions, self-serving special interest groups who are more inclined to advance their own power and influence rather than their fellow citizens' freedom, and savvy lobbyists who are paid by and do the work of the highest bidder rather than concern themselves with constitutional principles. Getting a law enacted without a grassroots army of like-minded citizens who can scare legislators into thinking they will not be re-elected if they do not vote your way, Jane would quickly find, is a tough endeavor indeed.

But Jane has also heard that in the United States there are certain things government cannot do, even if the legislature passes a law. Americans know that this is because of "the Constitution." But what many do not realize is that "the Constitution" does not just mean the U.S. Constitution; it also means *state* constitutions. These are designed to restrict the power of state and local governments just like the U.S. Constitution can contain government power at every level. As Oprah might have said: "*Every state gets a constitution!*"

So Jane flips through both the U.S. Constitution and her own state's constitution to see if they are of any help. Assume all the procedural requirements for legislation to be "a law" are in order: the bill restricting what Jane wants to do passed both houses of the legislature, started in the right house, was signed by the governor, etc. No help there. She then looks at what most Americans think about when they think of constitutions: the Bill of Rights. "Rights!" she says. "That law violates my rights! If my liberty is listed in the Bill of Rights then that law must be unconstitutional."

Let us summarize some of the rights that we supposed Jane might have exercised yesterday:

- The right to arise at the hour you wish.
- The right to eat what you think is best for you.
- The right to wear the clothes of your choice.
- The right to educate your child in the school of your choice.
- The right to earn a living.
- The right to collect stamps.
- The right to renovate your own home with your own hands.
- The right to have a dog.
- The right to play poker.
- The right to gather with friends after hours.
- The right to meditate on your own terms, without permission.

Some of these look pretty important. Education and working are high on that list. Some of them seem almost dumb: Do many folks care about stamp collecting anymore? But all of them are things that people do and are important to at least some of them. If the government banned those activities the people that do them would not be happy. Not just unhappy; they might be out of a job, out of an education, or out of a home.

So Jane reads through the bills of rights in the federal and her own state's constitutions to see what her rights are. Did her treasured liberty make the list?

Probably not. She sees all kinds of protections—speech, religion, searches, jury trial—in the federal Bill of Rights. She probably sees those and other ones in the state version: an "anti-monopoly" provision, perhaps, or protections on "freedom of conscience" that go beyond the First Amendment's protection of religious liberty. But she likely will not see anything protecting her own specific right. No state enumerates the right to get up at the time of your choosing. Or be out of your home after hours. Or improve your home with your own hands. Or eat what you think is best for you. Or collect stamps. A few explicitly protect the right to pursue an occupation, but not many.[1] And none explicitly protect one of the most central rights on our list: the right to send your child to the school of your choice. Somehow these important liberties, including the one she is fighting for, got left off.

"Wait," she replies. "I get that the rights listed in these bills of rights are important. We should protect freedom of speech, religion, and jury trials. But how about all the other liberties we need in life to pursue our happiness? What kind of a hatchet job did these constitutions' framers do if the government cannot ban a book but can require you to rise at 6 a.m.?" (And, for that matter, make you perform calisthenics in the public square, as there is no right to not do that either.) "They should have spent a little extra time listing them all!"

Depressed, she then notices near the end of each bill of rights something else. The federal version reads like this, and the state version is very similar: "The enumeration in the Constitution, of certain rights, shall not be construed to deny or disparage others retained by the people."

"Wow!" she exclaims. "This recognizes there are 'other' rights, like the right I am concerned about. That seems to mean that even if a right was 'left out,' it still has equal value with those that actually are listed in the Constitution. So even though a bill of rights does not include a right to earn a living, or a right to educate your child, or a right to collect whatever stamps you wish, the right is still out there and cannot be 'denied or disparaged' just because it did not make the first cut." Thus maybe she has a claim that her important liberty is being violated, after all. This last provision is kind of an "etcetera clause" for other rights. Right?

This book is the story of the answer to that question, or rather the answer to that question as it concerns state constitutions. Although many have argued (correctly, in the author's view) that the Ninth Amendment "means what it says" and protects rights not included in the Constitution, the federal courts have not agreed. Not only have the courts not agreed, but many scholars have argued that the Ninth Amendment actually does not do what it seems to do.[2] Although Jane would think it protects her rights, these scholars argue that it does something else that will not help her with whatever right she is worried about.

But what few people realize is that two-thirds of all state constitutions have the same kind of provision. Christened "Baby Ninth Amendments" by University of California-Berkeley law professor John Yoo, they are exactly that.[3] Although the term "Baby Ninth" is of recent vintage and has not been widely employed outside of a few scholarly legal articles, it is used in this book because just like the "baby FTC Acts" (state consumer protection laws in the mold of the Federal Trade Commission) the term encapsulates what these constitutional provisions are.[4] Even though most are not identical to the Ninth Amendment itself, they generally differ by just a word or two. For example, Nevada's "Baby Ninth" states, "This enumeration of rights shall not be construed to impair or deny others retained by the people."[5] The clause trades "impair" for the federal version's use of "disparage," but otherwise it is basically the same. All of these Baby Ninths were adopted after the Ninth Amendment itself. All of them come near the end, or at the end, of their state's bill of rights, like the Ninth. Each was plainly adopted with the Ninth Amendment itself in mind. The federal Constitution's Ninth is the mother of them all, and she has had quite a few babies.

What is different about the babies is, as we shall learn later in this book, that the arguments made by critics of the "it means what it says" view of the Ninth Amendment do not work when set upon the Baby Ninths. The various arrows launched at an expansive reading of the Ninth Amendment—that it is really about enumerated powers, or states' rights, or to ensure a balanced federal system, or only protects nonconstitutional rights—bounce off of Baby Ninths. The state constitutional versions truly mean that rights beyond those enumerated in a state constitution exist and should be protected at the same level as the enumerated ones. These nonlisted liberties are called "unenumerated" rights.

They are rights beyond those "enumerated" explicitly in the state's constitution. But even though not enumerated in the relevant constitution they are constitutional rights.

So, if Jane is in a state with a Baby Ninth, can she now march down to the courthouse and defend her unenumerated freedom?

She *should* be able to. But in her case she probably cannot. In most situations, when people in similar circumstances have tried to protect their rights that "got left out" of the state's bill of rights, their state's courts have come up with excuses why the Baby Ninth does not protect them. Not always, but most of the time courts have not come to the aid of people in her situation.

This book is here, however, to say there is hope.

The courts have generally not agreed, but Jane's fellow Americans who actually wrote our states' constitutions did. On sixty-six occasions in U.S. history, Americans have drafted a constitution that became the fundamental law of their state that included a Baby Ninth. Over and over again, the drafters, and the ratifiers, of those constitutions have agreed that the "other" rights not enumerated in a constitution should not be "denied or disparaged" or "impaired or denied," or what have you, just because those rights were not enumerated themselves. The right to go to work, choose one's child's school, tend one's garden, collect stamps, or associate with friends after hours is protected even though the constitution's framers did not list it explicitly.

But, wait, a critic may say: A constitution's drafters put rights in a bill of rights for a reason. After all, adding another right is just a line or two more. This Baby Ninth thing seems like a technical glitch. That a right is not "in" a constitution has to count for something. Why did they not just list those other "important" rights?

Because then a constitution would be the size of that thing we once called a phone book, and maybe larger. We have discussed just a few liberties here, but even those would add quite a bit to the size of a typical bill of rights. Imagine everything else people do that we think the government should not be able to arbitrarily infringe upon. From the very small (shoelaces or Velcro?) to the very large (buy a house or rent?), the infinite number of choices in life cannot be boiled down to a list that we can agree on and then apply to all future situations, secure that we have protected everything worth protecting.

America's Founding generation understood this well. Many opponents of adding a bill of rights to the original U.S. Constitution warned that if one were drafted and adopted it would imply (1) that those rights that were not included were not protected, *and* (2) that a comprehensive list including all rights was impractical anyway because of the limitless number of liberties that we would want to protect. To quote just one Founder, future Supreme Court justice James Iredell, speaking at the North Carolina ratifying convention: "Let any one make what collection or enumeration of rights he pleases, I will immediately mention twenty or thirty more rights not contained in it."[6] In other words, enumerate a right to wake up at 7 a.m. and you will leave out the right to wake up at 8 a.m. And even if you make rights a bit more general ("the right to get out of bed whenever you want") you will still leave out other important aspects of human activity. As we will learn, some argue that James Madison came up with a work-around to this problem. The Ninth Amendment recognizes this inherent limitation in enumerating all rights, and bars that enumeration from "deny[ing] or disparag[ing] others."

Now, whether you agree that that was Madison's intention or not (the author does, but many smart people disagree), the Ninth Amendment's language found its way into state constitutions over time. And not just once or twice, but over and over, and *over* again. The further our nation developed, the more popular these Baby Ninths became. Madison's (witting or unwitting) invention of protecting an infinite number of rights by saying we do not have to list them all has made its way into two-thirds of all state constitutions. And in all but a couple of instances, when states have adopted constitutions including Baby Ninths they have kept those Baby Ninths in later, newer constitutions.

Thus, Baby Ninth Amendments are not just out there in constitutional text. They are popular. Constitutional drafters recognize the inherent limitation of enumerating rights, and how that is a problem. Constitutional drafters recognize that governments come up with all kinds of harebrained schemes that might violate an activity no one previously thought worth enumerating as protected. And they have figured out a way to nevertheless protect us against those schemes.

Indeed, not only do constitutional drafters recognize this problem, but so do judges themselves. Almost no one actually believes that neither the U.S. Constitution or state constitutions protect *any* unenumerated rights. Time after time the U.S. Supreme Court, and state courts, have protected unenumerated rights of all kinds including (to make a short and incomplete list) rear one's children, associate with others, pursue the occupation of one's calling, engage in intimate activity, and go hunting.[7] Sometimes the courts come out and say a right is protected, and sometimes a restriction on an activity that is not enumerated as a constitutional right is found to be unconstitutional because the government cannot justify its restriction. Either way, the result is a protection of a right not found in a constitution.

But courts have rarely "found" these rights in Baby Ninths, let alone in the Ninth Amendment itself. Instead, they generally have "found" them in due process clauses or in the "penumbras" and "emanations" of enumerated rights such as the First Amendment's Free Speech Clause. They have often done this while a lonely Baby Ninth Amendment sits elsewhere in the state's bill of rights, waiting for someone to come along and interpret it. Thus a central message of this book is that instead of exercising the gymnastics sometimes necessary to protect unenumerated rights with parts of constitutions that seem ill-disposed to protect them, judges can simply apply the words of a state's Baby Ninth, which are well-disposed to protect unenumerated rights.

Therefore, if Jane is lucky enough to live in a state with a Baby Ninth Amendment, yet unlucky enough to face a law denying an unenumerated liberty, she *should* be able to use its language to protect her. This would protect her choice to arise at the hour she wishes, educate her children how she sees best, pursue her occupation, associate with her friends after hours, and collect stamps in the manner she is accustomed to.

But the fact remains that the courts have, by and large, not allowed this to happen. Why have courts failed to protect our rights with Baby Ninths? And why the disconnect between what courts do and what seems to have been the straightforward purpose of the Baby Ninths' drafters?

As in other areas of constitutional law, it appears that courts have ignored Baby Ninths or watered them down to triviality because they just do not like them. Judges get what a serious implementation of a Baby Ninth would do—protect a lot of liberties not included in the state's constitution—and balk at making that a reality.

This is not their choice to make. People often decry judges seizing power: "Government by Judiciary" in one professor's phrase.[8] What you hear less about is judges abdicating their responsibility to apply constitutional commands. In ignoring Baby Ninth Amendments, judges have abdicated a responsibility that the people have placed in their hands. An individual judge may love Baby Ninths, or may hate them and think them foolhardy. But that does not mean she can ignore them any more than she can ignore any other provision of governing law.

The following pages tell the story of how the framers of dozens of constitutions took Madison's words from the Ninth Amendment and put them into the foundational law of most of our states. Throughout almost every period of U.S. history, in every geographic region, and increasing in popularity as judicial fads and movements ebbed and flowed, Americans learned to embrace Baby Ninths and accept them as a standard way to protect their liberties. Despite this, judges generally have given them next to no recognition. There are exceptions, however, and seeing those exceptions will illustrate how Baby Ninths can protect our liberties when they are actually interpreted and followed.

This story is mostly historical, partly theoretical, but at bottom it is practical. It is a story of how Americans grew into not just unenumerated rights, but the realization that states and the people have unenumerated *powers* and that unenumerated rights are a way to protect against those powers. It is a story of a consensus that defies left and right, economic and personal, North and South, Black and white. It is a story of Americans recognizing the dangers that governments pose and expansively shackling those governments into the future. Consider that although most Americans say that what the Constitution and the Bill of Rights do is protect our rights, the text of those documents protect our rights by saying what government *cannot* do, through familiar turns of phrase such as "Congress shall not." In the Ninth Amendment itself it states, "The enumeration in the Constitution, of certain rights, *shall not* be construed to deny or disparage others retained by the people." In other words, in protecting our rights we often say what the government cannot do to us, not what we ourselves can do. Americans repeatedly agree to give the government *some* power, but not *all* power, and we will take care of the rest on our own, thank you very much.

In chapter 1 we will begin with the invention of state constitutions during the American Revolution, and then move on a few years to the framing of the Ninth Amendment itself. We will also take a look at what the Ninth Amendment might have meant at the time. To do this we will inquire into the Ninth's "original meaning," a term we will spend a little bit of time defining. We will look at the various approaches on what that meaning is and how various scholars disagree. Then we will look at the early years of the Republic and how constitutional drafters understood the relation of the states to the new federal government. This will include the birth of older siblings, of sorts, of the Baby Ninths: the Baby Tenths.

Then, in 1819, two states come on the scene: Alabama and Maine. Perhaps no two states were less alike in 1819, other than that they both were about to be admitted to the Union. But they turned out to have one thing in common: They adopted the first Baby Ninths. And then for several years they stood alone, raising the question of whether the grafting of the Ninth Amendment into state constitutions was some kind of historical oddity.

But that was not the case. In chapter 2 we will learn that in the years before the Civil War, Baby Ninths increased in popularity. And during and after the Civil War itself that popularity expanded, North and South, East and West. In chapter 3, as we rush into the Gilded Age and the twentieth century, we will learn that Baby Ninths were almost everywhere. Although the practice was not quite universal, if your territory was being admitted as a state during this period you generally put a Baby Ninth in its new constitution. It was the "American" thing to do. And so that trend continued in the twentieth century. When that century was concluded, two-thirds of all states had adopted these provisions. While tracing which states adopted Baby Ninths and when, we will also look at what the constitutional drafters themselves had to say. And, on the whole, they saw Baby Ninths as they read: they protect rights not enumerated in the state constitution at the same level as those rights that are enumerated.

But, after our sweep of history, in chapter 4 we will also look at what judges have had to say about Baby Ninths. And there the story is not so positive. Although a few courts at various times have interpreted them to provide real protections to real people, most of the time judges have either ignored Baby Ninths or rendered them paper tigers.

Next, in chapter 5, we will put the courts aside and make our independent assessment of what Baby Ninths mean and what they protect. To do this, we will re-examine what the Ninth Amendment itself actually means, applying the various approaches we looked at in chapter 1 to the Baby Ninths themselves. And we will come to the conclusion that only one view—that the Ninth Amendment protects individual rights—makes sense for Baby Ninths, whatever one's view on the Ninth Amendment itself might be.

That, however, leaves a further question: *what* individual rights? How do we know which rights Baby Ninths protect and which they do not? That thorny issue we will tackle in chapter 6. Here we will do a deep dive into how to apply Baby Ninths to real situations and how the word "retained" tells us much about what kinds of individual rights Baby Ninths (mostly) protect. In the end, we will be left with an optimistic message for our friend Jane: If the state violates a treasured liberty of hers, Jane might be protected even if that right is not "in" the state constitution. If her state has a Baby Ninth, it might protect the right anyway. And her state's judges have a duty to protect it. Baby Ninths do not allow Jane to do *anything* (they do not outlaw government, after all), but they do protect a lot of human flourishing where the state simply does not belong. That is why we have these things called "rights" in the first place.

In the final chapter we will take a step back and ask a different question: What do the facts that Baby Ninths exist in the first place and are in so many state constitutions tell us? Spoiler alert: that unenumerated rights are popular. In the author's view this is actually the biggest takeaway from this book. More than mechanisms for protecting unenumerated rights, Baby Ninths are evidence of the acceptance of unenumerated rights. Far from shunning them as devices of an imperial judiciary, the American people embrace unenumerated rights when they have a chance to write them into constitutions. Baby Ninths are evidence that judicial engagement—where courts use constitutions to prevent the enforcement of duly enacted laws—is something Americans want. It is just that judges are not so into the idea. But, as we will conclude, that is not a judge's decision to make.

———

Before we leave this introduction, though, we should address an issue that will arise later, so it is best to talk about it before we dive into the story. Some readers may be asking: Who benefits from unenumerated rights? Are they just an undemocratic mask for the powerful retaining their power?

In fact, unenumerated rights benefit everyone *except*, in some situations, those with political power. As we will discuss in the final chapter, Americans enshrine the protection of unenumerated rights in our constitutions because those with political power invariably will seek to abuse that power. Baby Ninths should be interpreted, as argued in chapters 5 and 6, to only protect your right to be free from the power of others, not so you can assert your power over others. Thus Jane's right to garden or right to earn a living does not mean she can receive a special favor from the state legislature or city hall. But it does mean that an abusive government, or government official, cannot deny her right without a good reason or single her out for abuse.

The powerful have access to special favors, or at a minimum the power to keep abusive officials out of their hair. They do this through various levers of influence, such as hiring lobbyists, providing or withholding endorsements, winning government contracts, forming trade associations, and other examples of flexing the heft of what we often call "special interest groups." Yes, those with power can also go to court and have laws declared unconstitutional because they violate unenumerated rights. But only in some rare cases, and even then it is a lot easier to simply hire a lobbyist. For the powerless, on the other hand, they often have "only one place of redress"[9]: the courts.

And the powerful do not just go to the legislature, to city hall, the governor's mansion, or the sheriff's office to assert their rights to be left alone. They also go and ask the government to violate other people's rights to give them special favors. And those special favors frequently deny the powerless their own rights to be left alone. Unenumerated rights are a mechanism that can correct some of the unjustness of this imbalance. But that can only happen if courts take unenumerated rights seriously.

Before we close this introduction, let's look at a couple of examples that illustrate how this dynamic bears out. And as a bonus, both examples are delicious.

That is because both involve food trucks. Recent years have seen all kinds of interest in food trucks. Reality TV shows and social media have been full of snazzy vans with all kinds of cuisine announcing their locations in tweets and attracting attention from celebrity chefs. Most food trucks, of course, are run by the non-rich-and-famous, people just trying to earn a living from selling a few lunches in a city's downtown, in the parking lot of a brewery, or outside a factory when a shift ends. Overlooked by the Hollywood attention, however, is that established restaurants feel threatened by the trucks' low overheads and popularity. Simply to protect their own revenue, their lobbies have pushed city ordinances restricting where food trucks can operate. Instead of trying to outcompete this new business model, many restaurants have tried to shut it down.

Which brings us to sunny Fort Pierce, Florida. There, restaurant owners did not like it that food trucks were parking downtown and offering food to hungry workers. Instead of trying to match prices or offer better meals than these upstart competitors, they went to city hall and convinced the city council to pass a proximity ban, forbidding food trucks from selling food within five hundred feet of any "brick and mortar" business that also sells food.[10] The law was not a regulation of city streets, but rather a blanket restriction; it did not matter if the food truck operated from a private parking lot with the permission of the lot's owner.[11] And the proximity ban did not apply to other brick and mortar restaurants. Instead, it was simply a ploy for restaurants to keep out new competition with an enthusiastic customer base.

That did not sit well with Benigno "Benny" Diaz. He ran a food truck, the Taco Trap, and wanted to drive into the city and serve the residents of and visitors to Fort Pierce. But the expansive restriction kept him out of the city's downtown. As he put it, there are six to seven restaurants on every block; staying five hundred feet away from all of them effectively meant the city was closed to his tiny business.[12] As an outsider with no clout at city hall he would have been hard-pressed to change the law, given that established insiders already successfully pushed for its adoption.

The law also did not sit well, it turned out, with the Florida Constitution. Benny joined with another food truck owner and sued in state court, arguing the law violated the state constitution's protection of the right to earn a living. And, as we will learn, although the odds are very strongly set against a lawsuit like that (and part of the point of this book is to make the odds much better), they won, with the court preliminarily enjoining the enforcement of the law.[13] The court found that the only possible reason for the law was to protect other businesses, and that that is not a legitimate use of state power. Later the city repealed the law rather than risk continuing to contest the lawsuit and lose.[14]

Diaz's victory, again, is a rare success story for unenumerated rights and state constitutions. A more typical one, involving the exact same issue of restaurants and food trucks, befell Laura Pekarik, owner of a Chicago food truck. As *Washington Post* columnist George Will described her in 2019, "Pekarik, a feisty 33-year-old single mother and embodiment of America's entrepreneurial itch, grew up in Chicago's suburbs and at age 24 began baking for the fun of it. Eventually, she invested her entire savings ($12,000) in a lime-green truck, called Cupcakes for Courage, from which she began selling."[15] The name of her food truck arose out of a time a few years earlier when she quit her former job and cared for her sister after she was diagnosed with non-Hodgkin lymphoma.[16] The time off was filled with the fun baking Will described. After starting her food truck business she committed to donating 10 percent of proceeds to charity. Much of it goes, as you might imagine, to cancer research.

Who did Laura and other small food truck entrepreneurs threaten? Chicago's long-established and politically savvy restaurant industry, apparently. In 2012, a city alderman who was the former head of the Illinois Restaurant Association pushed through a restriction on food trucks similar to Fort Pierce's, forbidding sales within two hundred feet of a "brick and mortar" business.[17] Given urban density, this effectively outlawed Cupcakes for Courage in large chunks of the city, including the lucrative Loop at the heart of Chicago's downtown.

With powerful interests like those at work on the city council, Laura's only hope was in court. And she made it all the way to the Illinois Supreme Court, arguing that the two-hundred-foot rule violated the Illinois Constitution. The court, however, did not think the constitution protected her against the restaurant lobby. Applying an extremely weak standard of review, it stated that it was fine for the city to prevent this charity-supporting single mother from competing against wealthy Loop restaurants. After all, it explained without embarrassment, the city was only trying "to balance the interests of food trucks with the need to promote neighborhood stability."[18] A more cynical observer might remark, "that's the Chicago way."

In one case, a state constitution's protection of unenumerated rights ensured a Hispanic man could keep earning a living. But in another, the state constitution failed, and a single mom striving to ensure that others do not have to go through the disease that almost killed her sister found no redress after a powerful lobby pushed her out of their supposed turf. And both of them had to overcome the incredible odds that are stacked against unenumerated rights in most cases. This book's mission is to demonstrate that those odds should be remarkably lower.

Although Baby Ninths were not raised in either case, both of these food truck's respective states have them in their constitutions. In Florida, Illinois, and many other states people like Benny and Laura should have courts ready to enforce Baby Ninths against the powerful who unjustly try and take their rights away. That is the promise of unenumerated rights and state constitutions. Now let us see where that promise comes from.

CHAPTER 1

The Path to Judicially Enforceable Unenumerated Rights

Baby Ninth Amendments did not emerge fully formed from a constitutional version of Zeus's head. A long series of historical building blocks were required before the idea of protecting unenumerated rights with an "etcetera clause" came into being. The Baby Ninths not only first needed the federal Ninth Amendment to survive spirited debate and ratification, but a series of antecedents had to be invented before they could make their way into the American constitutional milieu. This included state constitutions, judicial review, and the emergence of a mysterious set of Tenth Amendment siblings.

The Invention of State Constitutions and Declarations of Rights

States have had constitutions since before the U.S. Constitution was even a twinkle in James Madison's eye. The oldest still-operational written constitution in the world is Massachusetts's of 1780,[1] largely drafted by Madison's co-Founder John Adams. Indeed, even before the thirteen colonies declared their independence from Great Britain in July 1776, some of the states already had constitutions. New Hampshire adopted the first state constitution in January 1776.[2] Many others soon followed in the lead-up to the Declaration. Most notably for the present story,

Virginia adopted its first constitution in June 1776, including its "Declaration of Rights," arguably the nation's first bill of rights.

"Arguably" because written statements of fundamental law were nothing new for these state framers and their English ancestors. And some
English fundamental law not only applied in England, but in Great Britain's thirteen colonies. First among them would have been Magna Carta,
the attempt by English nobles to restrain the tyrannical King John in
1215. The 1215 version was quickly invalidated, but parts of future versions of Magna Carta were law in England from the thirteenth century
through 1776 (and, indeed, through today).[3] And there were many
other examples. One important one was the English Bill of Rights of
1689 (also often called the "Declaration of Rights"). In the eyes of most
(at least those who were not "Jacobite" usurpers), it helped settle the
legitimacy of the Glorious Revolution of 1688, including the supremacy
of Parliament over the Crown, and declared a number of liberties that
look very familiar today.[4] These include the rule against excessive bail,
excessive fines, and cruel and unusual punishments; the protection of
subjects to be free to petition the government without fear of reprisal;
and the right to keep arms for defense (well, for Protestants at least).[5]

In turn, Magna Carta and other protections of English law applied to
the colonies through various royal charters. For example, the First Charter of Virginia, issued in 1606 before English colonists had even arrived
at Jamestown, declared that the colonists and their descendants "shall
HAVE and enjoy all Liberties, Franchises, and Immunities, within any
of our [i.e., the King's] other Dominions, to all Intents and Purposes,
as if they had been abiding and born, within this our Realm of England,
or any other of our said Dominions."[6] Thus, a Virginian colonist could
later assert his rights under Magna Carta in Virginia as though he were
back in England itself. Later in the colonial period, documents such as
the Petition of Right of 1628 and the Bill of Rights of 1689 would also
apply to the colonists through similar language in the various charters
(although their legal status as enforceable law is a different story).

There are many other examples of documents that look a bit like
"constitutions" in world history. The revolutionary generation would
know the story of the Twelve Tables of the Roman Republic and the
republic's constitutional order.[7] They also would have been familiar with
the Hungarian Golden Bull of 1222, which, along with Magna Carta, was
one of the first examples in medieval Europe of placing written constitutional limits on the executive.[8] And, much closer to home, they would
know the colony of Connecticut's adoption, in 1639, of the Fundamen-

tal Orders. This document structured the legislative, executive, and judicial institutions of the colony.[9] As Connecticut was not an officially recognized colony at that point, the Fundamental Orders are notable in not mentioning the English Crown, but instead asserting their legitimacy as based on God and the people.

All these constitutional precedents influenced the revolutionaries of 1776. But at least for those that supposedly applied to them—such as Magna Carta and the English Bill of Rights—there were many imperfections to overcome. Most of these "parchment barriers" largely lacked what we today recognize as inherent in a written constitution. They often only restrained one set of governmental actors and could be changed through the ordinary lawmaking process. Magna Carta protected against the king's abuses, not Parliament's, and was first adopted before Parliament in any modern sense had come to be. Its later manifestations (including those that survive in law today) were technically just statutes that a majority vote of Parliament could repeal at any time.[10] The same was true of the English Bill of Rights; it was an important document, but one that future Parliaments could repeal at will. Furthermore, the colonial charters were only binding on the king, yet many of the colonists' grievances lay with Parliament, not with the Crown.[11]

What many early state constitutions did was establish rules for the administration of their newly independent governments that could not be changed like an ordinary "law" could be. They were a higher law that only the sovereign could amend or abolish. And in the view of these framers, the "sovereign" was not any one person—such as King George III—or even Parliament or the state legislature. It was "the people" themselves. And for "the people" to manifest their will, it was best if it was done in a certain way: through a constitutional convention.[12]

George Mason and the First Unenumerated Rights Clause

Virginia's constitutional convention of 1776 thought it prudent to not only set out rules for how its government was to operate free from royal direction, but to declare rights that its citizens enjoyed vis-à-vis that very government. Given the task of drafting a Declaration of Rights for the convention, George Mason enumerated dozens of liberties in his famous draft, from freedom of the press to the right to confront one's accuser in a criminal prosecution.[13] Section One was especially expansive in its application. After a few changes in the full convention it stated:

THAT all men are by nature equally free and independent, and have certain inherent rights, of which, when they enter into a state of society, they cannot, by any compact, deprive or divest their posterity; namely, the enjoyment of life and liberty, with the means of acquiring and possessing property, and pursuing and obtaining happiness and safety.[14]

These words became influential, as framers in other states picked them up and incorporated them into their budding declarations of rights. And most readers will notice that Mason's words sound a lot like the second paragraph of the Declaration of Independence itself, which famously declares that "all men are created equal, that they are endowed by their Creator with certain unalienable Rights, that among these are Life, Liberty and the pursuit of Happiness." This is not a coincidence. Thomas Jefferson took this fresh-off-the-press language from his colleague when he drafted the Declaration a few weeks later.[15]

Mason's invention, and its open-ended language, demonstrated the range to which a state's declaration of rights could go to protect liberty. The Virginia declaration included a number of fairly specific rights, such as freedom of religion ("all men are equally entitled to the free exercise of religion, according to the dictates of conscience") and civil jury trials ("That in controversies respecting property, and in suits between man and man, the ancient trial by jury is preferable to any other, and ought to be held sacred.").[16] These are helpful if you want to practice your religion or demand a jury. But not so much in other areas of life. No one who wants to assert a right to garden, for example, would realistically turn to these for protection. But the expansive language of Section One leaves a lot of room for the imagination. What does "pursuing and obtaining happiness and safety" mean? Does it include *anything* that makes one happy, and therefore protect against any law that inhibits pursuing and obtaining happiness? What about "the means of acquiring and possessing property?" Does that encompass the right to work an occupation? Because, after all, most of us need to work in order to "acquire" property. What about making stamp collections? They are "property" after all.

The story of Mason's Section One and all its many offspring (there are dozens of states today with a version of it in their own constitutions) is not the subject of our story here, although you can read about it in a fascinating article coauthored by Professor Steven Calabresi, who christens the clauses "Lockean Natural Rights Guarantees" after the natural rights philosopher John Locke.[17] But it is raised here to demonstrate that the idea of an expansive—arguably expansive enough to count as an "etcetera clause"—rights-protecting provision in a constitution was not novel by the time the Ninth Amendment came to be, and certainly not by the time the Baby Ninths were born. If the idea did not exist before Mason's draft, it certainly was a possibility afterward.

Declarations of rights in state constitutions grew popular after Virginia's example. By 1780, eleven of the thirteen original states (plus Vermont) had constitutions (Connecticut and Rhode Island would wait until well into the nineteenth century to adopt one). And by 1784, seven of those eleven (again, plus Vermont) had declarations of rights as part of their constitutions or adjacent to them.[18] Their popularity would weigh on the minds of "the people" when they were soon called upon to adopt another constitution *without* a bill of rights.

The Framing of the Ninth Amendment

With more than ten years of state constitutional experimentation under their belts, in 1787 the men who would become the framers of the U.S. Constitution met in Philadelphia to form a more perfect union. As the summer wore on, their tasks primarily were devoted to what the powers of the new federal government would be and how those powers would be divided among its branches. They gave little consideration to issues of individual rights,[19] unlike what had happened when many of the same framers had drafted their state constitutions over the previous eleven years. During the midst of the convention a call was made to add a bill of rights to the emerging constitution, but the motion failed amid the attendees' various pressures.[20] The delegates did, however, insert a few rights-protective clauses in the document's text, including guarantees against ex post facto laws, bills of attainder, prosecutions based on family ties, that is, "corruption of blood," and (applied to state governments only) a protection of "the obligations of contracts." Then, in the last days of the convention, the subject of a bill of rights was raised again. Perhaps largely from fatigue and a wish to present their almost-complete blueprint for a federal government to the people, the delegates voted the proposal down, even though George Mason (probably thinking of his Virginia handiwork) asserted they could bang a list out in just a few hours.[21]

But the issue of a constitutional list of rights (whether called a "declaration" or a "bill") was only to grow in importance when the draft constitution went to the states for ratification.

One of the biggest objections from those who opposed the document—the Antifederalists—was that it lacked a bill of rights.[22] Emphasizing the seemingly expansive reach of the powers given to the new government, the Antifederalists argued these powers could infringe on basic liberties such as the freedom of the press.[23]

The Constitution's proponents—the Federalists—countered that no bill of rights was needed because the new federal government was one of limited, enumerated powers.[24] The government did not have the power, for example, to limit the freedom of the press because such a power was not enumerated.[25] In making this argument, Federalists sometimes contrasted the proposed federal government with state governments, which were understood to have general powers.[26] A bill of rights made much more sense, argued the Federalists, in a state constitution because there the government's powers are so broad that fundamental liberties might be infringed. Enumerated powers themselves, however, protected the people's rights from the new federal government, again, because it stated what the central government was allowed to do, with the presumption that it could do no more than that.[27] The people had delegated certain powers to the new federal government, but had only delegated a few well-defined ones, none of which endangered the people's rights. Further, if a bill of rights were added to the Constitution, it would only protect a handful of rights, and it might imply that the federal government *does* have the power to infringe on unnamed ones.[28] After all, given the infinite number of actions people can take, no bill of rights can name them all. The right to wear a hat was even given as an example in one debate.[29]

The Antifederalists did not buy these arguments for several reasons. Two stand out.

First, the powers granted to the new government seemed broad. This was especially true in light of the Necessary and Proper Clause, which added flexibility to the enumerated powers of Article I, Section 8.[30] With the growth of federal power since the New Deal, the Antifederalists seem to have definitely won the argument on that point. Given how broad the power to regulate interstate commerce has been interpreted,[31] it almost seems silly to think that under that same understanding Congress's power does not also reach any subject protected by the Bill of Rights (such as the interstate—or intrastate—sale of books).

Second, the original Constitution itself actually did contain some rights, such as the prohibition on bills of attainder.[32] If there truly was a fear that the federal government's powers would be read to intrude upon rights not enumerated, then that fear already existed due to the handful of rights in the original text. Therefore, the Antifederalists retorted, an additional bill of rights could hardly make things worse.[33]

In the state ratifying conventions where the Constitution went to receive the states' approval, many delegates voted to accept the Constitution, but only after recommending amendments for the new Congress to adopt. Several states submitted these suggested changes. They included protections for such things as freedom of the press, religion, and trial by jury, substantive and procedural rights that in some cases eventually made their way into the first eight amendments to the Constitution.[34]

But there were other suggestions that sought to clarify the federal government's powers and to try to prevent the argument the Federalists feared: a limited set of rights that nullified other rights and/or expanded federal powers.[35]

Among those suggestions were several from the Virginia ratifying convention. It proposed twenty clauses to serve as a declaration of rights and twenty other clauses to limit the federal government's power. The seventeenth suggestion to the latter set of clauses read as follows:

> 17th. That those clauses which declare that Congress shall not exercise certain powers, be not interpreted, in any manner whatsoever, to extend the powers of Congress; but that they be construed either as making exceptions to the specified powers where this shall be the case, or otherwise, as inserted merely for greater caution.[36]

When the First Congress began its work, James Madison, now a Virginia congressman, had come around to the necessity of adopting a bill of rights, and he submitted several proposed amendments to the House. Two of them later became the Ninth and Tenth Amendments. They were, respectively, as follows:

> The exceptions, here or elsewhere in the constitution, made in favor of particular rights, shall not be so construed as to diminish the just importance of other rights retained by the people, or as to enlarge the powers delegated by the constitution; but either as actual limitations of such powers, or as inserted merely for greater caution.
>
> The powers not delegated by this constitution, nor prohibited by it to the States, are reserved to the States respectively.[37]

These were obviously influenced by Virginia's suggested Amendment Seventeen.[38] They were referred to a select committee in the House, which left the draft of the eventual Tenth Amendment unchanged, but edited quite a few words in the eventual Ninth Amendment. After the committee was done with its edits the now Ninth Amendment read as it does today, except it had a "this" instead of the first "the:"[39] "The enumeration in the Constitution of certain rights shall not be construed to deny or disparage others retained by the people."

Both draft amendments later changed in the Senate to their present versions, with the only substantive difference being the addition of "or to the people" in the Tenth.[40] They, and the rest of what came to be known many years later as the Bill of Rights, were then ratified by the requisite number of state legislatures over the next two years.

What Did the Ninth Amendment Mean When It Was Adopted?

That is the story of how the Ninth Amendment came to be. Scholars agree that these things happened. What the Ninth Amendment actually "meant" at the time, however, is a very different matter. There are a number of different arguments for what the Ninth Amendment meant at the time it was adopted, that is, what its "original meaning" was. Professor Randy Barnett at one point helpfully organized them into five broad models.[41] Since Professor Barnett categorized these, an important sixth model has been put forward by Professor, and former judge, Michael McConnell. All six are briefly outlined here. Further, although the focus of this book is on the "originalist" understandings of the Ninth, we will look at a couple of nonoriginalist points of view as well.

First, however, a brief word on what is meant by "original meaning."[42] The value of "original meaning" as a subject of constitutional interpretation has become an issue of rabid interest over the past few decades, and it shows no signs of abating as a crucible of controversy. There are quite a few shades of "originalism," and fans and critics of it from both left and right. Some think that whatever the "original meaning" of a provision of constitutional text is, that is how courts should interpret it. Others—often referred to as "living constitutionalists"—might think that what the text meant at the time it was adopted is an interesting question of history, but should not affect in any determining way how we interpret the provision today. Still others are all over the map in between. Whether or not one thinks it is a valid, or the only, method of constitutional interpretation, the takeaway for present purposes is that "original meaning"—or more exactly, "original public meaning"—means the meaning that language would have to the general public at the time it was produced. Thus, the "original public meaning" for language written in 1787 would be what a member of the general public would have understood that language to mean at that time.

Now to the models of the Ninth Amendment's original meaning. The first model of what the Ninth Amendment might have meant when it came into being is the state law rights model. Under this model, the Ninth Amendment simply tells us that rights enjoyed under state law "continue in force under the Constitution until modified or eliminated by state enactment, by federal preemption, or by a judicial determination of unconstitutionality."[43] The Ninth Amendment does not protect these rights from the federal government, it simply says the rights "continue in force" until changed or overridden. For example, state laws regulating the formation of contracts continue in force after the adoption of the Constitution, but might be pre-empted by federal legislation in the future.

The second model for the original meaning of the Ninth Amendment is the residual rights model. Here the Ninth Amendment prevents a specific argument: that Congress has broader powers than it otherwise would have if enumerated rights had not been placed in the Constitution.[44] Under this view, it could be supposed, for example, that because there is a prohibition on violating the freedom of the press, that means Congress actually would have a power to regulate the freedom of the press if it were not for the First Amendment. This would then imply that Congress has additional, unenumerated powers. Under this model, however, the Ninth Amendment makes unavailable that particular argument.

The third model, the individual rights model, is that the Ninth Amendment tells us that just because there are enumerated rights in the Constitution does not mean that there are not other rights, and that those rights should not be "denied or disparaged" just because they are, not enumerated.[45] Those rights receive *constitutional* protection because if they did not they would be "denied or disparaged" simply because they were unenumerated. What those rights *are* is a different question that scholars then subdivide themselves into. Libertarians, such as Randy Barnett, believe economic liberty is a protected unenumerated right, but that positive rights such as the right to an education are not.[46] Some left-of-center scholars, such as Dan Farber (who we should note is not himself an originalist), believe some negative rights are protected (although not economic liberty) but also that some positive rights, such as the right to an education, are too.[47] We will wade into these issues, in the context of Baby Ninth Amendments, in chapter 6.

The fourth model, the collective rights model, believes the amendment is a rule of construction that does protect rights, but collective rights of people in the states. A foremost example of such a collective right, put forward by Professor Akhil Amar, is the right of the people to alter or abolish their government.[48] Another is the right of a state's body politic to choose the policies it wants to adopt free from federal government interference.[49]

The fifth model is the federalism model. It is in some ways the flip side of the residual rights model. Here the Ninth Amendment works with the Tenth Amendment to limit the federal government to a narrow reading of its enumerated powers. Instead of fighting against a conclusion that the federal government has general, unenumerated powers, the federalism model has the Ninth Amendment fighting against a conclusion that the federal government has broad enumerated powers.[50] In other words, it fights against pretty much exactly how the post–New Deal Supreme Court has interpreted the Commerce Clause, allowing just about any regulation that has anything to do with commerce of any kind, which is basically any regulation.

The sixth model, that of Professor McConnell, pays close attention to the use of the word "retained" in the Ninth Amendment. McConnell argues the Ninth was adopted with the backdrop of the state of nature theory of philosopher John Locke. Under Locke's view—recognized as influential at the time of the American Revolution and the Constitution's framing—people have "natural rights" in the state of nature, the theoretical mode of living before people ever came together to form a government and establish civil society.[51] People discover that it benefits them to give up *some* of their rights in exchange for creating a government that will then allow them to live in greater security and achieve greater prosperity. Thus they form a society where they give up rights, such as the right to punish others for wronging them, and turn those rights over to their collective body, the government. But they by no means give up all natural rights. Those rights that they do not relinquish they "retain."

According to Professor McConnell, it was believed at the time of the framing of the Ninth Amendment that retained natural rights were protected, but that the government could infringe on them if the lawmaker—such as Parliament—explicitly made clear it was doing so.

This amounted to a rule of construction: courts were to read a statute as not infringing on retained natural rights unless it was clear that was its intent. When the Bill of Rights was adopted, some of those retained natural rights became constitutionalized; they were now protected *even if* Congress was clear it wanted to infringe them. For McConnell, the purpose of the Ninth Amendment is to make clear that just because some retained natural rights (and a few non-natural or positive rights, such as the right to a jury trial) are raised up to the constitutional level does not mean that other retained rights are suddenly meaningless. Instead, the Ninth Amendment tells us they have the same protection they had before the Bill of Rights was adopted: presumptions of liberty, but not constitutional protections of liberty.

It should be noted that some of these models do not necessarily contradict each other. For example, someone could hold that the Ninth Amendment both protects unenumerated individual rights and prevents a broad reading of the federal government's enumerated powers.

As is discussed later in this work, whichever view of the Ninth Amendment itself is right, the *only* originalist view that makes sense for Baby Ninth Amendments in state constitutions is the individual rights model. As we shall see, when that same language is found in the text of a *state* constitution, most of the other readings of the amendment's language do not make any sense. For example, states have general, not enumerated, powers, thus arguments about enumerated powers are beside the point. In addition, there is no sovereignty to share with another level of government. Cities and counties might have charters, but they are not sovereign, as the states are understood to be. Thus, there is no federalism problem of dual sovereignty to deal with. Further, although a fascinating application of Enlightenment natural rights theory, Professor McConnell's view is completely absent in later discussions of Baby Ninths, diminishing its status as the original meaning of them, even if he is right about the Ninth Amendment itself. Therefore, whatever one's views on the Ninth Amendment, when reviewing the history of how the Baby Ninths came to be, remember that asserted meanings of the Ninth Amendment itself do not always map well onto the Baby Ninths.

Other Than Originalists

While the focus of this book is on originalist understandings of the Ninth Amendment and of the Baby Ninths themselves, it is worth spending a brief digression here on other "nonoriginalist" views of the Ninth Amendment so we have a better idea of how it is seen. One such view is that of Professor Laurence Tribe. He thinks the Ninth Amendment is important, but only as a reminder that the fact that a right is not enumerated is not a reason to conclude it is not constitutionality protected. In this way he is essentially in league with the originalist proponents of the individual rights model, although not entirely and only in a general sense. He argues that the Ninth Amendment does not *itself* protect rights, but prevents the argument that a right is not protected because it is not enumerated:

> For, read properly, the ninth amendment *creates* no rights at all. There are *no* "ninth amendment rights" in the sense in which there are, for example, first amendment rights or fourth amendment rights. That there are individual rights fully derivable from no single provision but implicit in several, or in the structure of the Bill of Rights as a whole, is a proposition implicit in the ninth amendment. But that amendment is not itself the *fount* of any such rights, and it in no way obviates the need to argue that the Constitution does indeed impose upon government the particular limitation for which the advocate contends.[52]

Thus the Ninth Amendment itself does not protect a right, but tells us not to *not* find a right in the Constitution just because it is not specifically enumerated. The right to privacy still needs some kind of constitutional hook, although that hook might be the Due Process Clause of the Fourteenth Amendment, for example, even though the clause does not mention "privacy." In interpreting that clause, and other clauses, we should be mindful of their more expansive interpretations.

Meanwhile, Professor Sanford Levinson takes a modest view of the Ninth, which he also amusingly—and correctly—calls "the stepchild" of the Constitution.[53] After weighing various interpretations he suggests that using the Ninth as a kind of "remand" device might be in order. Under this idea, the courts would apply a kind of "suspensive veto" to some laws that seem to offend some kind of long-protected liberty and where it seems there was not a proper legislative assessment on the offending law's merits.[54] The legislature can then keep the law after "a sober second look."[55] Levinson does not argue that this *should* be the interpretation of the Ninth Amendment, only that it might be worthy of serious consideration as a way to operationalize the amendment's reference to unenumerated rights.

Finally, perhaps the most famous view of the Ninth Amendment is the only one ever seriously explored at the United States Supreme Court, Justice Arthur Goldberg's view as set forth in his concurrence in *Griswold v. Connecticut*. That case concerned a challenge to Connecticut's ban on the use of contraceptives, specifically in the context of married women trying to acquire them. The majority opinion by Justice William O. Douglas, in a famously imprecise passage, said "that specific guarantees in the Bill of Rights have penumbras, formed by emanations from those guarantees that help give them life and substance" and that from those penumbras and emanations the Court could locate a right to marital privacy that the contraception ban ran afoul of.[56] Justice Goldberg, joined by two other justices, wrote separately to say that while he agreed with the Court's ruling, he thought its decision to protect the right to marital privacy was better anchored in the Ninth Amendment. Although the Ninth did not directly protect the right (given that the Ninth was not a part of the Bill of Rights that had been found to apply to the states), Goldberg argued it nevertheless told the Court that there were other rights beyond just those in the Constitution that were protected.[57] And on the question of how to figure out what rights those other rights were, Goldberg, in a manner almost as imprecise as Justice Douglas, claimed we should look to our traditions and "conscience" as a people for which liberties are "fundamental."[58] Applying this test to Connecticut's contraception ban, he thought it failed and was unconstitutional.

In later unenumerated rights cases the Supreme Court has, for whatever reason, shied away from Justice Goldberg's suggestion. That has not prevented it from using tests looking to "traditions" and the like for "fundamental rights" worthy of its protection, such as in famous unenumerated rights cases like *Roe v. Wade* (abortion), *Troxel v. Granville* (parents' right to direct the upbringing of their children), or *Lawrence v. Texas* (right of same-sex intimate sexual conduct).[59] But in none of those or related cases has it invoked the Ninth Amendment beyond, at best, a passing reference. Thus, Justice Goldberg's undeveloped but interesting thoughts on the matter are the only more than transitory statements on the Ninth Amendment from the nation's highest court.

The Baby Tenths

Before moving on to how the Ninth Amendment birthed the Baby Ninths, we need to examine a couple of other issues. One, discussed in a few pages, is judicial review. Another is a mysterious and even more forgotten sibling of the Baby Ninths, what we will here call the "Baby Tenths." These shadowy figures crystallize the views of state sovereignty, constitutional authority, and constitutional rights that framers in the early Republic held. They are a key to understanding why a bill of rights might be crafted to encompass more rights than just those explicitly stated in one.

After a spring and summer of drafting the Bill of Rights, Congress sent the proposed amendments to the states on September 25, 1789. Meanwhile, Pennsylvania was gearing up for a constitutional convention to redraft its own constitution. The state had been living under its relatively "radical" constitution since it was adopted in the revolutionary fervor of 1776, and after much acrimony had finally come to a place where the elites of Pennsylvania society were about to tame the state's perceived democratic excesses.

The convention appointed various committees to redraft different articles of the previous Pennsylvania constitution, including the article constituting the state's declaration of rights. This committee was appointed on December 10, 1789,[60] and reported a draft on December 23, 1789.[61] The last clause of the new declaration of rights that this committee proposed looked similar to the then proposed amendment we now know as the Tenth Amendment. It read:

> To guard against transgressions of the high powers which we have delegated, we declare, that everything in this article is excepted out of the general powers of government, and shall forever remain inviolate.[62]

It appears that this collection of phrases was first put together in December 1789 at the Pennsylvania convention. The author has found no earlier examples in American constitutions of the "transgressions" or "excepted out" terminology. The language about delegation is, however, similar to the language in the then proposed Tenth Amendment: "The powers not delegated to the United States by the Constitution, nor prohibited by it to the States, are reserved to the States respectively, or to the people." Both speak of how the government the respective constitution concerns has been delegated certain powers. Thus, given the timing of this proposal and the federal Bill of Rights, this language seems at least inspired by the Tenth Amendment itself.

Indeed, the connection between the Tenth itself and this Baby Tenth becomes more apparent when considering the political circumstances at the convention. It appears the provision was meant to please Antifederalists as part of a series of compromises between Federalists and Antifederalists in reforming the prior Pennsylvania constitution: "If, as Federalists had argued, the states were the guarantors of individual rights, this statement [the Baby Tenth] would be a further protection against federal encroachments."[63] Today we might ask how this provision in a state constitution could protect against the federal government, especially given the Supremacy Clause of the U.S. Constitution, but it is plausible that at the time this would have been a compromise the two factions settled upon.

Although it seems to have been inspired by the Tenth Amendment, this provision was noticeably changed in a couple of ways. These demonstrate that its Pennsylvanian drafters understood the differences between the federal government and state governments and how those differences called out for different constitutional protections.

First, it refers to "high powers" and "general powers," not enumerated powers.[64] Powers *are* delegated, but those powers are "general" and are also recognized as of a "high" variety. Perhaps "the people" *could* have delegated only certain enumerated powers to the state government, like they have to the federal government, but instead they delegated "general powers." If they had delegated only enumerated powers then the undelegated powers would simply be reserved to "the people" individually, a state of semi-anarchy in a sense.

Second, what are held back from that delegation are not simply powers not delegated—which is what the Tenth Amendment says—but the powers, *any* powers, that intrude upon the rights in Pennsylvania's declaration of rights. This has an echo of the Federalists' now-discarded argument that a federal bill of rights was not needed because the enumerated powers did not include the power to violate fundamental liberties. Here, because the powers are "high" and "general," Pennsylvania's framers recognized there well might be "transgressions" against those liberties. Thus, to protect against any power being used to violate the rights in the declaration of rights, such rights-violating powers are expressly not delegated as part of those "general powers." It is not simply that the constitution affirmatively protects those rights, but that the power to violate them is not given to the state government in the first place. This, in a sense, was an answer to Hamilton's and the Federalists' promise that enumerated powers would not infringe on rights: we will not only spell those rights out, but explain that those powers do not extend to those rights at all. Pennsylvania's framers intended to hold up their liberties with a belt *and* pair of suspenders.

The Baby Tenth demonstrates a belief in popular sovereignty, something commonly held at the time of the U.S. Constitution's adoption. This view of the legitimacy of government asserts that sovereignty did not reside in the federal *or* state governments, but ultimately in the people themselves.[65] The people can delegate their sovereignty however they wish, either through énumerated powers (à la the federal government) or general powers (à la the states). They could also, presumably, delegate *no* powers to any government and live in complete anarchy. Pennsylvania's Baby Tenth asserts that the people are delegating quite broad powers that are in keeping with how "sovereign governments" generally operate, but that they are safeguarding some of their rights out of those powers. It is also worth remembering that Pennsylvania's declaration of rights contained (both before and after the constitution of 1790) a Lockean natural rights guarantee. Thus it could be argued that the Baby Tenth exempted out of the state's general powers the broad rights that the Lockean provision protected, such as the right to pursue happiness.[66] We will return to this idea in a moment when we discuss the role of judicial review.

The Pennsylvania convention voted to include the Baby Tenth language, and, as the convention continued, the language stayed in the various drafts. Meanwhile, the state legislature ratified what we now call the federal Bill of Rights on March 10, 1790.[67] A few months later, the state officially adopted its new constitution, including the Baby Tenth, on September 2, 1790.[68] The federal Bill of Rights was not actually adopted until December 15, 1791, with the Virginia legislature's ratification.[69]

After Pennsylvania's experience, Baby Tenths grew to be popular among constitution drafters. Conventions in Delaware (1792), Tennessee (1796), Kentucky (1799), Ohio (1802), Indiana (1816), and Mississippi (1817) included similar language in their revised or brand-new constitutions.[70] Often they were a conclusion to a bill of rights, not in a numbered clause but set forth at the end to then exempt out of the state's powers the preceding rights.[71]

At the same time, George Mason's Lockean natural rights guarantee continued to be popular. Versions of it specifying its various expansive protections of the rights to pursue happiness and acquire property had been adopted by seven states by 1818.[72] Therefore, by the early nineteenth century state constitutional drafters had learned to do two things: protect rights broadly through fairly open-ended constitutional language, and exempt rights out of the powers that the people extend to state governments. But some people wanted to take things a little further.

Judicial Review of Unenumerated Rights

Now that we have heard about the origins of the Baby Ninths' mother and siblings, but before we proceed to their actual birth, we should talk a little bit about how constitutional rights come up in the practical lives of the people and how that was viewed in the early Republic. Although constitutions are supposed to be interpreted and followed by all officers of government, the barrier a constitutional provision places on state actors typically arises in one forum: the courts. This is not to say that legislators, governors, police officers, etc., do not withhold from passing certain laws and abstaining from certain actions because they believe a constitutional provision forbids them. Or that structural provisions regulate the government in a way that no one questions and generally do not get to court, such as the requirement that a bill pass both houses of the legislature before becoming law. But where the rubber usually hits the road, and where the meaning of the constitution is publicly discussed, is in court where a party asserts that a law or an action is unconstitutional.

For the most part, that was as true in the late eighteenth and early nineteenth centuries as it is today. The institution of judicial review, where courts declare laws to be unconstitutional, goes back at least to this period. The absolute latest date where judicial review became a generally recognized tool of government is 1803, with the famous case of *Marbury v. Madison*. There is an incorrect but popular notion, not so much among scholars but among lawyers and the general public, that judicial review was "invented" by Chief Justice John Marshall in that case.[73] But the evidence demonstrates that judicial review in fact goes back earlier to at least the framing of the U.S. Constitution. And arguably, at least as an idea, back to inventive common law judges in England, especially Lord Edward Coke (pronounced "cook"). We'll start this review of judicial review with Coke and then work our way forward to Justice Marshall.

Coke had an astounding career of many different trades.[74] He served as judge, counsel for the Crown, member of Parliament, even court reporter. His biggest long-term impact was his magisterial compilation of the common law, his *Institutes*.[75] That work was the basis for the legal education of two centuries of lawyers—including many of the U.S. Constitution's framers—until William Blackstone's clearer prose (Coke's work was not exactly a page turner) passed it by. But he made many other contributions to Anglo-American law, among them to popularize the ability of judges to stand up to the executive when it violates the law, and perhaps even to Parliament as well.

When Coke served as a judge, and even as an advocate, he was involved in a few cases concerning the granting of monopolies, typically monopolies the Crown had granted to a favored subject. Examples include tailoring, the mining of saltpeter, the manufacture of playing cards, and the practice of medicine. Several times his cases determined that the monopoly in question was unlawful, enraging the Crown in the process.[76] It should be emphasized that most of these involved the question of whether the Crown itself had the authority to grant the monopoly without Parliament's permission. We would think of these today as administrative law cases: does the executive have the authority to act even though the legislature has not clearly stated it can? But they were still important victories over the Crown that the king did not take kindly to and where the courts defied the wishes of those in power to protect the liberties of the people.

One case in particular, *Doctor Bonham's Case*, arguably (and we need to emphasize "arguably") said something that was much more radical. Whether it actually inspired American ideas about judicial review is debated, and for present purposes it does not matter whether or not it did. But we will briefly review the case because it demonstrates what is at issue when we ask whether a court can defy an act of the legislature.

The case concerned Dr. Thomas Bonham's right to practice medicine. Although trained at both Oxford and Cambridge, when he moved to London the College of Physicians refused to admit him as a member.[77] He then went forward and began practicing in the city anyway. As Parliament had granted the college the power to punish nonmembers who practiced in London, the college had him arrested and imprisoned. Bonham's lawyers argued that Parliament only granted the college the power to prevent malpractice, not simply practicing without a license. Coke agreed, and on this ground Bonham won his case. But Coke went further. He stated that "the common law will control Acts of Parliament, and sometimes adjudge them to be utterly void; for when an act of Parliament is against common right and reason, or repugnant, or impossible to be performed, the common law will control it, and adjudge such an Act to be void." This was arguably dicta—reasoning that is not essential to decide the case—as many critics of the decision have long pointed out.[78] The licensing law did not need to be ruled void as the court also decided it did not apply to Bonham's situation. But even so, it appears to be an assertion that there are some laws that even Parliament cannot pass, laws that are against "common right and reason." In other words, there is a higher law than Parliament and the Crown.

Coke did not elaborate much on what that "common right and reason" was; England, of course, had no written constitution and so Coke seemed to not be making an argument about anything more than simply the strength of the common law. And, indeed, in the long run, this dicta was ignored by English jurists. It is an odd outlier in the grander evolution of English law toward Parliamentary supremacy.

In the colonies, however, there was a more receptive audience. How much of an impact Coke's dicta had on the Founding generation is a matter of great debate, and its importance can be overstated.[79] It seems to have been modest, most famously influencing lawyer James Otis in his attack on writs of assistance in a Boston trial in 1761.[80] But the overall jurisprudence of Coke and monopolies, both regarding the power of Parliament and the power of the Crown, gave the Founders a primer on the importance of judicial review. The point of retelling Dr. Bonham's story, and Coke's related cases, is not to say that Coke "invented" judicial review. But it is to demonstrate how the idea of judicial review, including judicial review applying a "higher law," was not alien to the framers of the early state constitutions and the U.S. Constitution itself if they wanted to draw inspiration from the past. This is particularly true in the "Revolutionary" times of 1776–1780, when the first state constitutions were adopted. And not long after that time—and the transfer of constitutional authority from one embracing Parliament to one embracing constitutions delegated from the people—judicial review of the constitutionality of duly enacted laws began to occur.

Although constitutional judicial review of statutes was controversial in the early Republic, it was not uncommon. One analysis counted thirty-one times a court held a statute unconstitutional even before *Marbury v. Madison.* "The sheer number of these decisions not only belies the notion that the institution of judicial review was created by Chief Justice Marshall in *Marbury,* it also reflects widespread acceptance and application of the doctrine."[81] Many of these concerned fairly clear examples of a law violating a specific constitutional command. For example, courts in New Hampshire found a 1785 law, the "Ten Pound Act," barring jury trials in actions for less than ten pounds in damages to be unconstitutional because the state constitution required a jury trial in "all suits" without a monetary qualification.[82] This does not mean that courts were aggressive in striking down laws, nor did they not give deference to the government in resolving constitutional disputes, especially when the issue was a close one. But it does mean that judicial review was a not uncommon feature of American constitutionalism by the early nineteenth century, and even in the eighteenth century before the Constitution itself was ratified.

And in the use of judicial review, there are indications of courts going beyond instances of clear violations of constitutional text, to readings of broad statements of principle or even invocations of natural justice. For example, a 1783 Massachusetts court found slavery to be incompatible with the state's Lockean natural rights guarantee that people are born "free and equal."[83] Another case, in 1793 in Virginia, declared that the state legislature could not discharge debts Virginians owed to British citizens, citing "the law of nature" among other authorities of common justice and going beyond constitutional text altogether.[84]

Thus, while states were adopting new constitutions—including new Baby Tenths—in the late eighteenth and early nineteenth centuries, the possibility that a court would use a constitution's language to find a law or action unconstitutional was by no means unknown. This included open-ended language, such as in Lockean natural rights guarantees, and even no constitutional language at all, as Lord Coke had tantalizingly come close to doing in *Doctor Bonham's Case*. The coming of *Marbury* in 1803 only accelerated this acceptance.

Therefore, if a state were to adopt a provision in its constitution with an open-ended commitment to unenumerated rights, it would be adopted with two things in mind. First, that constitutional provisions, including provisions in declarations of rights, are judicially enforceable and the constitutionality of legislation and other governmental action can be attacked in court. Second, that even when a law is not explicitly in tension with a constitutional provision, the law nevertheless can be declared unconstitutional. These understandings set the foundations for the coming of the Baby Ninths.

The Birth of the Baby Ninths

It was not until a full thirty years after Madison and his colleagues drafted the Ninth and Tenth Amendments that a state adopted language modeled after the Ninth. When it happened it attracted little fanfare. But it was to set a precedent for generations of American constitution drafting.

Congress created the Alabama Territory in 1817.[85] The territory soon moved toward statehood, and in 1819 Congress authorized a constitutional convention for the expected new state.[86] After the territory's counties elected delegates, they arrived in Huntsville, Alabama, in July 1819 to draft their new foundational document.[87]

One of the convention's first tasks was to appoint a committee to write a draft of the state constitution. It selected a group of fifteen men, chief among them the committee's chairman Clement Comer Clay, a future governor.[88] Of the fifteen, Clay and two others—plus one nondelegate, the territorial governor William Wyatt Bibb—were the resulting draft's "chief architects."[89] The committee was selected on July 6 and issued their draft constitution to the convention as a whole on July 13, after a mere week of constitution writing.[90] And somewhere in those seven days the concept known today as a Baby Ninth Amendment was born. Whether it was Clay, Bibb, or a random member of the committee who volunteered the idea of using the Ninth Amendment as a basis for part of Alabama's Constitution, we do not know. For some reason someone in their drafting room had an idea that had not been implemented in any state constitution up until that point.

The draft state constitution was later changed in some ways by the convention as a whole. It was, after all, simply a starting point. But the draft declaration of rights, Article I of the draft constitution, met little resistance in the convention.[91] Article I was largely modeled after next-door Mississippi's constitution of 1817. If one sets the declaration of rights from both documents side-by-side they are substantially identical, with only eight of Alabama's thirty provisions differing in substance from Mississippi's.[92]

So we know that the committee members were influenced by Mississippi's constitution, if only out of expediency. But we do not know much more than that.[93] A scant journal has survived with some clues on what was said in the convention as a whole, but on many topics the convention did not disagree with the committee's draft and had no comment on a constitutional provision.[94] When it came time for the Baby Ninth in the committee's draft, nary a word is recorded in the convention journal (as, indeed, was also true for most of the rights provisions).[95] This lack of discussion or recording of one is all too common a story for constitutional conventions. All legal historians have to work with are the constitutional texts themselves, and (if you are lucky) the drafting history. This is not always the case, but it was in Alabama in 1819.

What we do know is how the section differed from the section it seems to have been modeled on, the Baby Tenth of Article I of the Mississippi Constitution. That provision stated:

> To guard against transgressions of the high powers, herein delegated,
> We Declare that everything in this article is excepted out of the general powers of government, and shall forever remain inviolate; and

that all laws contrary thereto, or to the following provisions, shall be void.[96]

Alabama's had this language, but with a couple of additions. They are highlighted in the following:

This enumeration of certain rights shall not be construed to deny or disparage others retained by the people; and, to guard against *any encroachments on the rights herein retained*, or any transgression of any of the high powers herein delegated, we declare, that every thing in this article is excepted out of the general powers of government, and shall forever remain inviolate; and that all laws contrary thereto, or to the following provisions, shall be void.[97]

First, there is the language italicized for emphasis. This seems to come from the Indiana Constitution of 1816, which was the one state with a Baby Tenth that had used the emphasized language instead of the "transgressions" language before stating "we declare."[98] Alabama's committee apparently liked both introductory clauses, and joined them together.

But more importantly for present purposes, the committee also joined the bolded language. This can only have been taken from the Ninth Amendment itself, as no other constitutional document contained a provision with something like those words at that point.

Why did the committee put the Ninth Amendment in there? Unless some paper buried deep in an archive can be found, we cannot know directly. The fact that the provision as a whole already contained language from Mississippi's and Indiana's otherwise materially identical clauses provides a clue. Perhaps its drafters liked a belt-and-suspenders approach to protecting the declaration of rights, and threw in every clause they could find in prior constitutions to protect against state abuses. And perhaps someone on the committee had the idea that they should "except out" of the general powers of government not just those rights in the declaration of rights, but other rights as well. Thus, stating that those "other rights" cannot be denied or disparaged, plus excepting them (as they were "in this article" via the Baby Ninth language) along with the enumerated rights from the "general powers of government," would be the most comprehensive rights protection.

But perhaps, instead, a member of the committee liked the Ninth

Amendment itself and simply wanted a parallel provision in the state constitution. Coupling it with a Baby Tenth Amendment might seem to make sense—instead of making them separately numbered clauses—because they both are "all inclusive" provisions, covering rights and powers, respectively, that are not dealt with elsewhere. Using Indiana's language, they were natural together as they both used the word "retained" to describe the rest of the declaration of rights.

In any case, no one at the convention is recorded to have objected to this draft language. The constitution eventually ratified contained the same language. The state was then admitted to the Union later that year. A similar version of the provision, still with a Baby Ninth and a Baby Tenth, is in Alabama's constitution today, although the Baby Tenth has been significantly trimmed over the years.[99]

Maine's Baby Ninth

Alabama can rightfully call itself the first "Baby Ninth State." But not by much. Just three months after Alabama's drafting committee invented its Baby Ninth, Maine did a similar thing. In Maine, however, there apparently was no hunger for a Baby Tenth as well. So Maine had, and still has, the first stand-alone Baby Ninth.

For years the residents of what was then the District of Maine debated whether they should leave the Commonwealth of Massachusetts and create their own state. After a number of failed referenda on the subject, Maine's voters finally voted to become their own member of the Union.[100] To do so, of course, the prospective state needed its own constitution, and just like Alabama, they elected delegates to a constitutional convention. The convention began in October 1819. One of Maine's political leaders, William King, had planned for this moment for years and wanted to write a constitution anew, instead of copying from John Adams' Massachusetts Constitution of 1780.[101] But given the time constraints when the convention was actually called, the convention did begin with Massachusetts's version as a template, although many changes were then made.[102]

Maine's convention spun off the business of drafting various provisions of the constitution to different committees. The declaration of rights committee was composed of thirty-three members.[103] As in Alabama, no detailed record has been found of the committee's deliberations. There is a (non-exhaustive) journal of the convention's proceedings, but, as in Alabama, no remarks are recorded that were made about the Baby Ninth Amendment.[104]

The Baby Ninth was in the committee's draft declaration of rights and remained unchanged throughout the convention (and, indeed, is unchanged today). Much of the declaration of rights was taken from the Massachusetts Constitution, but the Baby Ninth, at the end of the document, was new. It read:

> The enumeration of certain rights shall not impair nor deny others retained by the people.[105]

This was similar, of course, to the actual Ninth Amendment, but different in a couple of interesting ways. First, instead of "deny or disparage" it says the enumeration of rights shall not "impair nor deny." "Impair" seems to ring with a stronger protection than "disparage."[106] Furthermore, the phrase "shall not be construed" is completely absent. In Maine, the Baby Ninth does not forbid a reader from construing the bill of rights to mean other rights can be denied or impaired, but says the enumeration of certain rights *itself* shall not impair or deny other rights. Perhaps this difference is immaterial, but perhaps it is meant to be a stronger clause than a "mere" rule of construction.

Maine then adopted its constitution and entered the Union in 1820 as part of the infamous Missouri Compromise.

A "Proto–Baby Ninth" in Tennessee?

Before we see where the examples of Alabama and Maine lead to, we must add an asterisk to this story and consider what happened in Tennessee in 1796. As noted above, along with other states that adopted constitutions in the years following Pennsylvania's 1790 constitution, Tennessee included a Baby Tenth in its first constitution of 1796.[107] Tennessee, however, included a phrase absent in Pennsylvania's and in those of the other states that adopted Baby Tenths before 1819. Its Baby Tenth stated, in relevant part,

> And to guard against transgressions of the high powers which we have delegated, We declare, that every thing in the bill of rights contained, *and every other right not hereby delegated,* is excepted out of the general powers of government, and shall for ever remain inviolate."[108]

For the most part this is a Baby Tenth. It uses the transgression language going back to Pennsylvania's original drafting. Then it reserves what is in the bill of rights to the people. This seems to functionally be the same thing as excepting those rights out of the "general powers of government" in other Baby Tenths.

Stuck in the middle of the language, however, is a reference to "every other right not hereby delegated." Delegating rights? The same sentence already speaks of *powers* that have been delegated, like the actual Tenth Amendment's reference to the delegation of powers. If that is true, then how are rights also delegated?

The answer is not entirely clear. It could be that "every other right" actually means powers of government. But that does not seem to work because "powers" was already used to mean powers of government, and "every other right" comes directly after a reference to the state's bill of rights. A more plausible reading is that "every other right not hereby delegated" means that there are *some* rights delegated over to the government, beyond those in the bill of rights, and that the people therefore do not have those rights anymore. But, of those "other" rights that are *not* "hereby delegated" they are "excepted out of the general powers of government" just as the rights enumerated in the bill of rights are. In other words, through the Tennessee Constitution the people have alienated some rights, but not the rights that are reserved to the people in the bill of rights *plus some others.* This accords well with Professor McConnell's discussion of how the Founding Era viewed constitution making through the prism of Lockean natural rights theory. Some rights are given over to the government, but some rights are retained. But unlike in his view of the Ninth Amendment (where the Amendment does not constitutionalize unenumerated rights) here those retained rights ("rights not hereby delegated") *are* constitutionalized, as they are excepted out of the general powers of government.

The provision is also different from a Baby Ninth because it does not talk about denying, disparaging, or impairing unenumerated rights. It just says that some unenumerated rights—that is, all unenumerated rights that are not delegated to the State of Tennessee—are reserved to the people. Perhaps the best way to describe it is as a weak or "proto" Baby Ninth. Some "other rights" *are* denied or disparaged because they are not enumerated, but the "other rights," the vast majority of the rights citizens of the state are supposed to enjoy, are protected in some way.

It appears this language was never litigated in a published case in

Tennessee during the thirty-nine years of the constitution's existence. Then, for good or bad, in the Tennessee Constitution of 1835 the "every other right" language was removed, although the rest of the Baby Tenth stayed in.[109]

————

As the 1820s began, two states had tried something new when it came to protecting the rights of citizens within their states from state intrusion. They referred to unspecified "retained" rights in their constitutions, and they stated that those rights cannot be, alternatively, "denied," "disparaged," or "impaired." And they did this with a common background understanding that rights in state constitutions can be enforced in court under a system of judicial review. Were these new additions going to be isolated experiments that perhaps die out a few years later—like Tennessee's language—or would they lead to more action, both in state constitutional conventions and in state courts? The answer came slowly, but steadily.

CHAPTER 2

The Growth of Baby Ninths
Before the Civil War

The arrival of the Baby Ninths in 1819 marked a new chapter in the emergence of unenumerated rights in America. Judicial review was firmly established, and although "etcetera clauses" protecting unenumerated rights arguably already existed, the Baby Ninths pushed this concept into new territory. But these babies had a long way to go before they came of age. This chapter follows them on their journey out of the nurseries of Alabama and Maine and through their antebellum growing pains up to the eve of the Civil War. Along the way we will see which states added these provisions to their constitutions, but also which states did not. We will look at states on "both sides" because in understanding the growth of Baby Ninths we want to see the full picture. Their growth was not sudden and steady, but plodding, halting, and yet in the end continuous.

We take this journey primarily through the lens of state constitutional conventions. Other than in the case of an amendment, a convention is when constitutional change most clearly happens. A convention, and subsequent adoption of a new constitution, demonstrates what the framers wanted to change about their fundamental protections at that time. And statements made at the convention—if we are lucky enough to have a record of them—tell us what those framers thought of their handicraft.

In this antebellum period, we will see how exactly a dozen states adopted Baby Ninths. And, most interestingly, we will see how four states—California, Ohio, Maryland, and Minnesota—discussed the meaning of Baby Ninths (or at least Baby Tenths) on their convention floors. These discussions tell us that the framers saw Baby Ninths as protecting individual rights. Indeed, objections to Baby Ninths and Baby Tenths (and there were a few) were not that these provisions would protect "too many" rights, but that they were not needed because unenumerated rights were protected *anyway*.

Early Fits and Starts

After their start in Alabama and Maine, Baby Ninths did not find any more homes in American constitutions for a few years. Massachusetts, New York, and Virginia, for example, all held constitutional conventions in the 1820s and early 1830s, where they either wholesale adopted new constitutions or made significant amendments.[1] But none of those states added Baby Ninths.[2] Also, Missouri joined the Union in 1821 and did not include a Baby Ninth in its constitution.[3] Delaware held a convention in 1831 for a new constitution from which no Baby Ninth came.[4] Mississippi did the same in 1832, and, as discussed in the last chapter, its neighbor Tennessee adopted a new constitution in 1835 and did not add a Baby Ninth (Tennessee even dropped its "proto-Baby Ninth").[5] In 1835 Michigan drafted what was to become its first constitution, but it too did not include a Baby Ninth.[6]

There is one partial exception to this "drought" in Baby Ninths after Alabama and Maine, though. In 1824 Rhode Island held a constitutional convention.[7] As we will see later, the state had no constitution at the time and would not have one until the 1840s. The constitution the convention drew up was submitted to the voters but rejected handily.[8] The draft constitution, however, contained a Baby Ninth, stating at the end of its bill of rights: "The enumeration of the foregoing rights shall not be construed to impair nor deny others retained by the people."[9]

But still, the Rhode Island draft did not pass. Thus in 1835 an observer might think it "cute" that Alabama and Maine had each experimented with making Madison's invention part of state constitutional law, but not worth much else because few other state constitutional framers had thought much about it or even noticed.

After 1835, however, things began to change. In 1836 Arkansas drafted a constitution and was admitted to the Union.[10] Arkansas's Declaration of Rights was similar in roughly half of its clauses to Alabama's, but with the rest often being quite different or changed in material ways.[11] In other words, it was not just a carbon copy. The last clause of the new declaration, however, was word-for-word exactly the same as Alabama's joint Baby Ninth/Baby Tenth clause quoted earlier.[12] As in Alabama and Maine, there is no record of any debate on the provision in the limited journal of the convention, so why Arkansas chose to adopt the provision is not clear. It was not simply inertia in copying Alabama's, however, because, again, the Arkansas delegates choose not to copy many of Alabama's other provisions.

And Arkansas was not the only example of creating something like a Baby Ninth in 1836. Outside the then United States, the new Republic of Texas adopted a constitution.[13] It was to be the country's fundamental law for nine years, until the State of Texas adopted a new constitution in 1845. At the opening of its declaration of rights, the constitution had a provision similar to Tennessee's 1796 Baby Tenth, including the "proto-Baby Ninth" discussed above (and obviously taken from it, as no other similar provisions existed).[14] But the clause did not last long, as it was removed in the 1845 constitution, when Texas entered the Union (although a Baby Tenth remained).[15] It appears this language was never litigated in the Texas Supreme Court during the nine years of the constitution's existence.

After Arkansas's and Texas's ("proto") Baby Ninths, Florida[16] and Pennsylvania both held constitutional conventions in 1838, but both did not include Baby Ninths in their resulting constitutions. Then, however, in the two decades before the Civil War, a number of states took Arkansas's lead. With each passing year it became more and more likely that if a state were going to either join the Union and write its first constitution, or simply redraft its present one, the state would end up with a Baby Ninth.

The next constitutional convention was in Rhode Island. Although the state's history as a colony goes back to the seventeenth century, and it (belatedly) ratified the U.S. Constitution in 1790, the state did not actually have a constitution until 1843, instead relying on its 1663 royal charter.[17] Arguably, however, its first constitution was actually adopted a couple of years earlier as part of the "Dorr Rebellion," a complicated and almost-quite-bloody episode where Rhode Island's old ruling elite were put under attack by a coalition of middle-class reformers and new immigrant laborers.[18] The two sides in the struggle held rival conventions in 1841, producing two proposed constitutions. The elite's constitution was defeated in a referendum, while the "People's Convention" proposed a constitution that was overwhelmingly adopted in an earlier statewide referendum that allowed many more voters because it rejected the state's strict suffrage rules requiring property owner-ship.[19] But this constitution was not recognized by the old elite who con-tinued to control the state government. Then, after defeating the populist forces lead by Thomas Dorr in a near-battle, the government held another convention in September 1842 that led to the state's first accepted constitu-tion, going into effect in early 1843.[20] This then served the state until a new constitution was ratified in 1986.

What is striking is that all three of these constitutions milling around Rhode Island from 1841 to 1843 included the same Baby Ninth: "The enumeration of the foregoing rights shall not be construed to impair or ['nor' in the People's Convention version] deny others retained by the people."[21] In other respects the constitutions are by no means identical, especially in voting rights, the primary basis for the Dorr Rebellion. But the Baby Ninth was agreeable enough to all sides that it made its way into all three constitutions. And, lest there be any doubt on where the inspiration for it came from, its text is virtually identical—including the idiosyncratic word "foregoing" instead of "certain"—to the failed 1824 state constitution.

In May and June 1844 New Jersey held a convention to redraft its constitution.[22] It was the state's first constitutional convention since 1776. The previous constitution, signed on July 2, 1776, had had no bill of rights (although a handful of individual rights dotted its scant paragraphs), so the framers of the 1844 bill of rights were in large part writing a new document.[23] And they included a Baby Ninth: "This enumeration of rights and privileges shall not be construed to impair or deny others retained by the people."[24] As the reader can see, the New Jerseyans followed the lead of Maine and Rhode Island by using "impair" instead of "disparage," and they also added "privileges" in addition to "rights."

After a Baby Ninth made its appearance in multiple constitutions in Rhode Island, another one did the same thing in Iowa. The then terri-tory of Iowa held a constitutional convention in October 1844, whose delegates settled on a draft that then went to the people for ratifica-tion.[25] The people, however, voted it down twice, leading to another convention in 1846.[26] That version was accepted by the people, and Iowa was then admitted as the twenty-ninth state later that year.[27] The 1846 version did not differ from the earlier one in many ways, and their bills of rights are almost identical.[28] Both had the same Baby Ninth: "This enumeration of rights shall not be construed to impair or deny others retained by the people."[29]

As we have seen, Texas declined to keep its (proto) Baby Ninth in

1845. Louisiana did not include a Baby Ninth in its new constitution of that year.[30] Two and three years later, respectively, both Illinois (to redo its constitution) and Wisconsin (to adopt its first) held conventions and did not include Baby Ninths in their constitutions either.[31]

California Dreaming

But even with a few states not adopting Baby Ninths, at this point the instruments were not going away. In 1849 California adopted a constitution with one.[32] And it is here, in the Golden State's first convention, that we finally have a record of what a state's delegates thought of a Baby Ninth's language.

We will only take a brief look at the California delegates' discussion. It proceeded in a confusing manner that is not worth a blow-by-blow account for present purposes. But a few of the delegates' remarks shed some light on views of the time about state constitutions, state powers, and unenumerated rights.

As in other state conventions, a committee performed the initial drafting of the bill of rights. The committee proposed a bill of rights with twenty clauses, eight of which it took from New York's constitution and the rest from Iowa's.[33] This included Iowa's Baby Ninth.[34] Again, Iowa's version is not a combined Baby Ninth/Baby Tenth like Alabama's and Arkansas's but very much like the Ninth Amendment itself: "This enumeration of rights shall not be construed to impair or deny others retained by the people."

After reviewing and voting on the other nineteen provisions, the convention came to the proposed Baby Ninth. Immediately, however, a delegate, W. M. Gwin, moved to replace the proposed "Iowan" provision with language identical to Alabama's and Arkansas's combined Baby Ninth/Baby Tenths.[35] This then led to another delegate, C. T. Botts, to move to amend Mr. Gwin's amendment with a still yet different provision. That provision—which Mr. Botts said he had drafted himself—read, "As constitutions are the instruments by which the powers of the people are delegated to their representatives, they ought to be construed strictly, and all powers, not expressly granted, should be taken to be reserved."[36] Mr. Botts claimed this would do the same work as Mr. Gwin's "Alabama version," but prided himself on the fact that it was not simply copied from another constitution.[37] Even in 1849, it seems, Californians needed to be noticed as different.

But careful readers will see that this provision in fact contained much stronger language than what it tried to amend. It seems to say that if the government of California does not have a power expressly authorized then the state cannot exercise it. This would be much more restrictive than the Baby Tenths we have discussed so far, because in those versions the only powers "reserved" are those that would violate enumerated rights and "other rights." Baby Tenths, after all, recognize that state governments have "general powers" of government, and not enumerated powers, in contrast to the federal government. Mr. Botts's version was much more like the Tenth Amendment itself—in fact, even stronger, as it used the words "expressly granted."

Another delegate took great exception to Mr. Botts's "amendment to the amendment." Delegate Robert Semple argued that such a provision is all well and good for the federal government, but that in a state constitution "[y]ou can only say what it [the government] shall not do."[38] Mr. Botts then retorted that, no, the state government only derives power from the state constitution, arguing that, "All the power committed to their hands is delegated to them through the Constitution. If it does not come through the Constitution, it does not come [sic] all."[39] Mr. Semple then responded with a very interesting distinction:

[Semple] was willing [to grant that], in forming this Constitution, that the powers not herein expressly delegated should be withheld. But by whom? By the State, or by the people in their individual capacity. It must be by the people in some capacity—either individual or legislative.[40]

Mr. Semple then strongly implied that the withholding of power should be in the people's legislative capacity, as "Wherever [the people] have not thus restricted their own power, they have a right to enact such laws as they please."[41] In other words, if powers are not delegated to the state government in the state constitution they still can be exercised by . . . the state government. This, of course, makes any "delegation" a misnomer. The government has a power if it is in the constitution and also has it if it is not.

Soon afterward, another delegate, L. W. Hastings, stepped forward with a statement that would be familiar to those in the First Congress. His language suggests he was speaking to the original proposed "Iowan" Baby Ninth. He argued that "there appeared to be no necessity for the article at all. Why declare that all rights not herein enumerated are reserved to the people? Would it not be true without such a declaration? Does the mere assertion make it any more true? Gentlemen seem to be afraid that if they omit one right the people will loose [*sic*] it altogether."[42]

At that point the "amendment to the amendment" was voted on and rejected, and then the original amendment of substituting Alabama's language was also rejected.[43] But the original proposal itself, taken from Iowa's Baby Ninth, was then adopted. Further, just before the vote on the "Alabama amendment" Mr. Semple stated that "upon a more careful examination of the amendment" there was not "any difference of opinion after all between himself and the gentleman from San Francisco [meaning Mr. Gwin]"[44] and he would vote for it after all.

We should not make too much of this often confusing, and relatively short, exchange, but we can glean a few things.

First, delegates were by no means of like mind on what powers state governments had. Some adamantly asserted the traditional view, discussed earlier, that state governments have general powers. Mr. Botts, however, believed that the coming state of California would only have the powers granted to it in the state constitution.

Second, there is a hint of a "collective rights" reading of Baby Ninths. Mr. Semple seemed to be forwarding a view that when powers are not delegated to the government, they are withheld by the people in their *legislative* capacity. Now, there are logical problems with that view; there is no difference between delegating the government power and the people legislatively retaining power. The "government" and "the people" in their legislative capacity are, of course, the same thing (in a democratic republic at least). Even so, this may have been Mr. Semple's understanding of the Baby Ninth or Baby Tenth language. Given the confusing nature of the amendments offered, and given that Mr. Semple is referring to powers not rights, however, it could be that his reasoning only applied to Mr. Botts's idiosyncratic amendment to the amendment and not the "Iowan" Baby Ninth itself. Since Semple later agreed with Mr. Gwin "after all" and voted for Mr. Gwin's "Alabaman" Baby Ninth, it may be that Semple simply was referring to the hastily drafted version of Mr. Botts.

Third, that Mr. Hastings' objection to the Baby Ninth—that it was not needed to protect unenumerated rights—was rejected suggests that at least a majority of the delegates[45] viewed the Baby Ninth as at least helpful, if not necessary, in protecting rights that are not listed in the bill of rights itself. This, of course, supports the individual rights reading of California's Baby Ninth. But the fact that Mr. Hastings believed that rights were protected *even if* they were not in the constitution via an unenumerated rights clause *also* supports an individual rights reading. His argument essentially was that state government power could not violate certain rights no matter what a bill of rights says, that is, no matter what rights it enumerates or whether it has unenumerated rights clause(s). Include a Baby Ninth or not, those rights are still protected. This is what he appeared to argue by saying that others feared that if a right was omitted then it would be lost altogether. He seems to say that, no, even if a right is left out of the constitution it still is reserved to the people and protected.

Maryland and Ohio

Over the next three years, 1849–1851, six states held constitutional conventions. None of them were new states. New states, of course, are more likely to experiment with constitutional provisions because there is no local, previous constitution to start with. Even so, two of these six states chose to add a Baby Ninth where their former state constitution lacked one. Those states were Maryland[46] and Ohio.[47] The other states during this time period, Indiana,[48] Kentucky,[49] Michigan,[50] and Virginia,[51] for whatever reason did not add Baby Ninths. Maryland and Ohio are valuable to our story because, like California, they kept records of their floor debates, and each discussed their Baby Ninths.

In Ohio's convention there are some hints of how the delegates viewed its new combined Baby Ninth/Baby Tenth. After the initial draft bill of rights came out of its committee, the proposed provision was laid before the full convention. Placed at the end of the bill of rights, it said, "This enumeration of powers shall not be construed to impair or deny others retained by the people, and all powers not herein delegated, remain with the people."[52] A delegate then made a motion, which passed without discussion, to replace the first "powers" with "rights," presumably to make the first clause read more like other Baby Ninths and the Ninth Amendment itself.[53] This amended version is what came to be Ohio's Baby Ninth/Baby Tenth, still in force today.

The most interesting thing about the initial draft is not that "powers" was, perhaps inadvertently, used instead of "rights" in the first clause. It is the form of the second clause. It reads like Mr. Botts's failed amendment in California, discussed above. It summarily states that if powers are not delegated through the constitution then they "remain with the people." This, again, is much stronger than other Baby Tenths, which recognized that the people were not delegating enumerated powers but general powers of government. Ohio's first Baby Tenth, in its 1802 constitution, was a bit different. It had stated, "To guard against the transgressions of the high powers, which we have delegated, we declare, that all powers, not hereby delegated, remain with the people."[54] This old version did seem to imply that Ohio's government rested on a principle of enumerated powers. But it was ambiguous because it at least implied that "high powers," which is an open-ended term, were being delegated.[55] The drafters of the 1851 version added a Baby Ninth to the front of the old Baby Tenth and then simplified it, deleting the "transgressions" clause. But the resulting text is not ambiguous like the 1802 version. It simply says that if powers are not delegated—whatever they are—then they remain with the people, that is, that like the federal government, the state government only has powers specified in the state constitution.

That this scheme of enumerated powers would turn traditional state government on its head was actually recognized later in the convention. During a debate about how the constitution should address the state's regulation of liquor, a delegate stated the following, which is worth quoting at length:

> The other day, upon another subject, I ventured to express the opinion, that there was an unlimited power exercised by the General Assembly, except in cases where they were so restrained, their power was unlimited.
>
> But, I was then reminded—and forcibly, too—that the closing section of the bill of rights, upon which we have passed, is in these words: "This enumeration of powers[56] shall not be construed to impair or deny others retained by the people, and all powers not herein delegated, remain with the people."
>
> Sir, I wish that were the practical construction of the instrument we are forming. It is a beautiful theory of the general government, "that all power not delegated to the United States by the Constitution, nor prohibited by it to the States, are reserved to the States respectively, and to the people." Here we have almost the same language applied to the general Assembly: but I hold that they have hitherto been treated as void and meaningless words. But gentlemen say all power not expressly delegated is reserved: and I yield on account of the importance of the principle. It becomes, at once, a fundamental, a seminal principle—a clear touch-stone, by which to bring the action of the Legislature to the test.[57]

The delegate, Mr. Taylor, then went on to explain that there actually was a grant of power to regulate liquor in the separate provision they were considering.[58] It appears no other delegate challenged him on his construction of Ohio's "Baby Tenth."

Mr. Taylor's remarks are impressive because he pointed out the revolutionary nature of Ohio's new Baby Tenth (if taken literally). Other than internal operations of government, the only powers actually delegated to the State of Ohio in the original 1851 constitution are to promote education (art. VI), support care for "the insane, blind, and deaf and dumb" (art. VII, sec. 1), provide for jails (art. VII, sec. 2), repel invasions and suppress insurrections through a militia (art. VIII, sec. 2; art. IX), provide for public works (art. VIII, sec. 12), tax (art. XII), and allow incorporations (art. XIII).[59] Although covering a large amount of what state governments engaged in in the mid-nineteenth century, this list lacks central functions such as protecting Ohio citizens from crime and prosecuting criminals. No one, obviously, believed the state lacked these powers, even though they were not delegated to the state in the text of the constitution.

It thus appears that Mr. Taylor's remarks on enumerating powers were not taken too seriously, either by other drafters of the 1851 constitution or by Ohio's subsequent courts and lawmakers.

What this reasoning about the Baby Tenth means for the Baby Ninth portion of the same sentence is unclear. If the Baby Tenth actually is not to be taken literally, does that mean the Baby Ninth should not be either? Or should the Baby Ninth play more of a role given that the Baby Tenth has no force—and thus does not exempt the state's bill of rights out of the legislature's power, unlike other Baby Tenths—and therefore should be read expansively? Whatever the answer, the delegates failed to discuss it.

Maryland's convention, on the other hand, tackled its new Baby Ninth head-on. It came to be through the concerted efforts of one delegate. During the floor debate on the new convention's declaration of rights, a Mr. Parke rose to offer a Baby Ninth for inclusion in the constitution. His exchange is worth quoting in full:

> The next question was on the amendment of which Mr. PARKE had heretofore given notice, and which he now offered in the words following:
>
> "Article 43. This enumeration of rights shall not be construed to impair or deny others retained by the people."

The amendment having being read.

Mr. PARKE said that it was a mere assertion that there were rights not enumerated in the declaration of rights, and that they were retained by the people. There could not, he thought, be any impropriety in its adoption.

Mr. SCHLEY invited the gentleman, (Mr. Parke) to specify what the non-enumerated rights were.

Mr. PARKE said it was impossible for him to do so. He presumed that they were very numerous—so much so as to render it impossible to include them in the bill of rights. A bill of rights, probably, might not be absolutely necessary, yet it was customary to have such a declaration. We all know that all the rights could not be set forth, and he thought it would be best to make a declaration that there were other rights which were not enumerated.

Mr. JENIFER thought that such a declaration would be entirely out of keeping in this place. If, as was conceded, the bill of rights took away no rights, of course every thing which was not taken away, remained.

The PRESIDENT, pro tem., stated the question.

Mr. KILGOUR asked the yeas and nays.

Mr. MERRICK said he hoped the gentleman, (Mr. Parke), would withdraw his amendment. It certainly was unnecessary. It could effect no great good, nor, indeed, could it do any harm.

Mr. PARKE said if it was the wish of the Convention that the amendment should be withdrawn, he, (Mr. Parke) would withdraw it. He did not see that it could make any great difference, whether the amendment was incorporated in the Constitution or not. He had seen it in other Constitutions—he had seen it in the Constitution of California. He was willing, however, to withdraw the amendment.

But, after a moment's reflection,

Mr. PARKE stated that he preferred to adhere to his amendment.

• • •

The question was then again taken on the amendment of Mr. PARKE, and was decided in the affirmative: ayes 30, noes 25.

So the amendment was adopted.[60]

This exchange demonstrates both Parke's reason for the proposed Baby Ninth (to assert that there were more rights retained by the people than just those in the state constitution) and also that in his view, and the objecting delegates' view, the Baby Ninth was not strictly necessary. This was because the people had the unenumerated rights the Baby Ninth referred to, as well as the actual enumerated rights, whether or not the Baby Ninth, or indeed the declaration of rights itself, was in the constitution.

This seems to fly in the face of the careful task of writing a constitution. If rights are protected whether or not they are placed in its text—either by enumeration or indirectly through a Baby Ninth or another unenumerated rights clause—then why include a declaration of rights at all? The answer might lie in clarifying what at least *some* rights were, even though the framers expected others to also remain protected. In any case, the opposition to Mr. Parke's amendment did not win and the people of Maryland to this day enjoy a Baby Ninth in their constitution.[61]

The Eve of War

Baby Ninths continued to become more and more popular as Civil War storm clouds began to brew. In 1852 Louisiana held a constitutional convention but failed to adopt a Baby Ninth.[62] But then things became interesting in Kansas, where the people were not served up with one, two, or even three possible constitutions, but four.

The so-called "Topeka Constitution" was drafted in Topeka, Kansas, in 1855. This was the first of four constitutions the differing parties in "Bleeding Kansas" had in the violent run-up to Kansas' statehood.[63] A convention of delegates committed to a free Kansas drafted the document, which they then presented to Congress but which Congress never accepted.[64] The Baby Ninth (with a short Baby Tenth) it proposed, in article I, section 22, declared, "This enumeration of rights shall not be construed to impair or deny others retained by the people; and all powers not herein delegated shall remain with the people."[65] The language is identical to Ohio's combined Baby Ninth/Baby Tenth.[66]

The Topeka Constitution was followed by the also unsuccessful "Lecompton Constitution," the convention that was held by a rival pro-slavery group in 1857.[67] It also had a combined Baby Ninth/Baby Tenth, but which was taken from the Alabama and Arkansas constitutions.[68]

The third Kansas constitution in its run-up to statehood was the "Leavenworth Constitution" of 1858, written by free-soil partisans.[69] It contained exactly the same combined Baby Ninth/Baby Tenth as the first Topeka Constitution.[70] It also never became law, but the fourth constitution, the "Wyandotte Constitution," did when the state finally joined the Union in 1861.[71] It also had exactly the same combined Baby Ninth/Baby Tenth as the previous two free-soil versions.[72]

What might be taken from this back-and-forth of Baby Ninths is that both sides of the slavery debate believed in using Baby Ninths to protect their liberties, but had different inspirations in doing so. Whether either side thought the Baby Ninth itself—in addition to other, more explicitly pro- or antislavery language in the various constitutions—was a tool in the aid of their cause on the slavery issue, we do not know. But the fact that one took its combined Baby Ninth/Baby Tenth from the free state of Ohio and the other from slave states of Arkansas and Alabama demonstrates that slavery may have been on their minds in selecting the clauses.

In 1857 Iowa held a constitutional convention and retained its Baby Ninth without change and without comment.[73] In the same year Oregon held its convention to draft its first constitution, and it included the following Baby Ninth: "This enumeration of rights and privileges shall not be construed to impair or deny others retained by the people."[74] Its wording is identical to New Jersey's, the first Baby Ninth to include the word "privileges."

Minnesota also held a constitutional convention in 1857.[75] In fact, it held two simultaneous conventions. Although delegates were elected for a single convention to draft a constitution for the territory's impending statehood, there was so much acrimony between the Republican and Democratic delegates that the two factions held their own rival "conventions" after the first day.[76] Each then produced a draft constitution and hammered out a compromise version in a conference committee of sorts.[77] Interestingly for our purposes, each party proposed a Baby Ninth. The Republican convention appears to have adopted it but then rescinded it.[78] The Democratic convention, however, adopted theirs without comment.[79] The Baby Ninth then survived the "conference committee" to make it into the final state constitution.[80]

Evidence of the chaotic nature of how Minnesota's constitution came to be is that its Baby Ninth ended up in the same section as one of its religious liberty provisions. The language in the actual constitution was (and still is) the same as that adopted in the Democratic convention: "The enumeration of rights in this constitution shall not deny or impair others retained by and inherent in the people."[81] In the actual constitution, but not in the draft from the Democratic Convention, the paragraph continues with several sentences concerning religion.

In the Republican convention there were two separate colloquies on whether to include its suggested Baby Ninth and a Baby Tenth (the latter of which was never adopted). Both exchanges are worth examining.

First, in the Committee of the Whole—*not* in the delegates' capacity as the convention itself—a delegate, Mr. Billings, moved to add a Baby Tenth. It was virtually identical, with just the difference of a word and some punctuation, to Mississippi's 1817 constitution.[82] It did not have any Baby Ninth language. He was then challenged and the debate went as follows:

> MR. MORGAN. It seems to me that such a section would not work very well, as some of our propositions in this Bill of Rights are affirmative and some are negative. It is a very unusual provision, and I must confess I do not see how it can operate.
>
> MR. PERKINS. I do not see the need of a section of this kind. It does not add any particular sanctity or obligation to the Constitution. That all enactments of the Legislature, in contravention to this Constitution, shall be void, is certainly a principle which cannot be gainsayed, and it need not be affirmed and reaffirmed. The acts of the Legislature which conflict with the Constitution must be void, and it seems to me folly to add a section of that kind.
>
> MR. WILSON. I certainly am opposed to that amendment, because, as has just been stated, the facts asserted in that section lie at the very foundation of all government. And the idea that the Constitution is above all law is something which needs no affirmation.
>
> MR. BILLINGS. My idea of the necessity of this section arose from the fact that we have in this preamble enumerated certain rights as belonging to the people. But there are still remaining with the people a large number of rights which we cannot enumerate, and to guard those unenumerated rights, I proposed that section.
>
> MR. WILSON. I think the section has just a contrary effect from what the gentleman intends.
>
> The amendment was withdrawn.[83]

This exchange tells us, explicitly, that Delegate Billings wanted to protect unenumerated rights: "to guard those unenumerated rights, I propose that section." How he went about that (a Baby Tenth, *not* a Baby Ninth) perhaps was not the most direct way to do so, and it is thus not surprising that Delegate Wilson pointed that out. A Baby Tenth may have a lot to recommend it, but it does not reference rights not already set forth in a constitution. But that Billings was trying to protect unenumerated rights demonstrates that at least one delegate had the concern of leaving them on the table.

Immediately after the discussion on the Baby Tenth, there followed this shorter exchange:

> MR. ALDRICH. I offer the following as an additional section:
>> "Sec.—The enumeration of the foregoing rights shall not be construed to impair or deny others retained by the people."
>
> MR. MORGAN. That is almost in the very language of the Constitution of the United States, which is in these words:
>> "The enumeration in the Constitution of certain rights shall not be construed to deny or disparage others retained by the people."
>
> The amendment was agreed to.[84]

(Remember, the "amendment was agreed to" by the Committee of the Whole. To be adopted by the convention would take another vote, which is discussed below.)

This last suggestion seems to have addressed Mr. Billings' concern. The pushback against the proposed Baby Tenth seems to have been an "anti-clutter" argument. It announced a completely accepted proposition (that the government has no power to exercise laws that violate the bill of rights, and that laws contrary to them and the constitution generally are void), which many felt was pointless to include. Further, the conversation between the sponsor, Delegate Billings, and Delegate Wilson indicates that the clause could be read to limit unenumerated rights, and therefore have the "contrary effect" to Billings' stated purpose of protecting unenumerated rights. It therefore seems unsurprising that the very next proposal was a Baby Ninth, to which there was no opposition. The transcript does not say whether the Baby Ninth was offered to answer Delegate Billings' statement about the need to "guard those unenumerated rights," but given the timing it seems to be the case.

The very next day the proposed bill of rights again came up for discussion, this time before the convention itself.[85] This exchange then followed concerning the very Baby Ninth the same delegates had just agreed to the day before:

> MR. SECOMBE. I think the language of that section should be slightly altered. I do not understand that the people are giving up any rights by declaring this Bill of Rights. The word "retain" was the

word used in the Constitution of the United States where the States did give up to the general government certain rights, and that word would be proper in case the people were giving up, by this bill, certain of their rights. I move to amend by striking out the word "retain" and insert the word "possessed."

• • •

MR. ALDRICH. It seems to me that the section is all right as it now stands. The object is to give a portion of the people's rights to the officers of the government, and to retain a portion. It strikes me that the word "retain" is a better word than "possess," and we certainly have some rights which we have not delegated to anybody, and which we will not delegate.

MR. SECOMBE. I do not understand that in this bill we delegate any of our rights to any person or body. We merely enunciate certain of the principal rights that we possess and we do not wish to have it understood by that enunciation, because we do not happen to mention certain others, that we have not got them.

MR. ALDRICH. We do not delegate them in the Bill of Rights, but we do in the Constitution before we get through.

The amendment to the section was not agreed to. [Meaning the substitution of the word "possess."]

MR. NORTH. I now hope the additional section will not be agreed to. It seems to me to be entirely unnecessary, to be meaningless, and that it can have no real force. In fact it amounts to nothing. In the Bill of Rights we simply set forth certain rights, but we do not propose to take any rights from anybody, and to say that the setting forth any rights we do not impair any rights we retain is surplusage and can have no effect in any manner. I do not think we should encumber our Bill of Rights with anything which does not have a direct, plain, and tangible meaning.

The amendment was not concurred in [meaning, the Baby Ninth failed].

Much could be unpacked from this exchange, but perhaps the most interesting is Delegate North's statement that "we do not propose to take any rights from anybody." From this statement, he seems to be arguing that the Minnesota Constitution does not take away anyone's rights.[86] Instead, the Bill of Rights "simply set[s] forth certain rights" but that does not mean other rights are not retained, that is, protected. Further, he argues that it would be surplusage to say the rights are retained. Again, therefore, as we had in previous debates, such as in Maryland, some delegates opposed a Baby Ninth *not* because it would be a "fountain" of judicially created rights of a dubious distinction, but because it was *not even needed* to protect unenumerated rights.

We will have more to say on this later, but this view probably strikes many readers as shocking. In modern times the general view is that constitutions do not protect rights unless they either are explicitly protected, or at least protected via an "etcetera clause," such as a Baby Ninth, due process clause, or some other language referring to unenumerated rights. In fact, the late Justice Antonin Scalia went so far as to say that there are rights the Ninth Amendment recognizes, but that judges are powerless to enforce them.[87] These nineteenth-century delegates turn that around; they agree that language similar to that of the Ninth Amendment recognizes rights, but that those rights are protected without it anyway. That is a very different view of the government's power to infringe on the rights of the people (or what those rights even are).

Court Cases on Baby Ninths Before the Civil War

Before we leave the story of Baby Ninths during the time before our country nearly split in two, we should take a look at what judges of that period were saying about these creatures. And it will not take long. That is because there were very few cases in the antebellum period that discussed Baby Ninths. Overall, the few cases that were handed down reflect the understanding of the delegates discussed above, including the delegates' differing interpretations of state powers. Thus, to the limited extent they provide a window into the antebellum understanding of Baby Ninths, they do reflect a consensus that Baby Ninths protected unenumerated individual rights. We will look at them now, and not in the later chapter about judicial attitudes to Baby Ninths after the Civil War. That is its own story, as it was when the judicial juices really started to flow (and, unfortunately at times, really started to become hostile to Baby Ninths).

By far the deepest treatment of a Baby Ninth in a judicial opinion before the Civil War is Alabama's *In re Dorsey* in 1838.[88] There, an applicant to the Alabama bar challenged a requirement that before being licensed he swear an oath that he had not previously engaged in a duel and would not do so in the future. Three different judges rendered opinions, and all three interpreted Alabama's combined Baby Ninth/Baby Tenth to protect individual rights.

First, Judge Goldthwaite stated that the enumerated rights in the state's Declaration of Rights are exceptions out of the general powers of state government. But, "as it was impossible, in the nature of things, to provide for every case of exception,—a general declaration was added, that the particular enumeration should not be construed to disparage or deny others retained by the people."[89] In other words, the Baby Ninth was an "etcetera clause" protecting rights that "it was impossible" to enumerate in full. And, in keeping with recognizing that the Alabama legislature had general, not enumerated, powers, Judge Goldthwaite went on to argue that the legislature was not "expressly prohibited" from enacting the oath requirement at issue in the case, but because the retroactive portion of the oath violated the state constitution's right to trial by jury, the oath requirement was unconstitutional.[90] Thus, Judge Goldthwaite did not invalidate the requirement via the Baby Ninth, but did state that the Baby Ninth protected rights of individuals (that is, rights like those actually enumerated in the state constitution).

Second, Judge Ormond began with a discussion of well-known natural rights opinions (or, at least what *he* viewed to be natural rights opinions), including Lord Coke's *Doctor Bonham's Case* and Justice Chase's opinion in *Calder v. Bull*.[91] He recognized the important question that these cases raised—whether courts have the power to declare laws invalid on the basis of natural principles of justice alone—but concluded that that question was academic in Alabama "because the people who formed the Constitution of Alabama, have provided by the organic law of the State, for the examination by the judiciary, of all laws having this tendency, whether expressly forbidden by the bill of rights or not."[92] By the last clause he meant the state's Baby Ninth, which he then went on to quote and examine, including the Baby Tenth portion. The clause, he argued, protected "any" rights, enumerated or not, and should be given a "large and liberal interpretation."[93] He then went on to examine various other portions of the Alabama Constitution, and concluded—without singling out one clause in particular—that the oath requirement was unconstitutional.[94]

Third, in his dissenting opinion, Chief Judge Collier concluded that the oath requirement was constitutional. In addressing the Baby Ninth claim, the Chief Judge argued that the Baby Tenth language indicated the state government had general powers not needing "express constitutional recognition."[95] It appears he thought this was Mr. Dorsey's argument—a powers, not a rights argument—and so did not address whether the provision protected Dorsey's right to practice law. Collier did, however, echoing Madison, also state that the clause "was doubtless inserted *ex majore cautela* [for greater caution]—lest it should be supposed that an article intended to embody certain fundamental rights of the citizen, should be construed as yielding up others, and throwing them into the general mass of governmental powers."[96] Thus, although not in the context of what he thought Dorsey's actual claim was, Collier did state that he thought the Baby Ninth/Baby Tenth protected unenumerated individual rights.

Therefore, all three judges, in addressing Alabama's Baby Ninth, concluded that it in some way protected unenumerated individual rights. They also believed that the state had general powers, not limited to enumerated powers, but that the rights in the bill of rights—including unenumerated rights—were exempted out of those general powers.

As helpful a case as *Dorsey* is to understanding the judiciary's views of Baby Ninths in the antebellum era, it unfortunately is by far the most helpful. A handful of other cases cite Baby Ninths but do so along with a number of other constitutional provisions and without any great elaboration on the Baby Ninth's meaning.

For example, in *Ex parte Martin*, the Arkansas Supreme Court considered whether the state's constitution mandated that just compensation be paid for the temporary flooding of land as part of a levee project.[97] Although the court considered the project a proper public use, the problem was that the legislature had not provided for compensation for affected landowners. Further, the state's constitution, unlike the U.S. Constitution and the constitutions of many other states, did not explicitly provide for just compensation for takings.[98] Thus, in this pre–Fourteenth Amendment case, the issue was whether anything else in the state constitution could provide compensation.

The *Martin* court took together the state's Lockean natural rights guarantee, Law of the Land Clause, *and* Baby Ninth, to "necessarily impl[y]" a just compensation requirement.[99] The court then reviewed several cases from other jurisdictions involving natural rights principles, including *Fletcher v. Peck*, the famous Contracts Clause case.[100] Unfortunately for our purposes, there was no further analysis of the Baby Ninth. In putting it together with the other clauses, however, the court clearly did invoke the Baby Ninth to demonstrate that the Arkansas Constitution protects individual rights other than those specifically enumerated in it.

In another case, *Billings v. Hall*, the California Supreme Court found an adverse possession statute unconstitutional, relying on, among other authorities, the state's Lockean natural rights guarantee.[101] A concurring justice also invoked the state's Baby Ninth, but only in conjunction with the Lockean natural rights guarantee.[102] This seems to indicate that at least for one justice, the content of the state's Baby Ninth was linked to the Lockean provision.[103]

And that is about all the case law on Baby Ninths there was for the antebellum period. From this very modest body of opinions we should hesitate to draw too much, but we definitely do see an understanding among these judges that Baby Ninths protected unenumerated individual rights. And because two cases concerned property rights and one the right to work in an occupation, the case law indicates that Baby Ninths were understood to protect economic liberty.

———————

On the eve of the Civil War, twelve states—(in order of appearance) Alabama, Maine, Arkansas, Rhode Island, New Jersey, Iowa, California, Ohio, Maryland, Minnesota, Oregon, and Kansas—had adopted Baby Ninths. What started as a couple of random experiments had turned into a trend. When the issue arose in constitutional conventions delegates debated not whether unenumerated rights should be protected, but whether Baby Ninths are even necessary to protect them. Just about everyone, if not everyone, who commented thought rights should be protected from government power in addition to those rights spelled out in constitutions. This consensus on open-ended constitutional language would only grow when the country was torn apart and stitched back together.

CHAPTER 3

Baby Ninths from the Civil War to Today

Baby Ninths were only getting started when Americans started fighting each other. During the Civil War, in constitutional conventions on both sides of the Confederacy's border, Americans kept adding unenumerated rights protections to their states' fundamental laws. And they kept on doing so during Reconstruction, and even after that. Through the rapid westward expansion of the late nineteenth and early twentieth centuries, constitutional framers again and again chose to include Baby Ninths in their handiwork. Further, this romance with Baby Ninths continued into the second half of the twentieth century, when many states redrafted those documents.

In this chapter we briefly explore this continued story of the growth of the popularity of Baby Ninths, beginning with the Civil War and continuing through the present. First we will see which states adopted Baby Ninths and when they did so, looking chronologically at different constitutional periods when different concerns animated the various constitutional drafters. Next, much as we did for the period before the Civil War, we will examine what delegates at constitutional conventions thought of these Baby Ninths. We will learn that one constant among these diverse states and Americans is that whatever else was buzzing around the nation at that moment, the framers kept working to protect unenumerated rights. And the further forward in time we go, the more Baby Ninth Amendments there are. By the end of their growth, when Illinois adopted a Baby Ninth in 1970, thirty-three states out of fifty had Baby

Ninths in their constitutions. At 66 percent of all states in the union, that is the highest ratio in U.S. history. No matter where you look in the timeline, Baby Ninths keep getting more popular.

The Civil War

Quite a number of states adopted constitutions in 1861. Their drafters had a lot of things on their minds, and Baby Ninth Amendments were fairly far down that list.

What was on their minds, of course, was secession and the protection of the institution of slavery. Of the eleven states that seceded from the Union in 1861, seven adopted new constitutions in that year. For the most part, those that already had Baby Ninths kept them, and those that lacked a provision did not add one. The exception was Georgia, which adopted the following language as article I, section 27 of its new constitution: "The enumeration of rights herein contained shall not be construed to deny to the people any inherent rights which they have hitherto enjoyed."[1]

Georgia's language was unique, as the reference to "inherent rights which they have hitherto enjoyed" is not found in any prior Baby Ninths. In contrast to other Baby Ninths, on its face it only applies to rights that existed prior to the constitution's adoption, and only rights that are "inherent." Are these different from "retained" rights that the Ninth Amendment and most other Baby Ninths refer to? "Retained" implies rights that already existed at the time the constitution was adopted. (If they did not, how could they be retained?) So perhaps in the end there is no meaningful distinction. This idiosyncratic language, with minor changes, is still found in Georgia's constitution of today. We will reflect more on the use of "inherent" and nonuse of "retained" in chapter 6, including the surrounding context of protecting slavery.

As for the other seceding states that adopted new constitutions, Alabama[2] and Arkansas[3] kept their Baby Ninths while Florida,[4] Louisiana,[5] South Carolina,[6] and Texas[7] did not adopt new ones.[8]

During the remainder of the war and in its immediate aftermath, a handful of non-Confederate states also adopted new constitutions. And as Union forces occupied Confederate states, some of those states held new constitutional conventions to reject their Confederate versions and recognize the supremacy of the Union and the abolition of slavery.[9] In these various conventions, a few Baby Ninths appeared.

West Virginia, Maryland, and Nevada all adopted new constitutions during the war. The Virginia counties that rejected secession and formed the new state of West Virginia did not adopt a Baby Ninth,[10] but neighboring Maryland kept its Baby Ninth.[11] Out west, the new state of Nevada held two constitutional conventions: one in 1863 and then another in 1864 after the territory's voters rejected the first constitution.[12] The Silver State included a Baby Ninth in each: "This enumeration of rights shall not be construed to impair or deny others retained by the people."[13] Missouri held a convention in early 1865, drafting what would be adopted as a new constitution, but did not include a Baby Ninth.[14]

Meanwhile, in 1864 both Arkansas and Louisiana, now largely in Union hands, adopted new constitutions. Arkansas once again kept its combined Baby Ninth/Baby Tenth without change,[15] and Louisiana once again did not include a Baby Ninth.[16] After the war drew to a close in 1865 more formerly rebellious states held conventions. Alabama kept its combined Baby Ninth/Baby Tenth without change,[17] while Florida[18] and South Carolina[19] drew up new constitutions that continued to not include a Baby Ninth. Georgia kept its new Baby Ninth from 1861, with minor changes in wording.[20]

Reconstruction

Constitutional conventions did not slow down with the close of the war. They were only getting started. The long and jagged process of ex-Confederate states being readmitted into the Union led to a flurry of constitutional drafting, the most intensive at any time in our history since the Founding Era. This was because of the Reconstruction Congress's directive that states had to, among other things, draft constitutions protecting suffrage for Black males and have those constitutions be ratified by a popular vote.[21] The constitutions the formerly Confederate states adopted in 1864 and 1865 were mostly considered to not qualify under these rules.[22] Thus, those states[23] went back to the drawing board to adopt the many constitutions ratified from 1867 to 1870.

In those "Black and Tan" conventions the various states obeyed Congress's orders and duly adopted new, compliant constitutions.[24] They also made, to varying degrees, other changes often made in constitutional conventions. Sometimes the changes were rather drastic, which is not surprising considering that many of the delegates were Union loyalists and Blacks.[25] This included the addition or deletion of Baby Ninths.

Alabama kept a Baby Ninth but dropped the Baby Tenth language that had accompanied it since 1819.[26] Arkansas deleted its combined Baby Ninth/Baby Tenth.[27] Florida added a Baby Ninth for the first time, and in the process deleted its Baby Tenth.[28] Georgia dropped its Baby Ninth.[29] Louisiana, however, added one.[30] Both North[31] and South Carolina[32] also did so. Closing out ex-Confederate states, Mississippi[33] and Virginia[34] also included new Baby Ninths, but Texas[35] and Tennessee[36] did not.

The end result of these mandated conventions, plus Tennessee (which technically did not need to adopt a new constitution under Congress's rules, but did anyway), is the deletion of a Baby Ninth by two states,[37] the adoption of new ones by six,[38] the keeping of a pre-existing Baby Ninth by one,[39] and the continued absence of one in two states.[40]

The surge in the use of Baby Ninths during Reconstruction—with six states adopting them for the first time—strongly indicates Baby Ninths were becoming a generally accepted tool for constitutional protection. Admittedly, that two states—Arkansas and Georgia—affirmatively took out Baby Ninths shows this was not universal.[41] But the trend is clear. It is also interesting to note that three ex-Confederate states dropped their Baby Tenths. Two of those did so while keeping a Baby Ninth (Alabama) or even adopting a new one (Florida). Perhaps this was because Baby Tenths were seen as being anti-Unionist, paralleling the Tenth Amendment itself? Although their texts do not mention, or even intimate, the federal government, it could be that anything reminding lawmakers of the Tenth Amendment (and its seeming limitations on federal power) was not a welcome reminder amid the work of Reconstruction.

We should note two other developments from the Reconstruction period. One was the admission into the Union of Nebraska, which included a Baby Ninth in its constitution.[42] The other was Maryland's retention of its Baby Ninth when it adopted a new constitution in 1867.[43] This means that by 1870, eighteen out of the thirty-seven states in the Union (including all ex-Confederate states), or just under half of all states, had Baby Ninths in their constitutions, the highest percentage up to that time.

The Gilded Age, 1870–1900

The roughly three decades after Reconstruction saw both the addition of many western states into the Union—along with their constitutions— and an avid interest of many established states in adopting new constitutions. During this period, states adopted twenty-five constitutions.[44] Of those, fifteen included Baby Ninths. Nine of these Baby Ninths were new. As of 1900, twenty-six states out of the forty-five in the Union, a solid majority, had Baby Ninths.

Constitution drafting remained very popular in the 1870s. In that decade, a few states redrafted their constitutions and did not adopt Baby Ninths: Illinois (1870),[45] West Virginia (1871),[46] Pennsylvania (1873),[47] and Texas (1876).[48] But these were in the minority. Colorado (1876) was admitted to the Union and included a Baby Ninth in its bill of rights.[49] The states of Alabama (1875),[50] Nebraska (1875),[51] California (1879),[52] and Louisiana (1879)[53] adopted new constitutions while keeping Baby Ninths. And Arkansas (1874),[54] Missouri (1875),[55] and Georgia (1877)[56] adopted new Baby Ninths. In fact, in the case of Arkansas and Georgia they *re*-adopted Baby Ninths, as their Reconstruction conventions had dropped prior versions.

The next decade witnessed the admission into the Union of a number of states after the razor-thin election of 1888.[57] A full six states were admitted in 1889 and 1890.[58] Four of them, Idaho,[59] Montana,[60] Washington State,[61] and Wyoming,[62] placed Baby Ninths in their new constitutions. Only North Dakota[63] and South Dakota[64] did not. Also, in 1886, Florida adopted a new constitution and kept its Baby Ninth.[65]

Convention delegates kept writing constitutions in the last decade of the century. In the 1890s, Mississippi[66] and Louisiana[67] kept their Baby Ninths, and the new state of Utah adopted one.[68] Kentucky[69] and Delaware[70] adopted new constitutions and did not add Baby Ninths, but each kept its pre-existing Baby Tenth. And in 1895, South Carolina mysteriously dropped its Baby Ninth,[71] even though it was included in committee drafts of the eventual declaration of rights during the convention.[72]

The Twentieth Century

The Gilded Age's enthusiasm for writing new constitutions kept going for a couple of decades into the twentieth century, but then finally petered out as states for the most part grew comfortable with their constitutions and Americans hit the challenges of depression and war. After World War II, however, constitution drafting had a bit of a renaissance, and this brought with it a continued enthusiasm for the adoption of Baby Ninths.

In the decade and a half before World War I, the states of Oklahoma,[73] Arizona,[74] and New Mexico[75] joined the Union.[76] All adopted

Baby Ninths. Meanwhile, Alabama,[77] Virginia,[78] and Louisiana[79] all held conventions and kept Baby Ninths in their new constitutions. Only Michigan adopted a revised constitution in this period and did not include a Baby Ninth in it.[80]

Louisiana held yet another constitutional convention in 1921, keeping its Baby Ninth.[81] But after that, no state adopted a new constitution until 1945.[82] That was the longest "drought" in constitutional adoption in American history before the current one, which has not seen a new constitution since Rhode Island's in 1986.[83] In fact, the 1930s—which, given the Great Depression, might have been thought to contain the seeds of tumultuous constitutional change at the state level—was the only decade before the 1990s to not witness any new state constitutions.[84]

When Americans turned their attention away from depression and war, however, they found that there was some constitution writing to be done. Georgia adopted a new constitution in 1945, keeping its Baby Ninth.[85] Missouri adopted its own new constitution in the same year, dropping the Baby Ninth it had added in 1875.[86] New Jersey, however, kept its Baby Ninth in its new constitution of 1947.[87]

Baby Ninths only got more popular in the second half of the century. The two new states of this period, Alaska[88] and Hawaii,[89] each put a Baby Ninth in their constitutions. Then, in the 1960s and 1970s a number of states rewrote their constitutions. When Michigan did so in 1963, it adopted a Baby Ninth for the first time.[90] Connecticut did not add one in 1965,[91] but Florida kept its in 1968.[92] Pennsylvania also adopted a new constitution in 1968, not adding a Baby Ninth, but keeping its Baby Tenth.[93] Then, in the 1970s a few more states adopted new constitutions. Illinois added a Baby Ninth in 1970,[94] while North Carolina[95] and Virginia[96] kept theirs in 1971. Montana kept its in 1972,[97] as did Louisiana in 1974,[98] Georgia in 1976[99] and again in 1983,[100] and Rhode Island in 1986, the last state as of this writing to adopt a new constitution.[101]

This leaves us today with thirty-three states out of fifty with a Baby Ninth. At 66 percent, that is the highest percentage in history of states in the Union having a Baby Ninth. Baby Ninths are more popular than ever before.

What the Delegates Said

As we saw in the previous chapter, of the many constitutional conventions that produced Baby Ninths before the Civil War, only four recorded substantive remarks about Baby Ninths.[102] For the period since that time the story is much the same. Only in the records of the conventions of Missouri (both 1875 and 1945), Virginia (1902), New Jersey (1947), Hawaii (1950), Michigan (1963), Illinois (1970), and Montana (1972) has the research for this book found anything substantive about what the delegates thought of their various Baby Ninths, and even then the comments were generally short. All in all, however, these comments demonstrate what the comments made before the Civil War demonstrated: that delegates believed Baby Ninths protected citizens' unenumerated rights and that—for the most part, but not exclusively—they believed those rights were individual rights.[103]

A couple of conventions thought a Baby Ninth hardly needed explanation at all because the provision's meaning was obvious. In the Hawaii convention of 1950 the Committee of the Whole reported the following about the proposed Baby Ninth: "Your Committee recommends the adoption of this section, which is self-explanatory."[104]

The Montana convention of 1972 was not too much more detailed, when one delegate stated:

> Mr. Chairman. I move that when this committee does arise and report, after having under consideration [the Baby Ninth], that it recommend the same be adopted. Mr. Chairman, this provision is the same as the one we had in our last–in our present Bill of Rights, Section 30, and it's also contained in the federal Bill of Rights. I think that it is completely self-explanatory. There are rights which are not enumerated which the people of Montana should not be denied. Thank you.[105]

To this Montana delegate, and the committee in Hawaii, Baby Ninths mean what they say: there are rights beyond those in the Bill of Rights, and they should not be denied just because they are not enumerated in the constitution. That is essentially what Professor Randy Barnett has argued about the Ninth Amendment itself.[106] There is no hidden "Straussian" meaning to be discerned; they mean what they say.

One other tidbit should be pointed out in the Montana delegate's remarks, though. He said, "There are rights which are not enumerated which the people of Montana *should not be denied.*" That last clause makes clear not just that the Baby Ninth means that there are rights in addition to those enumerated, but that those rights must be protected. That, of course, would include judicial protection, just as it does for enumerated rights.

A few other discussions of Baby Ninths added a bit more than these "self-explanatory" comments but arrived at the same conclusion on the provisions' meaning. In Missouri's 1875 convention, a delegate stated that the Baby Ninth "declares that while we have set out and enumerated certain specified rights as belonging to the people, the fact that we have declared that they possess those rights is not construed to mean that they do not possess other rights also retained by the people."[107]

A slightly different view of Baby Ninths is not that their meaning is obvious, but that they are superfluous because a bill of rights would not be read to deny unenumerated rights in the first place. This is the "minority view" of Baby Ninths during the antebellum period, discussed in the previous chapter. Under this view, a Baby Ninth is unneeded because, in effect, a Baby Ninth is already an "unwritten" part of the state's constitution.

A drafter of a committee report articulated this view at the 1902 Virginia constitutional convention. After quoting the proposed Baby Ninth's language, which was from the state's prior constitution, he said:

> I do not think they [the "rights enumerated"] would probably be construed in that way. I think the section is possibly one which the Bill of Rights would have been as strong without, but we found it there and we deemed it best to follow as far as possible the landmarks where they did not interfere with our ideas of what really was the true theory of our State government.[108]

Thus the delegate thought the Baby Ninth was not needed as a "savings clause" but included it anyway out of a sense of tradition.

In 1945, Missouri removed its Baby Ninth seventy years after adopting it. The reason given was similar to that voiced in Virginia in 1902. After it was left out of an initial draft, one delegate recommended reinserting the former Baby Ninth. He said that under the provision, "this previous enumeration of private rights are not necessarily all the rights to which the citizen is entitled to have protection in. We don't know what question of rights may arise sometime. Just because it has been left out of the Bill of Rights that doesn't mean that he is still entitled to that protection."[109]

To this explanation, one Missouri delegate answered, "Well, isn't that law anyway?"[110] By this, he and other objecting delegates meant that they considered unenumerated rights to be protected whether or not the Baby Ninth's language was included. One delegate even called the

Baby Ninth a "shot gun" clause, that is, a clause that spews out rights left out elsewhere.[111] Thus, this view was similar to the "minority view" from before the Civil War: Baby Ninths were not necessary because unenumerated rights were already constitutionally protected.

But this view continued to be in the minority. New Jersey's 1947 convention referred to the Baby Ninth on a couple of occasions to allay fears that the inclusion of some rights would defeat others. In a discussion of whether to include an antidiscrimination provision that specifically banned discrimination in the militia and public schools, one delegate stated:

> [T]here has been some fear that the enumeration of the two rights, the [freedom from discrimination in the] militia and the public schools, would impair the usefulness of the amendment which I have submitted. But we take care of that in paragraph 20: "This enumeration of rights and privileges shall not be construed to impair or deny others retained by the people." The enumeration—just by mentioning the militia and the public schools—does not impair other rights, as practically all members of the legal profession know.[112]

Thus the delegate here argued that just because the right to be free from discrimination in the militia and public schools is protected does not mean other rights, whatever they are, that are not mentioned are not also protected.[113]

New Jersey's 1947 convention also gave a hint at a different reading of its Baby Ninth. At one point, a New Jersey delegate was engaged in an effort to remove a reference to the right to collective bargaining, and he defended his effort by arguing that because of the Baby Ninth, the fact that the reference to collective bargaining was not in the constitution would not imply that the right was not protected.[114] Collective bargaining, of course, is not an individual right, but a collective and positive right[115] held by workers and against employers. If workers have a right to collectively bargain, that means employers are limited, in at least some regards, in their right to contract. Thus, this is a hint, however slight, that some people in 1947 may have perceived the Baby Ninth as protecting not just individual rights, but some kind of collective right as well.

Michigan did not adopt a Baby Ninth until its 1963 constitutional convention.[116] Its delegates had a few things to say about it, and in a new way not seen earlier in other conventions. First, the relevant committee's comment on the proposal was as follows:

This language is taken from the ninth amendment to the Constitution of the United States. The committee believes that its incorporation in the Michigan constitution will set up a sound state parallel. The language recognizes that no bill of rights can ever enumerate or guarantee all the rights of the people and that liberty under law is an ever growing and ever changing conception of a living society developing in a system of ordered liberty.[117]

Later on, one of the delegates said in support:

I think most of you will recognize—if you don't recognize, you should—that this is taken from the federal constitution. The enumeration of these rights shall not be construed to disparage others retained by the people. This is for perhaps 2 reasons. First, we cannot anticipate in any declaration or bill of rights all of the things which perhaps should be said. Second, we do not intend that the statements that we have made here as to the rights of our people shall be limited by the fact that we did not state something which has always been considered such a right.[118]

These comments make two important points. First, they echo Founding-Era conceptions of rights used to support the Ninth Amendment, which apply with at least equal, if not greater, force to Baby Ninths: that rights, by their nature, are not capable of being comprehensively enumerated, and therefore an "etcetera clause" is a way of protecting those rights not included. Second, these comments raise another idea: the rights the Baby Ninth protects are not necessarily the same at any one time. Because "liberty under law is an ever growing and ever changing conception of a living society," new rights may arise in the future, or at least be *recognized* in the future, that are not protected today.[119]

Whether these comments imply something like a "living constitutionalism" understanding of Michigan's Baby Ninth is unclear. Just because new rights arise in the future does not necessarily entail that the *meaning* of the Baby Ninth changes. Rather, the world changes and therefore the Baby Ninth applies to additional things. (For example, a right to be free from online censorship would have made no sense in 1900, but it makes perfect sense today.) But this is a slightly different understanding from earlier explanations of Baby Ninths, which seem to assume the rights that are protected are rights that were protected at the time the relevant constitution was adopted.[120] Indeed, as we discussed earlier, the word "retained" seems to imply that the rights a Baby Ninth protects are those the people possessed at the time the relevant constitution was adopted. If the "ever changing conception" of our society creates new protected rights that were not protected before, that stands in tension with the rights being "retained" ones. We will more fully explore the meaning of "retained" in chapter 6.

The state convention with some of the most commentary on a Baby Ninth is from the state that most recently adopted a new one: Illinois. In that state's 1970 constitutional convention, the Committee on Bill of Rights stated the following on what the provision's purpose was:

> This provision gives explicit recognition to the principle that the Bill of Rights is not an exhaustive catalog of a citizen's rights and immunities in respect to government action. The language is the same as the Ninth Amendment to the United States Constitution, except that "people" has been replaced by "individual citizens of this State."[121]

The drafters of the provision also stated that "[t]his new section acknowledges that the people have many rights that are not mentioned in this constitution. It states that these rights are not denied even though they are not enumerated."[122]

Both of these statements are fairly standard for the commentary we have seen on Baby Ninths so far. Essentially, they assert that "it means what it says." But the primary endorser of the provision, Delegate Pechous, had a more idiosyncratic view that is worth quoting at length:

> Mr. President, Chairman Gertz, and fellow delegates, it is my pleasure to present what I consider the least controversial section of the bill of rights. . . .
>
> This particular language was extracted by myself from the State of Washington Constitution, and it's identical also to the Ninth Amendment to the United States Constitution except for the following: Instead of the reference to the "retained by the people" in the Ninth Amendment, this particular section retains the rights to "the individual citizens of this state." And there is not a great deal of law in this particular section. . . .
>
> The concept of the Ninth Amendment language and what I would hope that this particular language would do for the state of Illinois would be that it would have no negative implication, and it could only have a possible positive implication in the future. And I think—at

least I tried to sell the committee on the idea—that when we consider the concept of dual sovereignty where an individual citizen is both a citizen of the United States and he is also a citizen of the state of Illinois and considering the relationship of the state sovereign to the federal sovereign, I think that this particular language could estab-lish—or re-establish—some concept of state sovereignty that has been eroded by federal action in the past.

It is the—as the report says, this particular language gives explicit recognition to the principle that though a number of rights are enu-merated and set out in the bill of rights that by no means is that to be construed as an exhaustive catalog or a maximum of the rights involved. Any rights that are not individually set out are still retained by the individual citizens of this state, so in the future, for instance, any question that might arise as to whether a particular matter is— falls within the state jurisdiction or if it is a federal question under the United States Constitution and governed by the supremacy clause, this particular section would set some guideline for retaining a right to the people of the state of Illinois—that is, the individual citizen— even though it is not set out and enumerated at some other point in the constitution.

The law that I have—I have one case on the application of the Ninth Amendment, and that is *Griswald* [*sic*] *v. the State of Kentucky— Connecticut,* pardon me. It is a 1965 United States Supreme Court case wherein the person, *Griswald* [*sic*], was arrested for disseminating birth control information to married couples, and it was asserted in the argument before the Supreme Court that even though there is no explicit recognition of the right of privacy in a marital state, that is a right so fundamental and so basic to a free society and free individu-als that it is inherent and recognized in the Ninth Amendment which says that even though the right is not set out that it is, in fact, retained. So that was the biggest case on the federal level.[123]

What Delegate Pechous was discussing here is a bit mysterious. He seemed to be arguing that the Baby Ninth would protect the state, or at least its individual citizens, from the federal government. That is simply not true given the U.S. Constitution's Supremacy Clause, a clause he himself acknowledges in these remarks.[124] This is a basic tenet of con-stitutional law that he seemed to be missing: state constitutions do not change the application of federal law in overriding state law depending on how they are written. And he did not seem to be making a collective rights or "states rights" argument, as he acknowledged that the text of the Baby Ninth applies only to "the individual citizen."[125] Thus this argument is a bit befuddling.[126]

It should be noted that he did accurately summarize the discussion of the Ninth Amendment in *Griswold v. Connecticut*, the seminal case about an unenumerated right to contraception we discussed in chapter 1. (Although he failed to say that it was only Justice Goldberg's three-justice concurrence that relied on the Ninth Amendment.)[127] Therefore, in invoking *Griswold* Pechous seemed to believe that the Baby Ninth language applies to individual rights.

So what to make of Pechous's speech? No one else spoke about the Illinois Baby Ninth, so this and the committee report is all we have to go on regarding what the delegates thought about it.[128] Although the particulars of some of what Pechous said are unsupportable, perhaps the charitable interpretation is that he saw the Baby Ninth as protecting both individual and collective rights, of some sort or another. How the collective rights would work is unclear, although, as explained in the next chapter, some courts over the years have tried to give Baby Ninths a collective rights meaning. But his invocation of *Griswold* indicates he was generally on board with the "standard" interpretation of Baby Ninths: they mean what they say. In doing so, he certainly seemed to think that Baby Ninths actively protect rights and that future litigants against the government could use this provision to have its power declared unconstitutional.

———

We have now breezed through almost two hundred years of Americans putting Baby Ninths in their own constitutions. From humble beginnings in Alabama and Maine, the practice spread to two-thirds of the states. Along the way we have heard from some of the Americans who inserted those clauses in their constitutions. And of those whose voices are recorded, they uniformly either thought Baby Ninths protect additional rights to just those enumerated in their constitutions, or, at the worst, were unnecessary because those rights were protected *anyway*. A few of those delegates were ambiguous, but none of them stated that the unenumerated rights Baby Ninths reference are *not* protected. And, given the plain meaning of Baby Ninths, this should not be surprising.

Yet we shall see that for the people whose job it is to actually protect rights when the government threatens them—judges—the plain meaning of Baby Ninths was anything but plain. Or, in some cases, was all *too* plain and therefore not to be enforced.

CHAPTER 4

Judges (Mostly) Haven't Agreed

In chapter 5 we will get down to brass tacks: What do Baby Ninths mean? How should they protect those important, unenumerated liberties we talked about in the introduction: the rights to raise our children, work an honest living, and collect stamps? But first we should see how the actual bodies that protect rights, at least in modern-day America—the courts—have interpreted Baby Ninths in the past. With this background we can better see (we hope) how Baby Ninths should be interpreted in the future.

And unlike in the antebellum period, when (as we saw in chapter 2) there were only a handful of cases interpreting Baby Ninths in any meaningful way, since 1860 the country has seen a fair amount of jurisprudence on Baby Ninths. We can only say "fair amount," though, because for provisions that are in two-thirds of all state constitutions and whose language potentially protects all kinds of regulated behavior, there is not nearly as much case law as one would expect. That being said, there is enough that we can say a few things about what judges think of Baby Ninths. Here we will not examine every case, but merely outline the various approaches courts have taken. We will see that while some courts have, at least at times, taken Baby Ninths seriously, for the most part they have not. When faced with the text their fellow citizens have drafted and ratified, judges have generally not taken those citizens' handiwork seriously and instead have looked the other way.

By and large, courts actually interpreting Baby Ninths have taken two approaches. One is to read them, in one way or another, as clauses applying to unenumerated individual rights.[1] That does not mean, however, that they are meaningfully used to protect those rights. Under this umbrella, questions such as what those rights are, how numerous they are, and what burden is placed on the government when it wants to infringe on those rights, receive various answers. And usually those answers mean that the level of protection individual rights receive is nominal. Thus courts often find Baby Ninths protect individual rights, but not all that much.

The other approach courts have taken is to say that Baby Ninths protect collective rights, that is, essentially, the right of the people to collectively govern themselves. As we have seen, and will examine more deeply in the next chapter, at the state level this is a nonsensical position to take. "The people," through the legislature, would have that power even if the Baby Ninth were not included in the first place, rendering it superfluous at best. Yet this view has cropped up at times in various state courts. The collective rights position has also sometimes arisen in the context of local government versus state government, and in that case, there is a little more justification for it (but only a little). Later we will take a brief look as to why that might be.

What follows is a survey of the various interpretations of Baby Ninths that courts have rendered. The interpretations vary in a number of ways, geographically and also temporally. It will not be surprising that most of the Baby Ninth cases protecting property rights, for example, are from prior to the New Deal, back when courts were more serious about protecting property rights under various constitutional provisions. Nor should it be surprising that most cases protecting what are today called "personal liberties" are from the past few decades. The interpretations of Baby Ninths have ebbed and flowed just as the interpretations of other constitutional provisions—including due process clauses, privileges or immunities clauses, and Lockean natural rights guarantees—have ebbed and flowed. But, unfortunately, there has been more ebb than flow.

Another point to keep in mind is that many Baby Ninth cases not only follow the larger judicial milieu of that time on what rights receive stronger protections than others and what level of scrutiny applies, but also often include other constitutional provisions in their analysis. A common tactic is a "grab bag" of sorts where the court cites the Baby Ninth but also cites a due process clause and other clauses of both the state constitution and the U.S. Constitution and then determines if the right in question is protected by them. These are less valuable, of course, as a resource on what Baby Ninths mean, as there is often little or no discussion about the Baby Ninth specifically. "Pure" Baby Ninth cases are more rare, but not unheard of. In the following, most will be cases that specifically addressed the relevant Baby Ninth itself. In any case, what *should* be different about Baby Ninths, because of the obviously different meaning their words hold, does not often translate into judges interpreting them differently from these other clauses.

Finally, a word about perspective. If someone read nothing on unenumerated rights other than this chapter, they would leave with the impression that Baby Ninths come up a lot in those kinds of cases. But that would be incorrect. There are oceans of cases involving unenumerated rights of some kind in states with Baby Ninths where Baby Ninths never come up. Due process clauses and equal protection clauses abound. For example, in Illinois since the 1970 constitution was adopted the Baby Ninth has been quoted *once* by a state appellate court, but those same courts have mentioned "substantive due process" literally *hundreds* of times.[2] For whatever reason, probably because it is in their comfort zone, state courts and the lawyers arguing to them use less-suited provisions, such as due process clauses, to evaluate unenumerated rights more than they use Baby Ninths. This is true both when courts find the government to be violating a right and when the court finds the argument to fail. We will not be discussing those cases here, as this book is not about state constitutional protection of unenumerated rights generally. But understanding that these cases exist is important. The main failure of judges (and lawyers) in enforcing Baby Ninths is not that they do not take Baby Ninths seriously when they interpret them (although that is often true). It is that Baby Ninths are not interpreted *at all* when unenumerated rights are at issue.

A Case Study in 1860s Iowa

Some of the earliest post-1860 cases on Baby Ninths come out of Iowa. In a series of opinions from 1862 through 1870 the justices of its Supreme Court jostled on how to interpret the state's Baby Ninth. They eventually concluded that the clause offers almost no protection, but along the way they demonstrated two polar-opposite views on what it means. Examining these cases in some detail will give us a preview of how courts interpreted Baby Ninths in later eras, and more broadly how they thought about unenumerated rights in general.

The first, *State ex rel. Burlington & M.R.R. Co. v. County of Wapello*,[3] is one of the fullest examinations of a Baby Ninth in any judicial opinion. The 1862 case concerned a challenge to a state law requiring counties to purchase railway stock.[4] In concluding that the law was unconstitutional because it forced taxpayers to become stock owners against their will, it primarily relied on what it called the "saving clause" of the Iowa Constitution, that is, the Baby Ninth.[5] The court raised the common idea that state legislatures have all powers not denied to them in a state constitution.[6] But it expressly said that the Iowa Constitution was different because of the Baby Ninth:

> The Constitution of Iowa seems to have been written upon entirely a different theory, and utters quite another language, the words of which must furnish the only criterion by which we are to determine the rightful exercise of a given power. . . .
>
> The object of this saving clause, we suppose, was to guard not only against the above construction given to bills of right, not containing any such reservation, but to bring these unenumerated rights retained by the people, founded equally, it may be, upon natural justice and common reason, as those that are specified within the censorship of courts of justice, when even they shall be assailed.[7]

The most striking thing about this language is not just that it interprets the Baby Ninth as protecting unenumerated rights, but that it finds the Baby Ninth to put unenumerated rights on equal footing with the rest of the state constitution. That is, of course, what the language of any Baby Ninth seems to say. But this opinion takes that at face value. We will see this is by no means always the case.

The Iowa court returned to its Baby Ninth a few years later in *Hanson v. Vernon*.[8] There, following the *County of Wapello* case, the majority relied upon a number of provisions in striking down a similar railway stock law, and it only included a passing reference to the Baby Ninth.[9] But it is an exchange between a concurrence and the dissent where things get interesting for our purposes.

First, in his concurrence, Justice Joseph M. Beck saw the Baby Ninth as so important that he termed it "an *unwritten Constitution*."[10] His sweeping defense of Baby Ninths is worth quoting at length:

> It cannot be maintained that the Constitution confers upon the State government absolute and unlimited legislative power, authorizing all laws affecting the rights and property of the people, not expressly

prohibited by that instrument. The people, in the formation of the Constitution, wisely reserved to themselves all rights unimpaired over which power is not delegated to the State government. Section 25 of the bill of rights provides that the enumeration of rights contained in the Constitution shall not be construed to impair or deny others retained by the people. There is, as it were, back of the written Constitution, an *unwritten Constitution*, if I may use the expression, which guarantees and well protects all the absolute rights of the people. The government can exercise no power to impair or deny them. Many of them may not be enumerated in the Constitution, nor preserved by express provisions thereof, notwithstanding they exist and are possessed by the people, free from governmental interference. The rights of property, and rights arising under the domestic relations of husband and wife, parent and child, &c., may not be preserved by express constitutional provisions, yet they exist in all their perfection, and no legislative enactment impairing them can be sustained.[11]

Second, the dissenting justice, Justice Chester C. Cole, had a very different take on the Baby Ninth. Among other things, the phrase "unwritten constitution" was not to his liking. His opinion is worth quoting at length as well, because it touches upon a deep objection to Baby Ninths that recurs up to the present day:

For myself, I think that this section of the Constitution does not provide or establish any additional or further limitation upon the legislative power. And, indeed, I think that if this section had been omitted entirely from the Constitution the fact it declares would have had just as potential an existence as it now has. In other words, that by a uniform rule of interpreting constitutions, they are construed as not denying or impairing rights retained by the people other than those enumerated in them.

But I deny, most confidently, that, under this provision, whether expressed or implied, courts of law may rightfully declare an act of the legislature unconstitutional and void, as being in conflict with it. To so hold, is to place the legislative department at the feet of the judicial, and to render the immediate representatives of the people powerless to protect them in their rights, or from the encroachments of judicial power. If the views of the majority are sound, then it is certainly true, that our Constitution does not define the powers of the respective departments of our government, but leaves them to the necessarily uncertain, and everchanging measurement of *judicial discretion*. And this, I think, fairly illustrates the two fundamental errors of the majority: First, in supposing that there is an unwritten Constitution by which courts may measure the legislative power; and second, in supposing that the courts are the only protectors, though not in any just sense the representatives, of the people; that the people must look to the courts and not to the legislature to relieve them from actual or supposed unwise legislation. It is well settled that a statute cannot be declared void on the ground of its violating fundamental principles of republican government, when it does not come in conflict with written constitutional provisions.[12]

The disagreement between these men comes down to a stark contrast: Justice Beck says the Baby Ninth is meaningful and requires judicial protection of rights, while Justice Cole says the Baby Ninth is superfluous and does not require judicial protection of rights because otherwise it would upend republican government. Justice Cole's conclusion is similar to Justice Scalia's remarks on the Ninth Amendment in *Troxel v. Granville*, where he concluded that the amendment did indeed refer to unenumerated rights, but that he, as a judge, was powerless to protect them.[13] Essentially, Justice Cole seems to understand what the Baby Ninth is trying to do and it scares the dickens out of him.

The holdings of *Hanson* and *County of Wapello* were not to last long. With new justices on the court, in 1870, the very next year, it reversed *Hanson* and held a modified, but similar, law constitutional.[14] There the court heavily relied on a doctrine of judicial restraint,[15] admonishing courts to uphold a law's constitutionality unless it is a "*plain, clear and palpable* violation of the *written* constitution."[16] But even that was not enough to distinguish *Hanson*, so the court also reinterpreted the Baby Ninth to give it a collective rights meaning.[17] It inquired what rights were "retained by the people," as the Baby Ninth says.[18] And it concluded that those were legislative rights, which, through certain provisions in the constitution, the people have collectively delegated in toto to the general assembly.[19] Thus the right that the Baby Ninth protects is the right to legislate via the state legislature.

As we shall see in the next chapter, this interpretation of a Baby Ninth makes no sense and truly does render it worthless. Among other reasons, the legislature already has legislative power without the Baby Ninth obliquely protecting that power. But in any case, this interpretation got the job done for the court majority in 1870 Iowa.[20]

Justice Beck, who was still on the court, dissented and pointed out that this reading of the Baby Ninth "totally destroys its force and effect."[21] He explained that the Iowa Bill of Rights "secures private as well as political rights, and that section 25 plainly implies that the people retain others beside those enumerated."[22] Thus, Justice Beck saw room in the Baby Ninth for both personal rights, such as property rights, and certain political rights, such as, presumably, a right to vote. He insisted, however, that those political rights cannot deny the personal rights, which the "right" to legislate could, of course, threaten to do.

After these early cases, reliance on Iowa's Baby Ninth largely dropped out of the state's jurisprudence. But the extreme, collective rights view has not held. Instead, the state supreme court's most recent articulation is that the Baby Ninth does protect unenumerated rights and that they are judicially enforceable, but those rights are only violated if the government action is "unreasonable."[23] This waters down its protection to a level far below other rights, even other unenumerated rights protected by due process (such as parental rights), that receive a higher level of scrutiny.[24] Thus Iowa's Baby Ninth is recognized as protecting unenumerated individual rights, but not in any meaningful way. Indeed, in a way where the enumeration of rights seems to "impair or deny others, retained by the people."

Early Uses of Baby Ninths to Protect Property Rights and Economic Liberties

A scattering of cases from the late nineteenth and early twentieth centuries relied on Baby Ninths to protect property rights and economic liberties, or at least recognized that a Baby Ninth protected them in principle, if not in the case at hand. These decisions came amidst a much larger corpus of jurisprudence concerning similar issues but under other constitutional provisions, including due process clauses and contract clauses. Therefore, the cases we will look at here are not evidence that Baby Ninths were broadly used to protect economic liberties and property rights during this time. But they do show that state courts sometimes turned to Baby Ninths instead of the more commonly known devices.

Coster v. Tide Water Co. was an 1866 New Jersey lower court case reviewing a law that required property owners to allow improvements on their land by a politically connected developer.[25] The court issued an injunction to stop the proceeding, holding that the law violated various constitutional provisions, including the Baby Ninth. It grouped the Baby Ninth with the state constitution's Lockean natural rights guarantee and stated that the two in tandem "show[] that the right of private property was made sacred by the constitution, to be invaded by no one, not even the legislative power, except where such control was expressly given by that instrument."[26]

With a similar use of Washington's Baby Ninth, in 1898 that state's supreme court held a restriction on mortgage foreclosures to be unconstitutional. In emphasizing that rights pre-exist the state and its constitution, it explained that "[a]s if to emphasize this principle, our constitution (section 30, art. 1) declares that 'the enumeration in this constitution of certain rights shall not be construed to deny others retained by the people.'"[27] A few years later, in 1902, the same court upheld an inheritance tax, but along the way recognized the Baby Ninth "is apparently the expression that the declaration of certain fundamental rights belonging to all individuals and made in the bill of rights shall not be construed to mean the abandonment of others not expressed, which inherently exist in all civilized and free states."[28] Among those rights were "[t]he right to hold property by use and acquire by labor or occupancy."[29]

These uses of Baby Ninths to recognize protection of unenumerated individual rights continued in 1908 in *State v. Williams*, where the North Carolina Supreme Court found a prohibition on importing liquor into a dry county for the possessor's private use to be unconstitutional.[30] The court relied on the Baby Ninth for the proposition that the "government should not by construction, implication, or otherwise deprive them of unenumerated, but 'inalienable, rights.'"[31] Likewise, in 1932 the Supreme Court of Oregon invalidated a zoning ordinance that forbade the local Catholic Archdiocese from opening a school.[32] The court found the right to own property "an inherent right" and protected by the state's Baby Ninth, because in crafting the provision, the constitution's drafters "covered the matter of inherent rights of the individual."[33]

A notable tying of a Baby Ninth to the wider jurisprudence of unenumerated rights came in 1937 in *City of Mobile v. Rouse*,[34] where the Alabama Supreme Court struck down a price-fixing law for barbers. The court cited Alabama's Baby Ninth and linked it to a famous passage from the U.S. Supreme Court's educational choice and substantive due process case, *Meyer v. Nebraska*, stating that liberty includes "'the right of the individual to contract, to engage in any of the common occupations of life,'" and to pursue a number of personal rights as well.[35] The use of *Meyer* is a bit surprising given that the U.S. Supreme Court's ruling was based on the Due Process Clause of the Fourteenth Amendment, while, on the contrary, the Alabama court did not rely on a due process clause in the state's constitution, but only on the Baby Ninth. This demonstrates an openness—never fully realized in Alabama or anywhere else—to use Baby Ninths to be the primary guardian of "core" unenumerated rights, such as those spelled out in *Meyer*, and not the less textual fit of a due process clause.

One of the last cases involving economic liberty or property rights from this period is the 1944 opinion *Thiede v. Town of Scandia Valley*.[36] *Thiede* provides one of the most poetic invocations of a Baby Ninth. In a case the court itself declared "reads like a sequel to Steinbeck's 'The Grapes of Wrath,'" it found the forcible removal of a family from their home to violate Magna Carta's protection of the homestead, which was in turn protected by Minnesota's Baby Ninth.[37]

After the close of the New Deal and World War II, cases tying Baby Ninths to economic liberties and property rights became more and more infrequent. A handful of later cases cite a Baby Ninth in addition to other provisions when striking down an economic regulation,[38] and there is at least one exception to this trend: where, in 1975, the Michigan Supreme Court struck down an exclusionary zoning rule as violating the Baby Ninth's protection of low-cost housing.[39] But for the most part, Baby Ninths have not been used since the New Deal era to strike down economic regulations or property restrictions.[40] Where Baby Ninths have been used, however, are in the areas of non-economic personal rights and criminal procedure, which we turn to now.

Personal Liberties

Baby Ninths speak broadly of "other" rights "retained by the people," not simply economic, personal, or procedural rights. So it should be no surprise that substantive and procedural, economic and non-economic liberties have been protected through Baby Ninths. The following gives a brief overview of how courts have recognized non-economic personal rights and also rights of criminal procedure.

One non-economic right continually recognized in American jurisprudence is the right of parents to direct the upbringing of their children.[41] This right is almost unique in modern constitutional law. It is completely unenumerated; neither the U.S. Constitution nor any state constitution explicitly protects it. Yet it enjoys support across the ideological spectrum. About the only right that compares is the right to travel, which also is widely unenumerated and widely respected and often protected. In the most important case at the U.S. Supreme Court in recent times that concerned parental rights, *Troxel v. Granville*, only one justice out of nine stated that the right is not protected by the Constitution.[42] And as recently as 2020, a number of conservative justices who otherwise are extremely dismissive of rights protected by "substantive due process" affirmed the right of parents to direct the education of their children, citing the case *Pierce v. Society of Sisters*, mentioned in our introduction, which relied upon a substantive reading of the Fourteenth Amendment's Due Process Clause.[43]

Therefore, because of its "bipartisan" nature, it may not be surprising that one of the rights most protected in recent years via Baby Ninth Amendments, although still infrequently, is the right of parents to raise their children. Although generally found to reside in other constitutional provisions, such as federal or state due process clauses, a few courts have protected this right via a Baby Ninth. And, interestingly, it seems to have picked up steam in recent years.

Going back to 1957, the Idaho Supreme Court recognized the right when it concluded that "the rights accorded to parenthood before the constitution was adopted" were rights "retained by the people" according to the state's Baby Ninth.[44] That case concerned a petition by a group of parents to move their neighborhood from one school district to another via a statutory process, but the underlying right of the parents to direct their children factored into how to view the request. The Utah Supreme Court used its Baby Ninth in a family law case in 1982.[45] There the legislature had made it easier for the state to terminate a parent's rights, and a mother of a four-year-old challenged the new standard in a termination proceeding. The court cited a number of provisions in stating that the right at issue was fundamental and constitutionally protected, including the Ninth Amendment itself. But it included the state's Baby Ninth in this mix also. This was then followed up by the Utah intermediate appellate court a few years later, quoting the previous case's language involving the Baby Ninth in upholding the right of an unmarried father to have access to his child.[46] In 1997 Minnesota's intermediate appellate court found the right to establish a home, a right related to the right of parents to raise their children, to be protected by the state's Baby Ninth. The case concerned whether an individual could be forcibly moved out of their home by a conservator.[47]

Louisiana's Supreme Court addressed the issue of adoption and the rights of unwed fathers in an interesting 1990 case, *In re Adoption of B.G.S.*[48] There, a juvenile woman gave birth and failed to list the nineteen-year-old unmarried father on the birth certificate. She gave up the child for adoption without telling the father, but the father found out and sought custody. The court found that it was unconstitutional for the state to fail to give notice to unwed fathers in the adoption proceedings, relying primarily upon the well-established due process cases emphasizing the right to raise one's child. The court went a step further, however, and invoked the state constitution, stating that in past cases "we have implicitly recognized that the reciprocal rights and obligations of natural parents and children are among those unenumerated rights retained by individuals pursuant to" Louisiana's Baby Ninth.[49]

Although these kinds of cases, addressing parental rights and invoking a Baby Ninth along with the other usual constitutional provisions, have been spotty in their frequency, there has been an interesting recent series of invocations of the Baby Ninth by one appellate judge in Georgia, Judge Stephen Dillard of the Georgia Court of Appeals.[50] In a number of cases upholding the rights of parents, Judge Dillard has concurred and expressed his displeasure at the behavior of child welfare services in overstepping their bounds and interfering in family relationships. For support the judge has invoked cases such as *Pierce* discussing parental rights and stated that juvenile courts must take this into account when construing relevant state statutes and making custody decisions. And when making these repeated pleas, Judge Dillard has cited many of the precedents and constitutional provisions discussed above, including Georgia's Baby Ninth. In at least one case at Georgia's Supreme Court, it seems the court followed Judge Dillard's lead in stating that the Baby Ninth "may well constitute another source" for the right to raise one's children.[51]

Lacking anything like the universal support of the right to raise one's child, the most controversial unenumerated right of the post–New Deal era is the right to privacy. It has appeared in a handful of Baby Ninth cases. Mississippi recognized a right to privacy under its Baby Ninth in a 1985 case concerning forced blood transfusions. The court ruled that due to her Jehovah's Witness faith, a woman could not be forced to receive a blood transfusion. It did so on state constitutional religious freedom grounds, but also because it would violate her right to privacy protected by the Baby Ninth.[52] The Mississippi court went on to extend the right to privacy to protect abortion in 1998.[53] The plaintiffs in *Pro-Choice Mississippi v. Fordice* challenged a set of abortion restrictions, including a twenty-four-hour waiting period, a minor's consent from both parents, and that the physician involved have completed a residency. They raised a host of constitutional clauses, including Mississippi's Baby Ninth. Unlike in many other "shotgun" cases, such as some discussed above, the court primarily relied upon the Baby Ninth in finding a right to bodily integrity, which in turn "is an implicit right to have an abortion."[54] It also explained, "The right to privacy, whether founded in common law or natural law, is constitutionally guaranteed under Article 3, § 32 [the Baby Ninth] of the Mississippi Constitution."[55] In the end, however, even though it recognized the right in question, the court subjected the restrictions to an "undue burden" standard and concluded they survived the challenge.

It is most ironic that in *Fordice* the Mississippi Supreme Court recognized a right to have an abortion given that a federal lawsuit, *Dobbs v. Jackson Women's Health Organization*,[56] challenging a vastly more restrictive abortion law—outlawing almost all abortions after 15 weeks of pregnancy—recently led the U.S. Supreme Court to overturn its 1973 decision *Roe v. Wade*.[57] Surprisingly, with *Roe* no longer protecting the right to an abortion, it appears that Mississippi abortion rights activists have not sought to use *Fordice* and the Baby Ninth in a state court challenge to the same law, at least as of this book going to press. This could be because of changes in the state court's composition since 1998 (although *Fordice* has not itself been overruled) or another tactical reason. Nationwide, however, as abortion rights litigation has now shifted to the states with *Roe*'s demise, we should expect to see Baby Ninths invoked and interpreted in the abortion rights area to a much greater extent.

Rounding out our survey of Baby Ninths and the right to privacy, Arkansas's Supreme Court—a year before the U.S. Supreme Court found a similar law unconstitutional under the Fourteenth Amendment's Due Process Clause in *Lawrence v. Texas*[58]—ruled that the state's ban on homosexual sodomy violated the right to privacy protected by a number of state constitutional provisions. Included in that mix was its Baby Ninth.[59]

Other personal rights that courts have protected via Baby Ninths are the right to wear one's hair long[60] and the earlier mentioned right to travel.[61] The protection of all these rights is entirely in accord with the concerns of some Founders that no bill of rights can list all the rights of man.[62]

Criminal Procedure

There are not many cases applying Baby Ninths to the area of criminal procedure, but a few do stand out. In *Buford v. State*, the Supreme Court of Mississippi in 1927 addressed a number of issues in an appeal of a conviction for illegal liquor sales.[63] One argument the defendant made was that he was not given a separate jury trial on each charge made against him. The court ruled that the state's Baby Ninth did not protect such a right, but tied the Baby Ninth to common law protections in deciphering its scope: "at common law there was no immunity from a trial for more than one offense at the same time which the Legislature could not by a statute abridge, and consequently such immunity or right is not within the reservation of rights contemplated by section 32 of the Constitution."[64] A few years later, in 1932, the court struck down a statute that repealed an insanity defense. The majority found the repeal unconstitutional under the state's due process clause,[65] but a three-justice concurrence also extended their reasoning to the Baby Ninth, stating that the provision prevents all three branches of government from denying or impairing "other rights inherent in, and retained by the people."[66]

Later the Supreme Court of New Jersey found a broad right against double jeopardy in the state constitution, relying both upon its Baby Ninth and Lockean natural rights guarantee.[67] The New Jersey Constitution only explicitly stated that no person shall be tried again after an acquittal. The court reasoned, however, citing Magna Carta, that the language of these unenumerated rights clauses incorporated the ancient understanding that no man shall be put in jeopardy twice.[68] This then extended to the case at hand, where the defendant had been previously convicted of a lesser charge. Because of that previous experience he was protected from a subsequent prosecution on a greater charge.[69]

In 1974, the Alaska Supreme Court used the state's Baby Ninth for a straightforward invocation of the right to represent oneself in court without an attorney.[70] Looking to the Treaty of Cession, where Russia ceded Alaska to the United States, and the Judiciary Act of 1789, the court found the right to self-representation to be "so long established and of such fundamental importance [that it] must be held to have been so retained" under the Baby Ninth.[71] The court cautioned that not "all statutory rights in existence at the time that Alaska was admitted to the Union" count as protected rights under the Baby Ninth, but that this right did in this case.[72] Also, in 2006 the Iowa Supreme Court examined whether a number of state constitutional provisions, including the Baby Ninth, limit pretrial detention. The court concluded that the clause applied but only to "unreasonable action," and the limits in question easily passed that standard.[73]

Scrutiny of Baby Ninths

The above pages demonstrate that on a number of occasions courts have found Baby Ninths to protect individual rights in a meaningful way. But the larger context tells us that the cases where the court ruled against the government, or at least subjected the government to meaningful scrutiny, have been the exception. Most of the time when Baby Ninths are recognized to protect individual rights, it turns out that the protection is paper-thin and the government easily wins. And, of course, there are the many other cases involving unenumerated rights where Baby Ninths do not even come up at all.

As with any rights mentioned in a constitution, just because a Baby Ninth protects an individual right does not mean that any law affecting that right will be ruled unconstitutional. Courts apply certain thresholds and burdens to enumerated rights such as free speech, religious freedom, and equal protection (generally called "scrutiny" in modern jurisprudence[74]), and the same is true of Baby Ninths. If the government satisfies that scrutiny, then the law is constitutional. If it fails, then the court finds the law to violate the right in question and the law is declared unconstitutional. In much constitutional litigation "scrutiny" is the biggest factor of all. Apply a high level of scrutiny and the government probably loses. Apply not much and the government almost certainly wins.

The use of scrutiny is unsurprising. It is not scrutiny itself that is a problem. It is the level of scrutiny. Despite what seems like clear language in Baby Ninths themselves—"impair, deny or disparage others retained by the people"—the scrutiny applied to Baby Ninths has generally been less probing than that applied to enumerated rights. In other words, rights protected by Baby Ninths are "denied and disparaged" because they are not enumerated. A few examples will illustrate this.

Perhaps the most brazen case is a 2002 opinion by Louisiana's intermediate appellate court. The court concluded that the government had not violated the state constitution by withholding certain documents.[75] Along the way it noted that not all rights are equally important, and it turned to the Baby Ninth to justify this conclusion: "Although recognizing innominate rights other than the enumerated constitutional rights, this provision implicitly accords those rights not specifically recognized by the Constitution less gravity than the enumerated rights."[76]

This is hard to square with the Louisiana Baby Ninth's command that the enumeration of rights "shall not deny or disparage" those innominate rights.[77] How this implicitly accords those rights "less gravity" is not developed any further by the opinion. The only logical way, it would seem, that this could be true would be if (today's) unenumerated rights already were less important before the constitution was written, and those rights that were more important all *just so happened* to be enumerated. Then the Baby Ninth could simply be a reminder not to "deny or disparage" the unenumerated rights any *more* than they already are. But this seems far-fetched when set against the commonsense reading of protecting other rights at a level equal to the enumerated rights, a reading that we have seen numerous drafters and even judges believe in.

In applying scrutiny to Baby Ninths, courts will often turn to the same "rational basis" protection often seen in other areas of law, such as non-fundamental rights protected by substantive due process.[78] Almost all the time, "rational basis" means "the government wins." It is a standard that in its purest form mandates judges to come up with reasons to support the constitutionality of a law, even when the government's lawyers have not. What's more, judges can simply make up facts that the legislature *might* have believed when it passed the law being challenged in an effort to render it constitutional. Thus, even if a Baby Ninth is held to protect a right, if that right only receives rational basis scrutiny, the right might as well not exist at all.

Thus, in a Minnesota case, the court assumed that the state's Baby Ninth protected a right to bear arms, but that the right "is not absolute" and therefore the state "may reasonably exercise its police power" in regulating the carrying of weapons.[79] It then went on to find, as generally happens when a "reasonable" or "rational basis" standard is applied, that the denial of a conceal carry permit was constitutional.[80] The court did not discuss, or even cite any authority, on why it should invoke this standard simply because the right at issue is not "absolute." Its lack of an explanation is quite puzzling. No right, even free speech, is an "absolute right," but just because they are not does not mean a version of the rational basis test applies to restrictions on them.

This same sleight-of-hand move, where a rational basis standard is applied despite "deny or disparage" language, appears in many other Baby Ninth cases.[81]

Collective Rights Interpretations of Baby Ninths

Despite the straightforward individual rights implications of Baby Ninths, which we will talk about in our next chapter, some courts have done their best to turn them into mere guarantors of the collective right of the people to govern themselves, or at least have added something like that on top of the protection of individual rights. Although not nearly as numerous as individual rights holdings, there are enough examples to raise questions about how judges are arriving at a collective rights understanding given the mismatch between the provisions' text and structure and collective rights themselves. We can divide them into two categories: one that essentially reads Baby Ninths as giving state legislatures more power, and one that only concerns local self-government in struggles with state government.

One of each kind of opinion came out of Oklahoma in the 1920s and 1930s. In *Ex parte Sales*, a corporation challenged a transportation licensing statute, raising a Baby Ninth claim.[82] The court turned the Baby Ninth inside-out in justifying the law's constitutionality with the following reasoning:

> There is nothing in the act in question which tends to deny, impair, or disparage any right retained under the Constitution by the people. The term "people," as used above, means the "public," and one of the rights thus specifically and securely reserved to the public is its right to regulate "public service corporations." The act in question seeks to do no more than to exercise this right.[83]

Of course, if this were true there would be no need for the Baby Ninth, as "the public," through the legislature, would already have the power to pass public service corporation legislation. This seemingly obvious problem was not addressed in the opinion, however.[84]

A few years later, in a local government case, the Supreme Court of Oklahoma again looked at its Baby Ninth in *Thomas v. Reid*.[85] There, a city council attempted to sell the city's power company and submitted the sale to a vote of its citizens. A majority voted in favor, but less than the 60 percent required by a state statute.[86] The constitutionality of the statute was then successfully challenged on the ground that a majority, not a supermajority, is all that can constitutionally be required of a city by the state.[87] The court ruled on a hodgepodge of provisions, many concerning home rule of cities, but at one point after quoting various other courts waxing on the right to local self-government, the opinion cited Oklahoma's Baby Ninth, stating that because of it, it is not "necessary for us to point to any particular constitutional provision that is violated."[88]

In addition to Oklahoma, the Supreme Court of Iowa has found a right to local self-government in its Baby Ninth,[89] as did Nebraska's supreme court.[90] Both of these cases concerned structural fights between local and state government on the appointment of officials, not local governments' powers to regulate individual citizens.

A Baby Ninth right to local self-government is more defensible than a Baby Ninth right for the state legislature to govern, as, after all, protecting local self-governments from overbearing state legislatures is a "right" that is sometimes placed in state constitutions, such as with home-rule protections. But it still is problematic as a right protected by Baby Ninths. As we will see in the next chapter, a state bill of rights, including the rights in a Baby Ninth, that included a right to local self-government would fully protect an individual against the state government in many ways (speech, search and seizure, religion, etc.), but it would not protect her against local governments as much because those local governments would have the right to self-government. This right to local self-government would, presumably, include a right to enact laws that might otherwise violate the state bill of rights if they were passed by the state legislature. So it would be an unenumerated right to violate a right. Which does not make a whole lot of sense.

But we should grant that perhaps this is different for conflicts between states and municipalities that do not affect individual rights, such as the sale of the power company in *Thomas*. In that case, perhaps there may be a small area for collective political rights alongside individual rights in interpreting Baby Ninths, but only where there is no conflict between those collective rights and individual rights.

But only perhaps. The other problem with a local right to self-government is that, as we saw in chapter 1, state governments are traditionally seen as sovereign because they represent the delegated sovereignty of the people in that state. This is the basis for the Baby Tenths, where the people delegate their powers to the state government but retain rights for themselves. But a unit of local government cannot claim the same "sovereignty" in that sense. Otherwise we would not just have "dual sovereignty" between the state and federal governments, but a bewildering level of "sovereignties" among all the often overlapping levels of local government, including cities, counties, water districts, etc. Thus it seems a bit odd that a nonsovereign city could tell its sovereign state—that is, the people of the state as a whole, delegated to its legislature—that it has a "retained" constitutional right (as Baby Ninths generally say) to some level of local governance.

In any case, we should leave open the possibility of some kind of collective self-governance being protected by a Baby Ninth, but we should conclude that it would be narrow and on shaky grounds.

CHAPTER 5

What Do Baby Ninths Mean?

For the whole of this book so far there have simmered under the surface two underlying assumptions that have occasionally bubbled up. But we cannot allow that simmering any longer, and the time has come to let those assumptions emerge and confront them. One is that what Baby Ninths are supposed to do is protect *individual* rights. The other is that Baby Ninths are *judicially* enforceable.

The first assumption means that Baby Ninths do not protect "collective rights," protect federalism, or protect against some other thing that is not a right an individual can possess. They do what they say and protect individual rights just like most of the rest of a state's bill of rights, the only difference being that the rights a Baby Ninth protects are not explicitly "in there." The second assumption means that if those rights are violated, Baby Ninths empower an individual to go to court to protect her unenumerated individual rights, just like she already can for a right that is "in" the same state constitution.

In this chapter we are going to finally address these assumptions head on and demonstrate why they are correct. To do that we will start with a quick review of what the framers of Baby Ninths envisioned them doing. And we will also take a look at another piece of evidence from the formation of Baby Ninths: Baby Tenths. We will consider what in their history indicates Baby Ninths are supposed to do.

Then we will move on to re-examine the models of interpreting the original meaning of the Ninth Amendment that we briefly looked at way back in chapter 1. As we said there, we are not taking a side on how the Ninth Amendment itself should be interpreted. But when applying those models to Baby Ninths, we shall see that the only interpretation of their original meaning that makes sense is that Baby Ninths protect individual rights, and they protect those rights at the same level that other rights are protected. And we will also review what we discussed in the last chapter, what the courts have said. Although the courts have generally ignored Baby Ninths, and often given them short shrift by applying far too weak a standard, when they address the subject they actually do find that Baby Ninths protect individual rights as opposed to collective rights. That supports the conclusion that the individual rights model is the best interpretation. Finally, we will address how the conclusion that Baby Ninths protect individual rights, in turn, means that, in contrast to what the courts have often said, the rights Baby Ninths protect must enjoy judicial protection in the same way as other, enumerated rights already do.

What *specifically* are those individual rights that are judicially enforceable? That is something we will get to in chapter 6.

What the Floor Debates Tell Us

From the transcripts of convention debates over the years, as discussed in chapters 2 and 3, we see essentially two positions, both of which viewed the rights Baby Ninths refer to as individual rights.

The minority view (at least in those states that adopted Baby Ninths) that some delegates held was that Baby Ninths were not needed because unenumerated rights *were already protected.* Various delegates voiced this concern, including in Maryland, Missouri, New Jersey, and Virginia. It appears these delegates thought there was a general understanding that state governments could not violate rights, whether or not they were specifically included in a constitution. The understanding seems to have been that governments did have certain powers, but those powers only extended to regulation that would not infringe on the people's liberties. Bills of rights were accepted by those who objected to Baby Ninths, but they thought Baby Ninths were not strictly speaking necessary because all rights, enumerated and unenumerated, were not within the government's power to violate. A Baby Ninth was just added verbiage unnecessarily bloating a constitution. This is analogous to the Federalists' argument that a Bill of Rights was not needed in the U.S. Constitution because the government did not have enumerated powers to violate rights. At the state level, it was argued, the same principle applies even in a government of unenumerated powers.

Given that those powers are unenumerated, however, it is unsurprising that this view was a minority one. The majority view (which we must call majority in light of the overwhelming number of conventions that adopted Baby Ninths after they were proposed, and therefore did not think them bloated verbiage[1]) was that *perhaps* a Baby Ninth was unnecessary, but it should be adopted anyway for greater caution.[2] The delegates wanted to make sure that their constitutions protected rights beyond those enumerated in their various bills of rights. So they added in these "etcetera" provisions forbidding any inference that a right is not protected just because it is not enumerated. But what is clear is *everybody* agreed that there were (1) other rights of worth in addition to those explicitly mentioned in a state bill of rights and (2) that the state government was in some way prohibited from violating those rights (although for the minority view it is a bit unclear what exactly that was: the state constitution itself, an understanding of limited delegation from the people, or some other principle). The controversy was whether these rights needed to be recognized with a Baby Ninth, or whether they were implicitly protected even without one.

As to what kind of rights these "other rights" were, the delegates' comments unmistakably suggest that they were similar to the rights the drafters actually did list in their bills of rights. Their remarks are never in the context of suggesting that these "other" rights "retained by the people" are of a totally different flavor than those they just enumerated. Instead the effort always seems to be an exercise of saying "etcetera." Thus, whatever a Baby Ninth protects, it is something like the freedom of speech, right to counsel, protection against unreasonable searches and seizures, freedom of religion, protection of contracts, etc., that actually are in the preceding bill of rights. And given that almost every right—not absolutely every one, but generally almost all of them—that actually is enumerated in a state bill of rights is an individual right, this suggests that according to many of the framers of Baby Ninths, the "other rights" of Baby Ninths cannot be too far afield from these enumerated individual rights. Thus, for example, it would be an error to argue that a "collective right" of the people to pass legislation is a right protected by a Baby Ninth because state bills of rights do not have similar collective rights in them. (We consider what to make of the few non-individual rights in state bills of rights later in this chapter.)

There are a few pieces of evidence from constitutional conventions that could be interpreted otherwise, but not many, and they are not very convincing. One is in California with Delegate Semple's statement regarding the people's "legislative capacity." But that quite confusing exchange seems to have concerned the proposed Baby Tenth, not a Baby Ninth. And that Semple later said he was fine with adopting the Baby Ninth is further evidence that Semple did not think a Baby Ninth provided for a collective right to pass legislation. Another was the reference in the New Jersey convention of 1947 to collective bargaining rights being protected by its Baby Ninth, among other rights. Now that statement did not imply that individual rights are *not* protected by the Baby Ninth (pardon the double negative), but it does open the door to collective rights; here, a right not against the government but a collective right of workers against their employer. And that statement is just that, one statement. Finally, there are the opaque comments made by Delegate Pechous at the Illinois convention where he talked both about individual rights and rights against the federal government. But perhaps his confusing remarks can just be chalked up to a misunderstanding of constitutional law, not the meaning of the Baby Ninth itself.

Therefore, overall there is a smidgen of evidence that some framers may have thought their Baby Ninth protected something other than individual rights. But the overwhelming evidence from those who actually drafted these provisions is that they protect individual rights, and that they probably do not protect some kind of collective rights as well.

What Baby Tenths Mean for Baby Ninths

Unlike the relative agreement among delegates on Baby Ninths, the little we have on delegates' views on Baby Tenths is more confused. Basically, one side held that state powers were, as Madison said, "numerous and indefinite,"[3] while the other believed that just like the federal government, states only had powers delegated to them in their constitutions. And although the latter approach seems to be a minority view, some state Baby Tenths, such as Ohio's, seem to have explicitly said just that. Other Baby Tenths, a large majority, instead recognize, or recognized, the "general powers" that the people had delegated to their state, although at the same time implying that state governments did not *have* to be constituted that way. The people delegated "general powers" but perhaps could have delegated enumerated powers. Because they did not, and because delegating general powers instead was a dangerous, although perhaps otherwise prudent, thing to do, the Baby Tenths wholly excepted bills of rights out of those general powers.[4]

The Baby Tenths inform our understanding of Baby Ninths in a couple of ways.

First, where the two are used together (as in Alabama, Arkansas, Kansas, and Ohio) the Baby Ninth appears to be protecting unenumerated rights alongside the exclusion of the bill of rights from the powers of the state government. It would be odd if the Baby Ninth language in those constitutions did not protect unenumerated individual rights. Then the explicit *enumerated* protection of various individual rights would stand alongside something referring to "rights" but not protecting individual rights, with the two kinds of rights not distinguished at all in the Baby Tenth's "except-out" language. For example, Alabama's original Baby Tenth protected against "any encroachments on the rights herein retained" without stating whether those "rights herein retained" are only enumerated ones or also the "retained" rights referred to in the Baby Ninth. Instead of contorting the text to not include unenumerated rights, the straightforward interpretation is that these joint Baby Ninths/ Baby Tenths protect both kinds of rights.[5] They provided a belt *and* a pair of suspenders. Unenumerated rights are protected in addition to the enumerated rights, and *all* of these rights are excepted out of the powers of government in the first place.

Second, if joint Baby Ninth/Baby Tenth provisions protect individual rights, it makes sense that similar Baby Ninth clauses in other states that do not have a Baby Tenth would also protect unenumerated individual rights. Those provisions just would not have anything to say about withholding power from government to transgress against rights, enumerated or not. That pair of Baby Tenth suspenders simply is not present. But the belt of the Baby Ninth is. The same basic Baby Ninth language is used in both types of clause, and the first such clause in any state constitution is Alabama's joint Baby Ninth/Baby Tenth.

One final thing should be said about Baby Tenths. As we have seen, some states rejected Baby Tenths, such as in Minnesota's Republican Convention, because they seem to say something entirely duplicative. Everybody knows that the government does not have the power to violate the constitution, so why bother saying so? Another possibility, however, exists for these clauses' purpose. Although the rule that the government cannot violate the constitution is, of course, a generally accepted truism of American law, by enacting Baby Tenths it could be that constitutional drafters were expanding the effect of bill of rights provisions, enumerated or unenumerated. For example, it could be that without a Baby Tenth a judge or legislator might err on the side of thinking a questionable law was constitutional. With a Baby Tenth, however, a thumb is placed on the side of protecting rights because the constitution's text recognizes the dangerous nature of the powers the people have delegated to the state. The provision is asking judges and legislators to err on the side of finding or considering the law unconstitutional if it impacts provisions in the bill of rights. This would in turn include unenumerated rights if the bill of rights in question contains a Baby Ninth or another unenumerated rights clause, such as a Lockean natural rights guarantee. And, given their shared genealogy with Baby Tenths, Baby Ninths themselves could be seen as a thumb on the side of protecting rights (we will say more about this thumb-on-the-scale business later).

Applying Ninth Amendment Interpretations to Baby Ninths: Do Any Make Sense at the State Level?

Thus, in assessing the evidence we have from the people who actually crafted Baby Ninths, signs point toward them protecting individual rights, not some other kind of rights. But this is not the be-all and end-all of constitutional interpretation. Most originalist scholars today hold that what a provision in a constitution "means" does not just come down to what the delegates at a convention intended it to mean. Instead, the more important question is what would the general public have understood the words in the constitution to mean at that time? The usual name for this is the "original public meaning." This should take into consideration what delegates said at their conventions, because those are examples of people contemporaneously interpreting the very text we are interested in. But other pieces of evidence—such as dictionaries of the time, contemporary treatises, other parts of the constitution in question, or other writings from the same linguistic community—are also valuable in discerning this public meaning.

Yet when we are dealing with Baby Ninths *as a group* we are not just asking what a certain phrase meant in a certain year. There are dozens of different years, spanning almost two centuries. Therefore, examining the various possible "original meanings" of Baby Ninths looks like it would pose quite a task, on top of the already difficult task of discerning one original meaning. Given the history of Baby Ninths, however, there may be a way we can "crack the code." The Ninth Amendment itself has already been extensively analyzed for its original meaning. Perhaps if we look at what the various ideas are on the Ninth Amendment it will clarify what the original public meaning might be for the later (sometimes much later) Baby Ninths. We can thus ask whether there is a reason to think Baby Ninths (or some Baby Ninths and not others) are any different. We can also then examine if the meaning of the words common to Baby Ninths have changed between 1819 (the first) and 1970 (the latest). (And to preview, it appears they have not changed very much.)

Which brings us back to the meaning of the Ninth Amendment. Let us apply the various originalist models discussed in chapter 1 regarding the Ninth Amendment to Baby Ninths and see how they fit. This way we can see whether each alternative take on the Ninth Amendment's original meaning illuminates what the public might have thought of a particular Baby Ninth. If it does not make sense then that probably is *not* what the original public meaning of the Baby Ninth is. Yet if it does make sense, then there is a good chance we have found something approaching the Baby Ninth's original public meaning. If need be, we can then adjust to a certain time, whether it is 1819 (Alabama's original constitution and Maine's current constitution) or 1970 (Illinois's current constitution). None of this implies, or is meant to imply, what the original public meaning of the Ninth Amendment itself actually is. All these various theories of its meaning are taken as good faith attempts to figure that problem out, but then used by applying them to similar language in a different document to see if they shed light on what the other provision itself means.

As we learned in chapter 1, these models of Ninth Amendment interpretation are the state law rights model, the residual rights model, the collective rights model, the federalism model, the inherent rights model, the rights retained model, and the individual rights model. Instead of starting with the individual rights model we will end with it, as part of its justification depends on contrasting it with the others.

State Law Rights Model

First, the state law rights model. To recap, this model argues that the Ninth Amendment simply guaranteed that the U.S. Constitution's enactment itself was not interpreted to change any state constitutional or common law rights, but did not prohibit the federal government from changing those rights in the future.

This interpretation makes no sense in a state constitution. Even assuming that the Ninth Amendment protected state constitutional rights from the creation of the U.S. Constitution, state constitutions themselves do not, of course, need a clause protecting their own rights that are set forth in the very same document. Further, if the worry is whether a new state constitution would disrupt the state's common law, there are many examples of that being done with much more direct language. For example, South Carolina's 1790 constitution promised that "The rights, privileges, immunities, and estates of both civil and religious societies, and corporate bodies, shall remain as if the constitution of this State had not been altered or amended."[6] This language protected the common law rights of various entities from disruption from the constitution's enactment, but it did not protect against later legislative changes. The language of Baby Ninths is far afield from this. To the extent that a Baby Ninth protects pre-existing rights, that is satisfied via the individual rights model, but it does not protect simply any pre-existing contractual right, but rights of a constitutional nature.

Residual Rights Model

Second, the residual rights model. It also does not work for interpreting Baby Ninths. Under this model, the Ninth Amendment is meant to nullify the argument that the federal government has powers in addition to those that the Constitution enumerates. The fear is that because some—but not all—rights are enumerated, powers might be understood to be unenumerated as well. For states, however, if the state government is understood to *already have* these feared unenumerated powers ("general powers" as Baby Tenths say), then it makes no sense that the framers of a state constitution would add a Baby Ninth so the government would not have them. And if states with Baby Ninths actually do not have general powers then those states have *massive* problems they need to start worrying about (such as amending their constitutions to give themselves the enumerated power to ban murder, something basic but, as we have seen, sometimes not explicitly delegated to state legislatures). In short, since state governments and constitutions are not premised on enumerated powers, the residual rights model is nonsensical in the context of Baby Ninths.

Collective Rights Model

Third, the collective rights model. Again, "collective rights" here means the right of the people as a body politic to govern itself, including its right to abolish its government. This includes the people's collective right to set policy, and the right to hold a constitutional convention to amend or replace its constitution.

It should be obvious why it does not make sense for a Baby Ninth Amendment to protect collective rights, with the caveat or two we discussed in the last chapter.

One reason Baby Ninths are incompatible with collective rights is that any "collective right" of the state's body politic to choose its own policies is already furthered through the constitution itself. Indeed, enacting a constitution itself would seem to be the supreme exercise of that collective right. By setting up a legislature, governor, etc., the people of the state are giving themselves "general powers" to adopt laws. And through whatever amendment or convention mechanism in the document, the people are allowing for future alteration or abandonment of the constitution. "Protecting" the power to enact laws by essentially saying (as a "collective Baby Ninth" would) that the bill of rights does not impair or deny the "right" to adopt new constitutions and enact laws would truly be an absurd use of constitutional text. It would almost be an "anti–Baby Tenth," essentially saying, "All the above enumerated rights actually do not matter." Indeed, a collective Baby Ninth reading would be even more absurd in a state like Alabama that, in 1819, had a Baby Tenth that excepted, among other rights, the rights in the Baby Ninth itself out of the general power of government.

Another reason the collective rights model does not make any sense for Baby Ninths is there is no relevant "collective" to protect other than the state as a whole. That is, Baby Ninths are not a good fit for protecting smaller "collectives," such as cities or counties. The collective rights view of the Ninth Amendment itself depends on the desire at the Founding for the states to retain sovereignty that many were afraid the new federal government would take away, or at least would threaten. Under this view the "rights" that the Ninth Amendment protects are to be exercised by the people in a *state* collectively. We have just explained why it makes no sense that a Baby Ninth protects a state's sovereignty. Below the level of a state itself, however, there is nothing that the collective rights view of the Ninth Amendment speaks to. On the county or city or even more local level there is no "sovereign entity" in the traditional understanding of sovereignty embodied in the U.S. Constitution and state constitutions. The one thing that might qualify as "sovereign" would be the individual herself, and an individual's sovereignty vis-à-vis the state and the federal government.[7] That is what bills of rights are generally about, of course: to protect individual sovereignty. But between the level of a state and of an individual there is no "sovereignty" under any traditional understanding, whether that be in 1791, 1819, or 1970. Sure, a city could call itself "sovereign" and thereby claim an unenumerated right to collective self-governance, but that would have no historical or textual basis. Also, if Baby Ninths, for example, protected the right of cities to adopt their own policies, that would mean that the same bill of rights would apply to the state government, but not apply (at least as much) to municipal governments because of their collective right, protected by the Baby Ninth, to enact policies that those explicit individual rights might otherwise impede. Yet state bills of rights do not make this distinction, although it would be easy to write into the text. Local governments do often have "home rule" provisions in state constitutions protecting their powers from state legislation, but that is hardly an issue to do with a bill of rights. For a Baby Ninth to actually be exempting local governments from other rights in a bill of rights would constitute a Rube Goldberg level of constitutional drafting.

Unfortunately, as we saw in the previous chapter, this has not prevented a handful of courts ruling exactly that, finding that Baby Ninths sometimes protect local governments and even state governments from judicial review of their actions.[8] Without restating too much of what was said in discussing those opinions, there is perhaps a smidgen of plausibility for the idea that a Baby Ninth protects a municipality against a state, but if such a collective right exists it is a limited one. But there is no plausibility for a collective right of either the state or a municipality to violate the rights of individuals. Further, regarding the statement in the New Jersey 1947 convention about a right to collectively bargain, given that bills of rights are generally understood to only apply to state action, there is little reason to think that one of the other rights retained by the people is a collective right that applies to private parties (employers). We can simply chalk that statement up to crafty rhetoric by the good delegate in question.

Federalism Model

Fourth, the federalism model. This model also does not make sense for an obvious reason. Again, under this model the Ninth Amendment is meant to nullify the argument that the federal government's enumerated powers should be read expansively where they do not intrude upon rights enumerated in the Constitution. As we just discussed, unlike the federal government, states (generally) do not have enumerated powers. Now we have seen that this was not a completely unanimous view in antebellum America. For those few who believed that states could only legislate according to powers enumerated in their state constitutions, then the force (such as it is) of the enumerated powers model could apply to Baby Ninths. (Although, again, the actual practice of state governments, such as exercising the unenumerated power to ban murder, heavily suggests otherwise.) But for the overwhelming majority of constitution drafters, judges, and legal scholars who believed their states had broad powers to legislate beyond the exact powers in their state constitution, then the federalism model of a Baby Ninth does not make any sense. And it makes even less sense in light of the Baby Tenths, most of which explicitly recognize broad unenumerated powers.

Rights Retained Model

Further we have the "rights retained" view of Professor Michael McConnell. Again, his thesis is that the Ninth Amendment is a rule of construction where rights "retained by the people" are not "constitutional rights" such as those in the first eight amendments to the Constitution, but are nevertheless rights that the Ninth Amendment reminds us to respect.[9] And functionally how that respect is to be carried out is as a rule of construction when interpreting whether a statute allows the government to infringe on such a right when the statute is ambiguous. Thus, the Ninth is akin to a rule of lenity: when interpreting a statute a court should read it to not restrict any of these rights "retained by the people," unless the restriction is explicit. But if it is explicit the government *can* restrict the right, unlike if it were an enumerated constitutional right such as the right to free speech.

As with the other models, this does not work when applied to state constitutions. This is not because it cannot inherently work. But there is no evidence that anyone connected to a Baby Ninth has ever espoused such a view. There is no evidence of its being made in any convention of any Baby Ninth. Indeed, there is no view in any opinion interpreting a Baby Ninth. Of course, there is not a whole lot of evidence of what the framers of Baby Ninths, and their contemporaries, thought of Baby Ninths. But it seems to say a lot that within that evidence, nothing is said about this fairly nuanced view of the language of the Ninth Amendment in the Baby Ninth context. And much of McConnell's justification for his view comes from eighteenth-century understandings of "retained rights" that he argues the framers of the Ninth would have implicitly understood. But Baby Ninths are not the same fly in amber. They were adopted and readopted in various states anywhere from 1819 to 1986. Although the words of the Baby Ninths do not vary much at all, we have no evidence that the background understanding of the rule of construction that McConnell puts forward—of construing statutes to not violate rights based in eighteenth-century Lockean theory—continued after the Founding period. We *do* have evidence that "rights retained" should be understood in a Lockean context on what rights any given Baby Ninth should refer to (we will discuss this in the next chapter), but not that it should be understood to provide a rule of construction about ambiguous statutory text. Instead it is much more likely that the various statements about Baby Ninths putting other rights on an even footing (not an almost-even footing, as McConnell argues) with enumerated rights—which we see repeatedly from before the Civil War to after the civil rights movement—capture their meaning. Further, purely from a textual standpoint Baby Ninths do not state anything about a canon of construction regarding ambiguity. They textually are about "construing" the constitution in question, but not construing ambiguous statutes.

Individual Rights Model

Thus, the above five models for interpreting the Ninth Amendment according to its original meaning do not fit Baby Ninths.

So what do Baby Ninths mean? From the available attempts to find an original public meaning of the Ninth Amendment itself, we are left with the individual rights model. Of course, it might not fit either, in which case we would need to keep searching for a way to explain the original public meaning of Baby Ninths.

Thankfully, however, the individual rights view does fit. Under this view, the "other rights" referred to in Baby Ninths are individual rights that the state cannot impair or deny simply because they are not contained in the state constitution's bill of rights. And, as long as one takes the (virtually universal) position that the state cannot impair or deny enumerated rights, this means that states also cannot impair or deny unenumerated rights. Otherwise the government could impair or deny the latter because they are not the former, precisely what Baby Ninths say cannot be done. Baby Ninths are "etcetera" clauses to protect the rights that a constitutional convention did not include because it is impossible to list all of them, even all of the important ones.

What the Courts Have Said

Now we should return to the courts and see how what they have said may affect our analysis. Case law may not be as important in determining the original public meaning of a constitutional provision as it would be for, say, a judge applying the common law. Unlike a judge looking purely to precedent, original meaning, by definition, does not change based upon subsequent interpretations.[10] For example, Justice Scalia explained for the Supreme Court in *Heller v. District of Columbia* that sources from "75 years after the ratification of the Second Amendment . . . do not provide as much insight into its original meaning as earlier sources."[11] He said this with regard to legislative sources, but the same reasoning applies to court rulings.

If a case is not too distant in time from the provision's adoption, however, the situation changes. It can then give a clue as to what the relevant linguistic community thought of a text's meaning, as judges are speakers in that community like everyone else. Further, given that Baby Ninths have been adopted throughout American history, a case in one state, even if many decades after its own constitution was adopted, may still be relevant to the meaning of a Baby Ninth only recently adopted in another state.

Although this book has had, and will have, many criticisms of how courts have interpreted Baby Ninths, on the central question of this chapter—what kinds of rights do Baby Ninths protect?—the case law interpreting them is broadly supportive of the conclusion that they protect individual rights. As the discussion in the previous chapter makes clear, when state courts have interpreted Baby Ninths they have generally said they protect unenumerated rights, and they generally have done so when individual rights are at issue. This is true both of those courts that actually found laws to violate the Baby Ninth and those that found the laws in question constitutional but nevertheless potentially unconstitutional if the standard of review (often rational basis) had been breached.[12] The handful of collective rights cases are just a handful. Further, courts have found Baby Ninths to protect individual rights from the 1830s through today, essentially covering the relevant periods of "original meaning" for the thirty-three different Baby Ninths we have today. On the questions of *which* individual rights Baby Ninths protect and (most importantly) at *what* standard of review, the courts have been more all over the place. As we saw, they often reserve Baby Ninths for favored rights (such as the right to privacy) and only apply a rational basis standard for others. But more often than not Baby Ninths are simply ignored in unenumerated rights cases. This, of course, says nothing (literally) about their original meaning.

Further, of the cases that have picked and chosen to protect some rights but not others, most of those cases have been relatively modern, paralleling the Supreme Court's post-*Griswold* jurisprudence.[13] Does that mean that the original meaning of relatively modern Baby Ninths, such as in Michigan (1963) and Illinois (1970) might be more like *Griswold*, but older provisions might be more like the more expansive meaning argued for in this book? Perhaps, although just because there were a few cases about Baby Ninths at a certain time does not necessarily control the meaning of the words. After all, the judges could have the meaning wrong and be swimming against the tide of language. We will explore these issues more in the next chapter.

Collective Rights That Are in State Bills of Rights

Before moving on we should address one lingering issue that arose earlier. Although the vast majority of provisions in state bills of rights protect individual rights, there are a non-negligible number of counterexamples. We stated above that they are outliers that should not change our understanding of Baby Ninths. But let us take a quick look at a few of them to better understand why.

Many state constitutions contain a provision speaking of the right of the people to exercise political power. For example, Maryland's Declaration of Rights states "That the People of this State have the sole and exclusive right of regulating the internal government and police thereof, as a free, sovereign and independent state."[14] Vermont has a verbose provision protecting the "right, in a legal way" of good government:

> That frequent recurrence to fundamental principles, and a firm
> adherence to justice, moderation, temperance, industry, and frugal-
> ity, are absolutely necessary to preserve the blessings of liberty, and

keep government free; the people ought, therefore to pay particular attention to these points, in the choice of officers and representatives, and have a right, in a legal way, to exact a due and constant regard to them, from their legislators and magistrates, in making and executing such laws as are necessary for the good government of the State.[15]

And Montana's briefly states "All political power is vested in and derived from the people. All government of right originates with the people, is founded upon their will only, and is instituted solely for the good of the whole."[16] One might call these provisions "republican form of government" clauses, or perhaps "popular sovereignty" clauses. They affirm the principle that the people are in control of the government (not a king or some other person or group) and that the purpose of the government is the public good, not private interests.

Similarly, but a bit differently, are provisions that protect a right to change the government, including even via a revolution. New Hampshire's is perhaps the most famous: "[W]henever the ends of government are perverted, and public liberty manifestly endangered, and all other means of redress are ineffectual, the people may, and of right ought to reform the old, or establish a new government. The doctrine of nonresistance against arbitrary power, and oppression, is absurd, slavish, and destructive of the good and happiness of mankind."[17] New Jersey's is a bit less threatening, but still along the same lines: "All political power is inherent in the people. Government is instituted for the protection, security, and benefit of the people, and they have the right at all times to alter or reform the same, whenever the public good may require it."[18] Similar provisions are in many constitutions, including those of Maryland,[19] Tennessee,[20] and Virginia.[21] And there are some other examples of collective rights scattered here and there. To name one, New Jersey protects the right of private employees to collectively bargain, and of public employees to organize and petition for grievances.[22]

Overwhelmingly, then, what these collective rights provisions protect is a right of the people, as a whole, to form a government, live under a government committed to the public good, and to get a new one if it fails to do so. That they are in a bill of rights that might have well over a dozen or two other individual rights in it cannot turn a Baby Ninth in the same list into a secret protection of other collective rights, such as a "right" to pass legislation. Although they are collective rights, the rights to a republican government and revolution against tyranny are hardly collective rights that diminish the scope of individual rights. The very opposite is true; they are rights that work with individual rights to protect the public good in a free society. Far from being a reason to suspect that Baby Ninths actually protect the "right" of legislative majorities to restrict liberty, these collective rights work in tandem with both enumerated and unenumerated individual rights to ensure good government.

Judges Enforcing Rights

In the next chapter we will examine what individual rights Baby Ninths protect. But some of you may have a lingering doubt that we should first meet head on. We briefly discussed it earlier, but it bears repeating. "Sure," a close reader of state constitutions might say, "these provisions do seem to apply to individual rights. But why do they *protect* those rights? Or more exactly, why do they mean that *judges* can or must protect those rights when they are invoked in court? Most Baby Ninths just strictly say what they say, that the enumeration of other rights cannot be *construed* to deny, disparage, or impair other rights, not that those other rights are actually protected by the state constitution." "Perhaps," the critic might continue, "Baby Ninths are a way to remind legislators that when they pass laws they need to worry about how those laws might violate unenumerated rights in addition to those actually in the text of the constitution. But this does not carry over to judges enforcing those unenumerated rights in an attack on those laws, in the same way that a judge could enforce an enumerated right against a statute, because that is not the design of Baby Ninths. They do not *protect* rights, they merely *remind* lawmakers that there are other rights out there, and that they should not forget about them by *construing* the state constitution to imply they do not matter."

Although this argument does not stand up upon analysis (see below on that), we should not dismiss it out of hand. With a couple of exceptions, including one of the originals (Maine's), Baby Ninths say that the enumeration of rights should not be "construed" to deny, impair, or disparage retained rights. They do not say "other rights retained by the people are hereby protected by this Constitution." *That* would be even clearer. It is not off the wall to argue that this "construe" language means that lawmakers should not forget about those rights because otherwise they might and not much more. It is one thing to remind a legislator who is enacting laws that her actions might violate certain unenumerated rights. But it is another thing, continues the argument, for a judge who is being asked to protect such a right. In protecting a right the judge is not construing or avoiding construing the state bill of rights. She is enforcing a constitutional command. But a Baby Ninth only seems to construe not to command. What does enforcing a right have to do with construction? When a judge enforces an enumerated right such as a reasonableness requirement for a search—as when she interprets a state analogue to the Fourth Amendment—she is not doing that because of any construction of the constitution other than a construction inherent in constitutional interpretation. She is simply enforcing a prohibition in the text of the constitution. So the way that a Baby Ninth is different, this argument might say, is that it is a guideline to not violate certain unenumerated rights, *but it is not a prohibition on doing so.*[23]

Although a good faith attempt to make sense of the "construe" command in a Baby Ninth, this argument does not work. It proves too much. Baby Ninths are a constitutional command against denying, impairing, or disparaging certain rights retained by the people because they are not enumerated. That much cannot be denied. And the fact that those rights are referred to by the text of the constitution means that the constitution is in some way trying to protect them. Otherwise the Baby Ninth would not be doing anything. It would be saying "Hey, there are other important rights out there! And you should not impair, deny, or disparage them just because they're not listed above! But if you do, that's ok because this isn't a prohibition on you doing that, just some friendly advice!" In other words, those unenumerated rights could be denied, impaired, and disrespected just as much as if the Baby Ninth did not exist in the first place. But because it *was* adopted, indeed, because it was placed in the bill of rights of the state constitution, of all places, it must mean something. And that means that that denial, impairment, and disrespect cannot happen because the constitution says so. That is the significance of a Baby Ninth: it constitutionalizes the principle that the state cannot impair, deny, or disparage certain unenumerated rights. And that impairment, etc., cannot occur because the state cannot say to a judge, "Your honor, that right which the defendant says we are violating is not enumerated in the constitution, so you must rule that we are acting constitutionally."

The Baby Ninth forbids the judge from honoring that argument. If the judge agreed and ruled for the state, he would be *construing* the constitution to not protect a certain right because other rights were enumerated but it was not. That unenumerated right would be impaired, denied, or disparaged. Therefore, the only way the judge can act constitutionally is to not construe the right to not be protected because it is not enumerated (sorry for the triple negative, but it actually is necessary there). Note that this does not mean the judge should construe the right to be protected because it is not enumerated. As we will discuss in the next chapter, Baby Ninths do not protect *every* unenumerated right imaginable, even every individual right. But the right can be under the constitution's protection even though it is not enumerated, and that is because, at bottom, if it were not, the Baby Ninth would not be doing anything. It would simply be advice for legislators. But in mandating (Baby Ninths say "shall" not "please take under consideration") certain rights not be impaired, denied, or disparaged, it is not advice. And that means it is actively protecting unenumerated rights.

This then leads to judges. A judge must protect unenumerated rights when they are properly invoked just like she must for enumerated rights. This is because otherwise they would be impaired, denied, or disparaged because they are not enumerated. Just as a Baby Ninth protects unenumerated rights even though they are not enumerated, it requires judges to protect them just as they protect enumerated rights.

Original Public Meaning vs. Nonoriginalists

So now we (hopefully) have come to a point where all of us can agree that the original public meaning of Baby Ninths is that they protect unenumerated individual rights and that they are judicially enforceable. But you might respond, "So what? What do I care what the constitution meant whenever it was adopted. I care about what it means today." And that opens up a *big* issue about constitutional interpretation, namely how do we interpret constitutions? Do we worry about what the provision in question meant at the time it was adopted, or what it means at the time it is interpreted? And if the relevant time is today, what matters for how it is interpreted? Even then, many of the arguments we discussed above weigh in favor of an individual rights interpretation. Baby Ninths are still embedded within bills of rights overwhelmingly containing individual rights, and federalism and collective rights interpretations still lack coherence. Under some theories of constitutional interpretation, however, it could be that the language of Baby Ninths should nevertheless be interpreted in other ways. After all, we could interpret the language of Baby Ninths to mean collective rights, or animal rights, or all kinds of other "rights" if we really set our minds to it. If the constitutional theory you are working under demands that you interpret constitutional text to protect "social justice" (or, more exactly, whatever your idea is of the meaning of "social justice") then it could be that you interpret "other rights retained by the people" to include the right to collectively bargain, or the right of the legislature to pass laws overriding enumerated rights, etc. Maybe what rights are protected depends on what groups "need" protection at the present time, and thus the rights could even change over time, depending on what judges think.

Thus those who do not subscribe to originalism as the proper mode of constitutional interpretation could argue that Baby Ninths mean something else based upon another set of criteria: pure textualism, or the social mores of the present day, or some other standard. Indeed, on some level, if you want to interpret a text to mean what you think a constitution *should* protect, it is hard to argue about this. In that case, we may just have to agree to disagree on how to figure out what Baby Ninths mean. Whether originalism is the proper method of constitutional interpretation or not is not the question presented in this book, and many brilliant scholars—on various sides of the question—have attempted to answer it in books of their own. But if we are to use an originalist framework to interpret Baby Ninths, indeed, more basically, if we are to simply ask as a historical matter what they meant at the time they were adopted even if that does not matter for what they mean today, then there must be some meaning that they had at that time (a time which varies, of course, for each provision). And the author hopes he has demonstrated above that the individual rights model is by far the best account of that meaning.

In fact, even for those who are not "hard core originalists" but still think the history and meaning of words at the time constitutions are adopted should count for something in interpreting those constitutions, it is hoped that the above discussion is of value. What we have done is to apply the available models for what the Ninth Amendment meant at the time it was adopted to what Baby Ninths meant at the various times they were adopted. And although we should leave open the possibility that a better model may come along (or even multiple models, for different state constitutions at different times), the theoretical and contemporaneous evidence heavily leads us to believe that this whole enterprise is not that complicated. Drafters of state constitutions wanted to protect more rights than just those set forth in their constitutions, and so they put in these "etcetera clauses." They wanted them judicially protected. And they were not talking about collective rights, but individual rights.

Finally, one might ask, why did they use this language from the Ninth Amendment? After all, as we said above, they could have been a *bit* clearer, such as "There are other rights in addition to the above, and they are protected to the same extent as the above, and you can go into court and have them protected at the same level as the above." Well, perhaps for reasons of poetry (that example is not very inspiring language, is it?), but more likely because it was in the U.S. Constitution already; delegates used this "off the shelf" clause and repackaged it again and again. And that is what we are left with. Language in thirty-three states that protects individual rights beyond just those enumerated, and is judicially enforceable.

But *which* individual rights? Let us turn to that now.

CHAPTER 6

What Individual Rights Do
Baby Ninths Protect?

How about we go back to the introduction of this book and the various "rights" we were worried Jane's state legislature might imperil? To name just a few, there were the rights to earn a living, to garden, to go out after hours, and to collect stamps. If Baby Ninths protect individual rights, do they protect *these* individual rights? And if so, what others do they also protect? And whatever "Baby Ninth rights" we are talking about, how protected are they? After all, even highly protected rights, like the right to criticize the government, are not absolutely protected. For example, the White House press secretary does not have an absolute right to publicly criticize the president and keep her job; the right to "free speech" goes far, but not that far. To facilitate the protection of rights in a non-absolute way, judges generally use something we have talked about in previous chapters: levels of scrutiny. These vary between "strict" scrutiny (extremely hard cases for the government to win), to a "rational basis" level of scrutiny (which are extremely easy for the government to win), to something in between. As we saw in reviewing the (limited) Baby Ninth case law in chapter 4, this can be as important as whether the right is nominally protected in the first place. Thus we have two important questions: What rights do Baby Ninths protect, and how protected are those rights, that is, what level of scrutiny do they receive?

We will find out in this chapter that, generally, Baby Ninths should protect all the rights from the introduction (even stamp collecting) and protect them in a real way that puts the burden on the state to justify restrictions on them. And they protect a lot of other rights as well. Of course, given the infinite number of rights out there (that is why we have Baby Ninths in the first place), we will not have space to name them all here. Even a long appendix would be a waste of time. But generally Baby Ninths protect a lot of individual rights.

This does not mean, however, that Baby Ninths protect *all* individual rights. There are good reasons to think some kinds of "individual rights" are not protected by Baby Ninths. There are two large areas where the protection of certain rights are in question: rights that we give up when we form a government, that is, rights we do not "retain," and positive rights, that is, rights to have the government to *do* something *for* us rather than *not* do something *to* us. And although this is true for almost all versions of Baby Ninths in the various state constitutions that have them, there are a couple of nuances for Baby Ninths that are worded a bit differently.

After exploring what individual rights Baby Ninths protect, we will apply the Baby Ninths to real-world problems where people could use their help. In doing so we will see, as we touched on in the introduction, how Baby Ninths may be especially useful for the politically and economically powerless. Bringing the protections of unenumerated liberties to those who generally lack a voice in the halls of power may be the greatest benefit of adding "etcetera" to us declaring our rights. We will look at a few examples, including immigrant entrepreneurs, the homeless, and those who just want do something as simple as grow their own food.

What Is Being "Retained"?

We will begin with the text of an actual Baby Ninth Amendment. One of the oldest Baby Ninths in a constitution that is still in place today is Article I, Section 20, of Ohio's 1851 constitution:

> This enumeration of rights shall not be construed to impair or deny others retained by the people.[1]

Ohio's Baby Ninth is a fairly standard example of what is found in state constitutions. As we have seen in our sweep through their history, although various versions are worded a bit differently—for example, like Ohio, most use "impair" in addition to, or instead of, "deny" or "disparage"—almost all Baby Ninths follow the Ninth Amendment itself in structure. Most importantly, they use its most important language: the words "others" or "other rights" and "retained." Just two Baby Ninths do not use "retained": Georgia's and Virginia's.[2] And only Georgia's does not include "others" or "other" in reference to rights (although it is in the title to the provision). Further, Georgia's uses the arguably similar "inherent" in place of "retained." And a couple other states add "and inherent" to "retained" (Minnesota and Mississippi). Whether these quirky outliers should be thought of any differently from the others we can leave to the end of this chapter. In the meantime, though, we can rest assured that at least as a textual matter, our analysis of Ohio's 1851 constitutional text will be relevant to an interpretation of the Baby Ninths in most, if not all, other states that have one.

What does the text of Ohio's Baby Ninth tell us? That the people are "retain[ing]" "other" rights. What does "retain" mean here? Here's a clue: If rights can be *retained*, they also can be *given up*. And the text does not say "all" rights that are not enumerated are retained, only "others." How do we tell which is which?

This is the question that makes or breaks whether Baby Ninths make a difference or are merely cosmetic window dressing. We must remember the Enlightenment understanding of rights that are "retained" from the time of the Ninth Amendment itself. Social contract theory tells us that individuals give up certain things in order to form a society. But they retain others. Thomas Hobbes, an English philosopher who preceded John Locke, argued that individuals give *everything* up, delegating all their rights to a central "Leviathan" who then rules as an absolute dictator for the good of the people.[3] A Baby Ninth does not make much sense to a Hobbesian. "Retain" rights? But we are giving them all up!

Thankfully, Locke and others influential upon the Founders had a much narrower view, arguing that there were certain "inalienable" rights individuals do not give up. ("Inalienable" meaning that these rights cannot be taken away from or given away by their possessor.) What they most importantly do give up are the right to punish others for violating their own rights, that is, violent retribution, and corresponding rights to be free from supporting the government, that is, paying taxes that fund the handling of retribution, thereby securing retained rights. Thus, in a social contract, the state's police force and criminal justice system substitute for an individual's inherent right to retribution. Punishing someone for violating your rights, such as punishing someone who has previously assaulted you, is something you can do in a state of nature but cannot in a society, as then the government holds that right, not you. And in order to allow that government to function, you also give up the right to resist the taking of some of your rights, especially property rights, that is, taxation to fund the government that punishes others who violate your rights. In addition, there are, at least arguably, a few other associated liberties you give up, such as the right to be free from serving on a jury (which allows retribution to function more fairly).

Locke also at times suggests that the people give up other rights, although nothing nearly as sweeping as Hobbes' recommendations, in order to further the "public good."[4] We can leave it to Lockean scholars to debate the finer points of this. Whatever additional rights are given up (if any), however, it seems clear that Locke meant them in a limited context to protect the public, but beyond simple crime fighting and punishment. For example, storing large amounts of dynamite in your apartment might be something the Lockean social contract would allow the state to regulate for obvious public safety reasons.

Locke himself had detailed arguments about all of this.[5] Other theorists that were read at the Founding also believed in the validity of a social contract, or at least that government constitutes a compact of the people of some kind (setting the idealized state of nature aside), and a resulting mix of alienable and inalienable rights.[6] And we saw in chapter 1 how Lockean language, that George Mason likely directly lifted from Locke's own pages, had made its way into many state constitutions by the time the Ninth Amendment was crafted.

Therefore, in 1791 America, with the background of the Framers' revolutionary philosophies and the codification of Locke's own philosophy into state constitutional law, it is easy to imagine Locke's view of the social contract as applying to the Ninth Amendment. Further, the word "retained" does not make a lot of sense without social contract theory.[7] In addition, if the whole point of the Ninth Amendment is to cover the innumerable exercises of liberty that the drafters of a bill of rights do not have room or time to cover, it should not be a limited list of rights that are being "retained." If most exercises of liberty are given up to the state, the promised "etcetera" of the Ninth Amendment seems quite short. Thus the "retaining" is a large amount of "retaining," not just a few rights that could not quite make the enumeration.

This same analysis is even more applicable to the Baby Ninths themselves. We have seen how whatever the uncertainty with the Ninth Amendment, Baby Ninths were indeed "etcetera clauses." Although later framers of Baby Ninths may not have been the connoisseurs of seventeenth- and eighteenth-century social contract theory like some of the framers and ratifiers of the Ninth Amendment, they did deliberately choose to use its language, with that theory as its original backdrop. They used the word "retained," which has obvious social contract meanings that were still part of the public's understanding of that word at the time, and still are today.[8]

As we will discuss in a moment, this is not to say that all Baby Ninths perfectly impose John Locke's views on natural rights on their respective state governments. It just means that we can start with a Lockean understanding of what rights are given up and what rights are retained when the people form a government. (We will challenge this Lockean understanding of "retained" later in this chapter but end up settling on it. That can wait a moment.) Locke's specific influence upon the Founders is a heavily contested topic, as is the debate about *which* of his works were more influential and whether it was more his epistemology in *An Essay Concerning Human Understanding* than his social contract theory in his *Second Treatise of Government*.[9] More broadly, however, social contract theory, and the concept of giving up some rights and retaining others— even if not out of a state of nature but simply through real people forming social compacts—was "in the water," as it were, during the American Revolution and the Founding. Exact views on these matters differed, of course, but the general view of some rights as inalienable was widespread. The point to take away here is that the word "retained" signals this understanding of rights. Whether the framers of a Baby Ninth had Locke himself in mind is beside the point.

Baby Ninths protect individual rights in a libertarian way. A Lockean reading of a Baby Ninth is that just about every negative liberty other than those we give up for retribution, such as punishing criminals and resisting taxation, is "retained," and those retained rights cannot be protected any less than enumerated rights are. Now we should admit that something about this seems a bit aggressive. For example, Illinois adopted a new Baby Ninth in its 1970 constitution. Did Illinois citizens in 1970 really mean to place strict libertarian limits on any state regulation of consensual private behavior? This seems anomalous when placed against the wide range of governmental regulation that Illinois and its local governments wielded both before and after that constitution's adoption, from occupational licensing to zoning to environmental regulation. The same is true of past adoptions of Baby Ninths. Indeed, no state in American history has had the near-libertarian utopia that Locke's understanding arguably envisions. So it is hard to conclude that the meaning of Baby Ninths is that any limit on individual liberty is unconstitutional.

But we do not have to. Baby Ninths should be understood to protect all negative liberties, just as the Lockean understanding of the word "retained" implies. That does not mean, however, that they guarantee a night-watchman state where government deals with nothing other than crime and punishment. Just as other constitutional rights do not completely preclude governmental intervention, but limit it to where the government has a good reason to act, the same is true of Baby Ninths. How can this work? Through the scrutiny we have already discussed in this book.

Real Scrutiny for Real (But Unenumerated) Rights

As we learned in previous chapters, a constitutional right may "exist," but if the scrutiny a judge applies to it is not meaningful the right does not do anyone any good. Set the scrutiny low enough and the government can always justify what it is doing, no matter how silly the excuse. But set the scrutiny at a meaningful level, where the government must justify its actions with actual evidence, but not so high that it never can, then the right protects people while allowing the government to act beyond the role of a simple crime fighter. It allows for the people to have much more freedom than Hobbes would, but also allows for the state to wield more power than Locke might allot.

Applying real scrutiny, but scrutiny the government can surmount if it has a good reason, is not radical. It is therefore easy to square with the people of Illinois adopting a rule like that in 1970. Or Alabama in 1819 or New Mexico in 1911. Baby Ninths should be seen as protecting all the negative liberties we discussed in the introduction to this book—the rights to earn a living, garden, socialize, send your children to the school of your choice, or collect stamps—but the government can nevertheless be allowed to restrict those rights if it has a genuinely good reason. For example, the government cannot prevent you from planting tomatoes, but it can prevent you from using a certain type of insecticide that it has solid evidence can cause cancer. It cannot force you to spend time and money on training that is not related to your occupation to get a license to work, but it can force electricians to carry liability insurance. And it cannot forbid you from using birth control, but it can forbid a specific type of birth control if the evidence demonstrates it is dangerous. This type of scrutiny can then parallel the similar scrutiny applied to many (although, alas, not all) enumerated rights, such as the rights to free speech and to practice one's religion, in line with Baby Ninths' commands to not "impair," "deny," or "disparage" unenumerated rights just because other rights are enumerated.

This is close to what Randy Barnett calls "the presumption of liberty" in interpreting the Ninth Amendment. Under his view, all actions that do not harm others are presumed to be protected by the Ninth Amendment, but the government can counter that presumption with evidence that its regulation is needed to protect public health, safety, and welfare.[10] Barnett argues that the Ninth Amendment itself cannot be interpreted as an originalist matter to protect certain types of rights because the text's meaning does not supply that answer. But the presumption of liberty is a construction of the text that fills in that gap.

Whatever differences there are in how the approach taken here might vary from the presumption of liberty are not important for present purposes. What matters is that interpreting Baby Ninths to cover all Lockean negative liberties with a meaningful level of scrutiny, but one the government can still overcome with bona fide evidence and public-spirited purpose, allows them to function and be true to their original public meaning, while not, at the same time, mandating a night-watchman state.

Positive Rights in the Ninth Amendment?

That does not, however, end the story. We have been talking about what "individual rights" Baby Ninths actually protect, but so far entirely in the context of Lockean negative rights, that is, rights to keep the government from doing something to you. That makes sense considering that the key word in Baby Ninths, "retained," is inherently Lockean. But we have not seriously discussed whether that word could also include *positive* rights, rights to make the government do something *for* you. Although some readers may think "Why bother? Everybody knows 'retained' only refers to negative rights," as we will see below there is a sense where that is not true. Additionally, this question is worth pursuing because many rights advocated today are positive rights. If Baby Ninths are going to become more of a staple of jurisprudence, positive rights are going to rear their head sooner rather than later. Thus, although the following few sections may seem like a bit of a long detour, it is an important one for us to take so that we have a full understanding of the implications of Baby Ninths when the question of positive rights inevitably comes up.

In the end we will see that Baby Ninths do not protect positive rights, although we will leave the door slightly ajar for a positive right or two to come in. There potentially may be exceptions, but those exceptions are few.

Negative rights are rights Americans are most familiar with and that most high-profile constitutional cases are about. Familiar examples include the right to free speech, the right to practice your religion, and the right to work the occupation of your calling. Some of the cases using Baby Ninths that we discussed earlier concerned rights like these. In fact, all the rights that we discussed in the introduction are negative rights. For example, one of those rights was the right to garden. When we say something like "the right to garden" we generally mean it in a negative rights context. It does not mean a right to have the government do things for you. Now there conceivably could be a positive right to garden, and in that case the government would need to act in some way in order for that right to become a reality, such as giving people an "allotment" of land to plant vegetables, as some European governments do. But to try and exercise her *negative* right to garden, a gardener just needs the government to not punish her for, say, planting vegetables in her front yard. An allotment might help someone exercise that right, but the negative right itself is simply leaving the gardener alone. The same is true of a right to practice a religion. The government could help you exercise a *positive* right to practice by building you a church, but that is not the right we generally mean when we talk about religious liberty.

Positive rights to garden and worship do not come up that often, but positive rights that are often discussed are a right to a basic level of income or a right to housing. Some have called for courts to recognize these as constitutionally protected rights. To the author's knowledge, no state constitution, and definitely not the federal constitution, protects these rights or has been interpreted to contain them. But there are many individual positive rights that courts *have* found to exist, and that are much less controversial. For example, many state constitutions explicitly guarantee a right to a K-12 education.[11] If you asked Americans today "is the right to receive a state-funded primary education a constitutional right," many would say "yes," and they would often be correct (although they might confusingly believe that the right is in the federal constitution). Even less controversially, there are a lot of things the government is constitutionally required to do *for* you if it is *already* trying to do bad things to you. Most obviously, if it wants to lock you up, it must provide you with certain procedures. These include a jury trial, a speedy trial, a chance to make your defense and to see evidence the prosecution has against you, etc. All of these are "positive rights," in that they are things the government must do *for* you, although they are in the context of where the government is doing bad things to you in the first place. And the courts have held that even when the government is doing things not as serious as criminal punishment, but still important, such as firing you from your government job, it must provide certain procedures and justifications, otherwise it violates the constitutional right to due process.[12]

Before moving to whether Baby Ninths protect positive rights, let us first address whether the Ninth Amendment itself protects positive rights. As we have seen, scholars of the Ninth Amendment who have examined what the words of the Amendment meant at the time it was adopted, and who interpret it as protecting individual rights, generally agree that it referred (maybe not directly *protected*, but at least referred) to Lockean, negative rights. Most of the analysis of these scholars focuses, correctly, on what rights are "retained," and what to "retain" a right even means. For example, Randy Barnett and Michael McConnell argue that "retained rights" is language straight out of the natural rights tradition of John Locke and allied thinkers.[13] In the Lockean understanding the only rights that existed prior to the government being formed were negative rights. This is true essentially by definition. Someone cannot have a right to a basic income if no government or other institution even exists to provide that income. Perhaps government could *create* a right to a basic income, but then it would not be a right that had been "retained." Barnett and McConnell also agree that positive rights, such as the rights of the criminally accused, were by no means considered unimportant by the framers of the Ninth Amendment, but they were not considered rights "retained" by the people.[14]

But not everyone agrees with this assessment. Another scholar, Lochlan Shelfer, provides a strong argument that at the time the Ninth Amendment was adopted, "retained" rights also referred to well-established positive, procedural rights such as a jury trial in civil cases.[15] He does not do this by appealing to John Locke. Instead he looks at how people considering the Ninth Amendment's adoption discussed it. For example, there was a vociferous defense of the civil jury in Antifederalist literature when the Constitution was being adopted, and this included discussion of the Ninth Amendment itself. Whether the Ninth Amendment refers to the right to a civil jury did not later become an issue because the Seventh Amendment, adopted at the same time as the Ninth, explicitly protects that right. But Shelfer argues that before that became clear, one of the justifications for the Ninth Amendment by Antifederalists was that it would include a civil jury trial right, and therefore that it was understood to not refer purely to Lockean natural rights.

Of course, from a philosophical perspective it does not matter what the people thought "retain" meant when the Ninth Amendment was adopted. One can make a good argument that it simply does not make sense for "the people" to "retain" a right to a civil jury from a social contract perspective. But our concern is not philosophy. Instead, it is the legal interpretation of constitutional text. And if the ordinary public meaning of "retain" included positive rights like the civil jury at the time the text was adopted, then we—and judges enforcing the original meaning of the text—are stuck with that.

The present discussion does not mean to settle this disagreement about the Ninth Amendment itself once and for all. We will leave that to these various, able scholars. The takeaway, however, is that *for the most part*, the Ninth Amendment was understood at the time it was adopted to refer to negative rights, but there is a possibility for some application to certain positive rights. There is no evidence from the time, however, that it would apply *beyond* long-accepted positive procedural rights in the Anglo-American legal tradition and extend to rights such as a basic income, health care, etc. So perhaps we can call this originalist understanding of individual rights that the Ninth Amendment protects to be "Lockean rights, plus." Shelfer's point is well taken: A Lockean understanding of the word "retained" is not necessarily the *only* understanding from 1791, and we will see that the same could be true of later times, such as 1819 Alabama or 1970 Illinois. But we will also see that in the end it is hard to make the case for "Lockean rights, plus," even though some people at the time that the Ninth Amendment or a Baby Ninth was adopted might have believed that is what the provision meant.

Therefore, if we assume the Ninth Amendment itself protects individual rights (remember, that is not a question this book is trying to settle), and we interpret it from an originalist framework, it seems clear those individual rights are the Lockean negative rights we discussed earlier, plus just maybe a few "old English" positive ones of the civil jury variety. The latter are not rights people "retain" in an abstract social contract, but they are arguably encompassed within the meaning of "retain" at the time of the Ninth Amendment's adoption.

The question for us is, do those boundaries foreclosing most positive rights apply to Baby Ninths? And might that be different for Alabama's Baby Ninth in 1819 versus Illinois's in 1970?

Positive Rights in Baby Ninths?

In the abstract there is no reason an open-ended provision in a state constitution could not protect positive rights. We should fully recognize that constitutions often *do* provide for positive rights that many of us would not want in them. Indeed, the constitutions of other countries sometimes provide for a right to a basic income and many other benefits.[16] In other words, just because you like limited government and do not like guaranteeing that the government will do things for people does not mean that a constitution agrees with you. Continuing on this theme, one reason to keep most positive rights out of constitutions is that they are hugely problematic to enforce. (Witness the serial litigation in many states to better fund public education and the mixed results it has brought to actual educational outcomes.[17]) But just because they are hard to enforce does not mean they do not exist, or even that they are not designed to be enforced by the courts.

And it is not like positive constitutional rights are a recent innovation. Many state constitutions have guaranteed an education since the mid-nineteenth century. The constitutional conventions issuing these educational guarantees, and other positive guarantees, were often also writing Baby Ninths.[18] Putting aside the precise meaning of the words of Baby Ninths for a moment, who is to say that an open-ended constitutional clause could not have meant positive rights of certain kinds? And looking at the text of Baby Ninths specifically, the original meaning of "retained" of course included Lockean negative rights. But was it broad enough—perhaps by 1819, 1851, 1911, or 1970—to *also* include positive rights, especially after people started writing those kinds of rights directly into those very same constitutions?

The answer is "no," the Baby Ninth was not broad enough. But to get to this answer we are going to run a thought experiment. We need to turn to the history of whenever the Baby Ninth in question was adopted, from the point of view of an actual drafter at a constitutional convention and also consider the timing of rights being "retained." The enumeration of rights in that state constitution, the Baby Ninth tells us, cannot be construed to impair or deny other rights that the people already had and did not give up. But *when* did that "giving up" take place? In our discussion of Lockean negative rights we ignored this question, assuming the "retaining" and "giving up" is made at some idealized time when the people formed a social contract. But once we start inquiring, that becomes a bit unclear.

Thinking of Ohio's 1851 constitution, for example, it seems the giving up could either apply to some point in the past when "the people" referred to by the provision formed a social contract *or* to 1851 itself. Locke's view of a social contract is a bit of what lawyers call a "legal fiction." Yes, of course, it can happen that people come together to form governments (as in 1776 or 1787, for example), but when they do that they are not stepping straight out of an idealized state of nature where anything goes. Thus, the "rights bargain," of giving up some rights but retaining others, is either simply an abstraction or, perhaps quite differently, it refers to something that actually took place with the adoption of the 1851 Ohio Constitution. It makes sense that the "ordinary meaning" of "retained" in 1851 would be exactly that: a present-tense verb describing what "the people" are doing in adopting the new constitution. This "contemporaneous retaining" would also be true, of course, of other Baby Ninths, such as Maine's in 1819 or Illinois's in 1970.

Understanding the "retaining" as occurring at the time of a particular constitution's adoption also makes sense once we consider the other language in the Baby Ninth. It refers to "*this* enumeration of rights," that is, the list of rights just above it in the same article of the same constitution. The Baby Ninth then requires that particular enumeration not be construed to impair or deny certain other rights that are "retained." That sounds like something happening at the time the specific constitution is adopted, not just something that any old group of civilized people would do. The enumeration itself is certainly going on when the constitution is being adopted. If the "retaining" were not also, it would seem to be an odd fit, where something that is going on now (enumerating) cannot be used to deny something that already happened (retaining) at an idealized and unknowable point in the past.

Indeed, this view of "retaining" (as happening at the same time as the enumerating) comes out in some of the convention materials we previously reviewed. The delegate's speech for the Illinois Constitution of 1970 used "retain" in the present tense, stating that the proposed provision "retains the rights" of individuals.[19] And a delegate at the Minnesota Republican convention said, "The object is to give a portion of the people's rights to the officers of the government, and to retain a portion."[20] That certainly sounds like the people of 1857 Minnesota were delegating rights and retaining rights then and there, not at some point in the past.

Positive Law for Positive Rights in Baby Ninths?

In the end, however, seeing the "retaining" as happening at the same time the constitution is adopted does not work. It may be what certain constitution writers thought at the time, but as a matter of the language's meaning it cannot stand. Otherwise the Baby Ninth becomes absurd and unworkable.

If the "retaining" is going on at the time a constitution is adopted, that raises *another* thorny question. What kind of rights did Alabamans have in 1819, or Ohioans in 1851, or Illinoisans in 1970, etc., and are those the rights that are (or even can be) given up or retained? We do not mean here what kinds of rights they had as human beings, in the Lockean sense. We mean if you went to court what kinds of "rights" would be recognized. On a practical level, what rights did the people have to either give up or retain at the time they adopted their respective Baby Ninth?

We have already established that the people had Lockean natural rights whenever a Baby Ninth containing the word "retained" was enacted. But what about just ordinary "rights" people at those particular times possessed as a matter of positive law, that is based on what written constitutions, statutes, policies, etc. existed at the time? (And just to clarify, "positive law" should not be confused with "positive rights.")

Looking at positive law will greatly vary, of course, depending on the particular state and the particular time. A specific example may help clarify what we are looking at. We will again look at Ohio and the adoption of the 1851 constitution.

At that time, Ohioans enjoyed the protection of the former constitution of 1802. This constitution protected several positive rights, including rights to "trial by jury" (ambiguous as to whether it included civil juries), a speedy trial, open courts for civil wrongs, and several others.[21] Further, there were arguably other "rights" guaranteed by statute. For instance, by 1851 various pieces of Ohio legislation provided for a state-sponsored primary education.[22] Every state will have the same story regarding its Baby Ninth, of course. Most had previous constitutions (whether state or territorial; Rhode Island had a previous colonial charter) and existing state or territorial legislation.

Are these previous constitutional and statutory rights "retained" and therefore protected by the new Baby Ninth? This gets a bit metaphysical. Taking Ohio, in one sense the rights of the 1802 constitution ceased to exist as rights in *that* constitution once the 1851 version, containing the Baby Ninth, superseded it. After all, once the 1802 constitution ceased to exist, it stands to reason its "rights" ceased to exist (those rights might still exist in a different sense, but not as *constitutional* rights of positive law). Now, in the case of Ohio, to a large extent this was academic, because most of the rights in the former constitution were restated in the latter. This often has been the story for states adopting new constitutions, as bills of rights are not tinkered with nearly as much as the rest of the document. But if some rights are left out of a new constitution, would they still be "retained" by the people, even though they were no longer enforceable under the old constitution? Or would they truly cease to exist as positive law, because the old constitution ceased to exist, and the people would not "retain" them?

To help think this through, we can continue to use Ohio as an example because it interestingly actually had a positive right (that is a right guaranteeing that the government do something for citizens) that did not survive the change in constitutions: the right of associations of people "to receive letters of incorporation, to enable them to hold estates, real and personal, for the support of their schools, academies, colleges, universities, and for other purposes."[23] Although its outer contours are a bit unclear (what does "for other purposes" mean?), the central reason for this enumerated right in the 1802 constitution was obviously to assist in the formation of nonprofit corporations to help organize and fund various kinds of schools. The right to organize and give money to a school is a negative right, but receiving "letters of incorporation" to facilitate funding of schools is a positive right. It is an entitlement for the government to give you protected legal status (as corporate charters do not exist in any state of nature).

In the 1851 Ohio Constitution this right disappears. There are general provisions that *allow* the legislature to pass laws that let people incorporate (with nothing specific about schools), but nothing explicitly making it a constitutional right.[24] Thus, constitutionally speaking, a civic-minded group that wanted to form some kind of corporation to provide for a school had a constitutional right to do so between 1802 and 1851, but did not have that *enumerated* constitutional right after 1851.

But in, say, 1852, did Ohioans have a "retained" constitutional right to keep receiving letters of incorporation to fund schools? Again, just as with other rights that might be imagined, it could be argued that the Baby Ninth commands that just because there are enumerated rights does not mean the right to incorporate to fund schools does not exist and is not constitutionally protected. And it is undeniably a right that Ohioans used to have. So how could it not be a right the people "retained"?

To add one more thought, say the Ohio legislature had passed a law in 1849 guaranteeing a minimum level of income. And the statute actually called the support it guaranteed a "right." This would be a positive right of positive law just as much as the right to letters of incorporation, it just would be a statutory "right" not a constitutional "right." And then assume the Ohio legislature repealed the statute in 1852. Is that a "right" the people "retained" in 1851? It was a "right" in some sense at the time the Baby Ninth was adopted. Without the Baby Ninth, like all rights of positive law, it could be repealed. But with the Baby Ninth, does that make it different?

And now let us take this to the level of the absurd. Suppose in 1849 the legislature passed a law stating that everyone has a "right" to a pony. It is then repealed in 1852. Does the Baby Ninth nevertheless perpetually guarantee Ohioans a right to a small horse?

You can see where this is going. Just because people have a "right" in positive law (however nominal the item at issue is a "right") at the time a Baby Ninth and its surrounding enumeration of rights is adopted does not mean that the Baby Ninth then protects that "right." Otherwise the Baby Ninth would, in effect, freeze in time all "rights" that happened to exist in constitutions, statutes, ordinances, policies, etc., at that moment. It would be a one-way ratchet, forever protecting all these "rights," however misguided they later turn out to be.

It therefore seems that "retained" cannot be referring to rights of positive law, whether constitutional, statutory, or otherwise, because it leads to an absurd result. (Again, just to be clear, by "positive law" we do not mean the same thing as "positive rights.") Any positive "right," however minor or misconceived, that exists at the time the Baby Ninth is adopted would continue to exist in the future even if the positive law creating those positive rights were repealed.

However, if "retained" does not cover rights of positive law but the "retention" does occur at the time its constitution is adopted (and not in some theoretical social contract past), what does it relate to at all?

The only thing it can relate to that makes sense is a *reaffirmation* of a Lockean social contract. It is a social contract made by "the people" as people who, being people, have Lockean natural rights. This is distinct from Ohioans in 1851, or Alabamans in 1819, etc., bargaining away the rights they *happen to have* under positive law at that particular time. Thus, even though a Baby Ninth concerns rights being "retained" *at that time*, they are rights that individuals do not give up *at any time* to form ("reconstitute" might be the better way of putting it in this context) a free government. They are rights you have if there is no government around *and* that you keep after setting the new government up. Again, none of this means that the "state of nature" is or was an actual thing in 1819 Alabama, 1851 Ohio, or 1970 Illinois, or at any point in the past. It is just a useful idea to draw upon given the Lockean term "retained" that is used in Baby Ninths, and the absurdities we run into if it applies to all kinds of "rights" of positive law that happen to exist in law at the time a Baby Ninth is adopted. Thus, in the end, although the context of 1819, 1851, or 1970 is different from 1791, positive rights under positive law—such as the right to an education—that the people might have had at the time of adoption simply are not covered by "retained," even though at first glance that seems to be covered by the ordinary meaning of that word.

Another way to think about this is that on the floor of the 1851 Ohio convention, or the conventions for the 1819 Alabama Constitution or 1970 Illinois Constitution, or any other that adopted a Baby Ninth, the delegates are not delegating and exchanging whatever rights of the people they happen to have from their prior constitution and statutes. They are delegating and exchanging whatever rights the people have as free human beings, whatever their prior system of government said about them. The rights they had to delegate and retain are not different if their current state government was a welfare state with a massive charter of positive rights, a repressive regime where there were no recognized rights of any kind, or a utopian fantasy straight out of Robert Nozick's *Anarchy, State, and Utopia.*

But what about the idea of "Lockean social contract, plus" that we saw might apply to the Ninth Amendment, protecting some positive rights such as the right to a civil jury trial? Although we should interpret the present tense the delegates use in referring to Baby Ninths in an abstract sense (otherwise we get the absurd result of protecting all positive "rights"), it is hard to deny that many delegates and commentators did not strictly limit their understanding of Baby Ninths to Lockean rights.

We have two choices on that matter. First, we could conclude that taking a Baby Ninth beyond the Lockean context simply does not fit with the "retained" language of Baby Ninths, and that such an understanding is simply wrong and was wrong at the time of the Ninth Amendment as well. "Retained" means Lockean rights, we would say, and you just cannot include any positive rights even if many readers of a provision at the time it was adopted had an understanding that it did include some. In other words we would say although some readers understood "retained" to include some positive rights (the civil jury example demonstrates that at least some did for the Ninth Amendment), they did not realize how this would lead to absurd results, and so that cannot be the term's original meaning. Second, however, what if we found a middle way that did not lead to an absurd result, but still had room for some positive rights? One way this could be done is to join a social contract understanding of Baby Ninths with what we can call a "traditions" understanding. In the case of the Ninth Amendment, this would allow for *some* positive rights, but only if they were rights that were long understood as protected under the English common law system. The same could be true for Baby Ninths as well.

The problem is, it is hard to come up with such a "middle way."

At first blush, a perfectly justifiable reading of a Baby Ninth by an ordinary citizen following its adoption could be: "Oh, I'm glad they did that. It will protect our fundamental liberties that we have thus far enjoyed." This citizen might not have been immersed in Lockean social contract theory and not read "retained" in an idealized social contract sense. Indeed, this would likely be true of the delegates who we have seen talk about their "retained" rights when discussing proposed Baby Ninths. Thus to them a reading that might have made sense is that the new constitution protected some rights beyond purely negative ones, but that it appropriately did not protect any random "right" that the prior constitution or statutes had. In that way, the citizen and the delegate would read the Baby Ninth to "just make sense."

Although well-meaning, this approach could easily collapse back into looking at what rights were recognized by former constitutions and statutes and therefore lead to the same problems we just discussed. How best to look at what "makes sense" other than looking at what laws there are? The Baby Ninth does not say "fundamental rights, including a few really important positive ones." It just says "rights." It is hard to square this circle. Nevertheless, we should leave open the possibility that it *could* be done. After all, an understanding that "rights" in a Baby Ninth encompasses a historical understanding of long-recognized positive rights has been accepted by some well-meaning jurists. For example, we discussed in chapter 4 how the New Jersey Supreme Court used its Baby Ninth to protect the right against double jeopardy in criminal prosecutions, and how the Alaska Supreme Court interpreted its Baby Ninth to protect the right to represent oneself in court. Both courts looked at historical understandings of whether the asserted rights were protected. Indeed, this historical understanding could be used to prevent a Baby Ninth from going too far away from its Lockean language and include too many positive rights. Luckily it is not up to us to conclusively solve that problem now. We should merely leave it open as a possibility, but one that would need to be fairly limited lest the Baby Ninth expand far beyond being an "etcetera clause" to a freezing in place of all positive legislation.

Thus we have an answer on whether Baby Ninths (at least the huge majority that are written like Ohio's) protect any unenumerated positive rights: probably not, but if so in a limited way.

Odd-Man-Out Ninths

Before turning to the wider implications of Baby Ninths' protection of unenumerated rights, we should address something left open a few pages back. What about those Baby Ninths that are not worded like all the others? Well it turns out that they perhaps should be interpreted differently, but only slightly. Minnesota and Mississippi have the words "and inherent" after "retained," but that is not a huge difference. It seems that language would narrow the potential rights from all those that are "retained" to those that are *also* "inherent," but since all negative liberties would be "inherent" anyway (otherwise they would not be "state of nature" liberties), the word might not be doing much work. It could be read, however, as more definitively excluding any positive rights we have spoken of, such as a right to a civil jury, as those sound less "inherent." So, at most, it seems Minnesota and Mississippi might exclude whatever positive rights Baby Ninths could otherwise protect.

Further, Virginia does not mention "retained" rights at all, simply stating "The rights enumerated in this Bill of Rights shall not be construed to limit other rights of the people not therein expressed." Without the limitation of "retained" rights, does this mean that the Virginian Baby Ninth protects God-knows-what "rights" of any kind? Not necessarily, but it does take the analysis beyond just the social contract context. Virginia's constitution has the benefit of also containing a Lockean natural rights guarantee, which, if you remember from earlier (and as the name implies), essentially enshrines a social contract view of rights into the constitution anyway. It perhaps would be incongruous if an understanding of the Baby Ninth would go too far beyond this context.

That leaves Georgia. As we noted when discussing its origins, Georgia's provision is unique: "The enumeration of rights herein contained as a part of this Constitution shall not be construed to deny to the people any inherent rights which they may have hitherto enjoyed." This provision has been in various constitutions (Georgia has had quite a few in its history) since its Confederate constitution, the last time being with its most recent constitution of 1983, although it was dropped in 1868 and added back in 1877. Unlike the others, this is a Baby Ninth explicitly tying itself to rights enjoyed at the time it was adopted. There is no social contract language. But that does not mean that it goes down the absurd route of protecting random statutory "rights" that we spoke of before, as it only refers to "inherent" rights. And, as with Minnesota and Mississippi, "inherent rights" seems to refer to negative liberties, although only those that the people "may have hitherto enjoyed." A fair reading of that last language is that if at the time the constitution was adopted an "inherent right" was *not* being enjoyed (presumably because the state had regulated it or even banned its exercise) then it is not protected. Which would make it of more limited protection than other Baby Ninths, none of which say they only apply to rights that were being "enjoyed" at the time of adoption.

We should note one more thing about Georgia. There is a huge question of whether the timing of the Baby Ninth's original adoption was connected to its idiosyncratic wording, given that it was adopted as the state seceded from the Union in an effort to protect the institution of slavery. Perhaps "inherent rights which they may have hitherto enjoyed" was a thinly veiled reference to the rights of slaveholders. The author knows of no evidence of this one way or the other, but the timing makes it extremely plausible. The new constitution sought to protect slavery in other ways as well.

But does this matter for the people of Georgia today? Although the language of the Baby Ninth is essentially the same in the most recent, 1983, constitution as it was in the 1861 version, a lot has changed. Most importantly, the original public meaning of 1983 did not have the rights of current slaveholders as a backdrop. Not only were the two constitutions different, but there had been several in between them, including one (the Reconstruction constitution of 1868) that lacked a Baby Ninth altogether. Thus we should not see Georgia's current Baby Ninth as protecting slaveholders and therefore illegitimate in some way. But we should not deny that motivation as a historical question.

How Do Baby Ninths Work in Practice?

We now have our answer on what Baby Ninths mean: They protect individual, negative rights beyond those enumerated in the rest of a state's constitution. (We are leaving aside the discrepancies in the four states with slightly different language.) And they protect those rights by subjecting the state's actions to meaningful scrutiny, where the government can only act if it is doing so in the public interest and has real evidence that its actions are warranted. That scrutiny does not necessarily need to be "strict," but it needs to be meaningful enough that it is not the mere window dressing of the modern rational basis test.

Okay, so what does that mean in practice? First of all, it means legislators, city council members, governors, mayors, state agency commissioners, zoning board members, and others who make and enforce state laws and regulations need to remember that there are rights beyond just those enumerated in their state constitution's bill of rights that they need to be aware of when they exercise their powers. Now some readers, especially those who have worked in a state legislature, may be laughing. Why? Because politicians rarely take notice of *enumerated* rights already. But much of this is because of the abdication of judges in enforcing those rights. One of the few areas where policymakers take note of constitutional law is free speech.[25] That is because judges actually enforce the Free Speech Clause of the First Amendment at a meaningful level. Congress members and legislators will debate whether a proposal violates the First Amendment because they know that judges take it seriously.

The same is not true of other rights, even some enumerated rights. For example, the Supreme Court has applied a form of the rational basis test to the Public Use Clause of the Fifth Amendment and allowed cities to take people's homes and give the land to another private party, usually a wealthy developer, simply on the hope that the new use will lead to higher property tax revenues.[26] That this has happened literally thousands of times in recent decades demonstrates that city council members are not generally interpreting the Public Use Clause on their own.[27] If they did one would expect that some city councilors would conclude that even though they want to use eminent domain for economic development as a policy matter they are constitutionally forbidden from doing so. After all, the case that allowed this interpretation of the Public Use Clause was only decided five-to-four. Instead, however, city council members simply move forward with the constitutional interpretation the Court's majority left them. We should expect the same regarding their interpretation of Baby Ninths until judges begin enforcing them with real scrutiny and to more rights than the handful of favored ones that a handful of courts recognize today.

Thus the interpretation of Baby Ninths argued for in this book is going to come up where constitutional rights usually come up: in court. People like our friend Jane from the introduction can ask a judge to protect their unenumerated rights when state or local governments infringe upon them, either by going to court to challenge a law as a plaintiff, or as a defendant when the government tries to fine them, take their property away, or lock them up. They can raise the rights we discussed—earn a living, meet with friends, meditate, collect stamps—and many others. And then the government needs to come back with real evidence that the infringement on their rights is needed to protect public health and safety. Instead of turning to other constitutional clauses that many see as ill-suited to protect rights not explicitly in a constitution, such as due process clauses, they can raise these "etcetera clauses" designed for exactly this situation.

Bringing Power to the Powerless

Applying Baby Ninths in this way would help anyone burdened with an unjustifiable restriction on their liberty, rich or poor, of whatever color. But as we pointed out with the stories of food truck entrepreneurs in the introduction, it is important to emphasize that many on the margins of society would find this tool particularly helpful in fighting injustice. That already has been the case with unenumerated rights when they *have* been enforced. If Baby Ninths are to be interpreted as argued here, however, we will have a lot more help for those lacking wealth and political power.

Readers familiar with constitutional history may object here and argue that unenumerated rights have actually benefited the powerful. Pointing to the "*Lochner* era" of the early twentieth century, they might bring up the 1905 case *Lochner v. New York*[28] itself, where the Supreme Court found a maximum hours law for bakers to be unconstitutional. (In fact, the story of *Lochner*, where unionized bakeries pushed for the maximum hours provision as a way to compete against less industrialized immigrant bakeries, is much more complicated than the traditional narrative.[29] But it is not necessary to analyze that here.) Or a case like *Coppage v. Kansas*,[30] where a law preventing employers from forbidding their employees from joining a union was found to violate the Fourteenth Amendment. Both of these were cases where the government had passed a law that at least some powerful people disagreed with.

But given that powerful people are, almost by definition, better able to use the government to their advantage, it should be unsurprising that there are plenty of examples of the reverse: of the *powerless* going to court to prevent the government from violating their unenumerated rights. The powerless are more often going to be on the losing side of political disputes. We discussed in the introduction the 1925 case of *Pierce v. Society of Sisters*, where the Supreme Court found unconstitutional the state of Oregon's attempt to keep parents from choosing where to educate their children. The act was motivated by anti-Catholic and anti-immigrant paranoia (including from the Ku Klux Klan), where anti-communist and nativist supporters wanted to bar groups such as the Society of Sisters from teaching children.[31] Another example, which *Pierce* relied on, was *Meyer v. Nebraska*, where the Supreme Court found unconstitutional a law that forbade Nebraskan elementary school children from learning any language other than English.[32] This, of course, prevented recent immigrants from using formal education to teach their children the language of their home cultures.

Since the time of *Pierce* and *Meyer*, when in the New Deal rights revolution the Supreme Court put all but a few favored unenumerated rights to the rational basis test, it has been harder to find examples of courts protecting unenumerated rights. But there are some, including the subset of state courts that actually have used Baby Ninths discussed in chapter 4.[33] One was the case of the food truck owners in Fort Pierce, Florida, discussed in the introduction. Another, from federal court, that can illuminate what Baby Ninths might do is that of Jestina Clayton, who we also briefly mentioned in the introduction.

Jestina (whose full name is Jestina Sunkarie Bangura-Clayton) is an immigrant from Sierra Leone who learned traditional African-style hair braiding as a child.[34] After settling in Salt Lake City, Utah, she began braiding hair for her two daughters, but also for others as a way to supplement her family's income. But then she learned an unpleasant fact. In Utah, as in many other states, simply braiding hair constituted the practice of cosmetology, which required a license.[35] Obtaining a license required two thousand hours of training in cosmetology school costing thousands of dollars in tuition, followed by an exam. And in none—none!—of those thousands of hours or in the various questions asked in the exam was African-style hair braiding taught or tested. Other than some generic sanitation instructions, the entire licensing scheme was irrelevant to someone like Jestina who wanted to practice African-style hair braiding. Jestina did not want to cut hair, give women perms, or provide French curls. She just wanted to braid hair. But to practice one craft, she had to train to do the others. Jestina even went to the state cosmetology board about this disconnect, but they told her their hands were tied under the law, which the legislature failed to change.[36]

Jestina went to federal court and argued it was unconstitutional to require her to obtain a license to do a job for which the license was almost completely irrelevant. And in 2012, unlike with the overwhelming majority of others in recent decades who have tried to protect their unenumerated rights under the Fourteenth Amendment, the court agreed. It stated that "Utah's regulations do not advance public health and safety when applied to Jestina because Utah has irrationally squeezed 'two professions into a single, identical mold,' by treating hair braiders—who perform a very distinct set of services—as if they were cosmetologists."[37]

Readers might respond to Jestina's story by asking what is the big deal with Baby Ninths if people like Jestina can just win in federal court under the U.S. Constitution? Well, if the Fourteenth Amendment, or indeed if the Utah Constitution's due process clause, were interpreted like this book argues Baby Ninths should be, then it would be a bit of an academic question (although Baby Ninths, because they are specifically designed to protect unenumerated rights, are still arguably a better fit than a due process clause). But we live in the world where the U.S. Supreme Court has consigned most rights to the rational basis test, and state courts have generally followed its lead. Jestina's victory is rare. The U.S. Court of Appeals for the Eighth Circuit upheld a similar Missouri law just a few years later in a challenge by a different group of African-style hair braiders. Faced with the same kind of outrageous disconnect of education and examination to actual practice as in Utah, the court waved its hands and said, "the State 'may exact a needless, wasteful requirement in many cases,' which may 'not be in every respect logically consistent with its aims' but still be 'constitutional.'"[38] The quotations within that quote are from the paragon of modern rational basis law, the Supreme Court's 1955 decision of *Williamson v. Lee Optical.* Setting aside the merits of that decision, this book's central point is that entrepreneurs like Jestina should be able to use Utah's Baby Ninth to protect their rights instead of having to slay the modern federal rational basis test. This protection could also extend to all kinds of occupations that the marginalized practice and that are often burdened with nonsensical and protectionist barriers, including eyebrow threading[39] (another beauty technique, primarily practiced in the United States by South Asian immigrants), child care (where regulators are sometimes now requiring a college education to provide daycare[40]), and tree trimming,[41] to name a few.

Another challenge often facing those without political or economic power is simply finding a place to live. Modern land-use law has played a huge role in driving up the cost of housing by making it more expensive to build more housing units and by limiting where multifamily structures can be built.[42] That, of course, makes it harder for someone already struggling to get by to find a place to pay rent or a mortgage. But it even makes it hard to provide housing for free. For example, the Catherine H. Barber Homeless Shelter was the only such shelter in North Wilkesboro, North Carolina.[43] It had to find a new home, and a benefactor donated his former two-story dental office to the charity. The property met all the requirements under the zoning code to operate as a shelter. But it still needed a conditional use permit from the city. And that permit was denied by the land use board for unclear reasons. The chairwoman of the board even said, "I think the issue here is that it meets the zoning requirements, but that doesn't mean it belongs here."[44] The shelter went to court, but its battle would have been a lot easier with a Baby Ninth (which North Carolina has) with real scrutiny (which it lacks).[45]

Further, it is not just economic rights that Baby Ninths could protect. Remember how Jane liked to garden? In the introduction we also met Hermine Ricketts, a Jamaican immigrant who lived with her husband, Tom, in Miami Shores, Florida.[46] Hermine had a beautiful vegetable garden in the front of their house. Unfortunately for her, however, their city banned vegetable gardens in front yards. Vegetables were legal to grow in backyards, and growing flowers and *fruit* was legal in front yards, but vegetables in the front could land you in trouble. And they got in trouble with the city. So they sued in state court. The lawsuit argued that the ban violated their right to garden. The attorneys on the case did not invoke Florida's Baby Ninth, but it did use other provisions in the state's constitution that have been interpreted in the past to protect unenumerated liberties.

Hermine and Tom lost in court. Applying the most rational basis of rational basis standards, the Florida Court of Appeals ruled that the ban was a way of furthering the city's interests in protecting aestheti-cally pleasing neighborhoods, and therefore constitutional.[47] The court made no real analysis of whether vegetables actually hurt or threaten anyone when in a front yard, as opposed to other plants, or any other facts for that matter. It was enough that perhaps the city council might have thought this was a good idea, quipping that it was rational to ban "the cultivation of plants to be eaten as part of a meal, as opposed to the cultivation of plants for ornamental reasons."

Whether in Hermine's case, the homeless shelter's case, Jestina's case, or anyone else's, under the approach we have discussed here the court would have started not with a presumption that the law must be constitutional, but by recognizing that the right at issue is an exercise of individual liberty that the state constitution protects as a "right" that the people "retain." It would then assess whatever argument the govern-ment made on why that right must be restricted in this case, but would demand actual evidence of a problem and a connection between what the law did and a remedy to that problem. Jestina's case would come out the same way as it did, semi-miraculously, in federal court, although it would not seem miraculous but normal. And in Hermine's case the city would fail to demonstrate that planting kale in the front of one's house will harm the good citizens of Miami Shores.

Finally, what about the stamps? If a state passed a law regulating the collection of a certain stamp because it had real evidence that the stamp contained poisonous chemicals that would make someone who touched it sick, well, then that sounds like a regulation that very well might be constitutional. But if it just outright banned stamp collecting or made it subject to a license that only stamp collection industry insiders were eligible for? Then that silly law would be unconstitutional under a Baby Ninth. That is the way Baby Ninths should work. Providing the people with real protections of the unenumerated liberties they have retained.

Is that the end of the story? Almost. We have explored what Baby Ninths mean and what they should do for people's lives in practice. But there is a larger lesson here too. The very fact that Americans across the centuries, and across the land, have adopted Baby Ninths tells us some-thing else. And we will turn to that lesson now.

What Do Baby Ninths Tell Us?

Baby Ninths protect individual rights, and citizens in the states that have one should be able to use their Baby Ninth to protect themselves from state and local government. Is that all there is to this story? Almost. We have learned the substance of what Baby Ninths mean and how they could be better used in the service of liberty. But the mere fact that Baby Ninths exist raises a further question, perhaps the most interesting one of all in this tale: What does their presence tell us about our constitutional order itself? We end this book by learning that it tells us *a lot*.

Love 'Em or Hate 'Em, "the People" Like Baby Ninths

During a period of 150 years, from 1819 to 1970, Americans added Baby Ninth Amendments to the constitutions of thirty-three states, with a couple more states, Missouri and South Carolina, plus the "proto-Baby Ninths" of Tennessee and Texas, joining the party for a time. That means that today the residents of two-thirds of all states live in a place where their constitutional representatives decided to adopt constitutional language that affirmatively protects unenumerated rights. Counting (1) conventions and other constitution-writing bodies (a handful used the legislature or a "constitutional commission") that included a Baby

Ninth for the first time in a state's history, and (2) conventions and other constitution-writing bodies that simply kept or re-inserted a Baby Ninth from a state's prior constitution, Americans have included a Baby Ninth in a constitution sixty-six times. As we have learned from the statements made at constitutional conventions, and the text of Baby Ninths themselves, there is no reason to think that the various delegates' purpose in adopting them was anything other than to protect individual rights, including protecting individual rights through the judiciary. Inspired in some way by James Madison, they understood that constitutions cannot enumerate all rights that need to be protected, so they included a safety, "etcetera" clause. They did this time and time again, from all different ideologies, in all different time periods, in all different geographic areas of the country, from Maine to Hawaii, Alaska to Florida. The first two states to adopt one, Alabama and Maine, could not have been more different in 1819 America, yet each of them independently wanted this "etcetera" protection.

Given contemporary (and not just contemporary) rhetoric on unenumerated rights—much of it scornful, dismissive, and often at best defensive—one would think unenumerated rights are not really "American." Some liberal or (take your pick) libertarian plot to impose an elite view of society on an unwilling public via raw judicial power. An aberration in constitutional law for "activist judges" to wield when their purpose suits them. Few of these critics completely shun unenumerated rights (even Justice Scalia did not!), but the consensus among most judges and scholars seems to be that they are best locked away in a liquor cabinet, only to be brought out on your favorite holidays.

But the glaring evidence of actual constitutions and actual constitution writing makes it clear that unenumerated rights are not the hard alcohol of our constitutional order. At least judging by what "the people" put *in* their constitutions, unenumerated rights are more like water, orange juice, or at worst Diet Coke. Americans adopt Baby Ninths over, and over, and over again. In short, Baby Ninths tell us that unenumerated rights are *popular*. Judges do not so much thwart the will of "the people" when they use Baby Ninths to find laws unconstitutional, but instead thwart the people's constitutions when they interpret Baby Ninths out of functional existence.

And this does not even include other examples of constitutional acceptance of unenumerated rights, such as the Lockean natural rights guarantees we met earlier. When Americans write constitutions they do not carefully craft bills of rights to only include certain narrow subjects and then state "do not read these too broadly so as to impede Democracy." Far from it. They even go as far as including Baby Tenths in some constitutions, taking rights completely out of the power of the legislature to come close to infringing on them in the first place.

When Americans write constitutions they include unenumerated rights. Many judges and scholars may not like that, but as those same judges and scholars are famous for declaring it is not their decision to make; it is "the people's"!

Further, the repeated choices to include unenumerated rights provisions in constitutions are not the artifact of an earlier era long before the rise of modern social and economic legislation. Even in constitutions written since the New Deal—when the full power of the administrative state was in full view—Americans have adopted unenumerated rights provisions with no "when in doubt protect the police power from judicial scrutiny" provisos. When Americans actually write constitutions, they protect rights over legislation. Far from judicial review being an elite's (whether that be a leftist cultural elite or a right-wing property-owning elite) method of rejecting what "the people" want, it is a democratic method of protecting those same "people's" desires.

How Do We Know Baby Ninths Are Popular?

Now a critic might argue that just because Baby Ninths are in a lot of state constitutions does not mean they are "popular." After all, there are a lot of laws in a lot of states that most people are unaware of. Perhaps people might be in favor of Baby Ninths if they were brought to their attention, but then again maybe not. Lots of states have overbearing cosmetology laws like those discussed in the previous chapter, but most people likely know little about them and very well might not like them if they learned more.

This is a fair point. But it does not take into account the way state constitutions are adopted and it also proves too much.

First, laws passed in state legislatures, or in Congress for that matter, only represent public opinion in a very disconnected and theoretical (at best) sense. Lobbyists and narrowly interested groups are heavily involved in legislative drafting, and when legislators run for election only a small part of potential legislation is part of the conversation with voters.[1] This is what it means to have a republican form of government, as opposed to a pure democracy, especially with an active government of many laws like we have today.

But constitutions are a bit different. Constitutional conventions are not simple legislative bodies with their eyes on run-of-the-mill legislation. What they are writing may stick around for dozens or even hundreds of years. Thus it is harder for delegates to conventions to predict how various constitutional provisions will affect the interest groups they care about. Further, as constitutional conventions are infrequent affairs, delegates are not looking to please special interest groups that they may be depending on to help them with re-election. That does not mean delegates will instead turn to channeling the wishes of the voters who send them to the convention, but they will be more independent to think for themselves as citizens rather than as interest-group-captured politicians. And this is not to say that delegates at conventions are saintly compared to legislators; there are many examples of various interest groups backing different factions of delegates at constitutional conventions. But it does mean that some of the dysfunction of the normal legislative process does not track onto the constitution-writing process.[2]

Second, given how ignorant people are of state constitutions, this criticism could apply to *anything* in a constitution, which demonstrates that it proves too much. Many Americans may not know that their state has a constitution, let alone anything about individual provisions in their state's constitution, but even they likely will be familiar with the freedom of speech, free exercise of religion, and the right against unreasonable searches and seizures, for example. It is fair to say these rights are popular, and we can safely say that their presence in virtually all state constitutions reflects that popularity. But that does not mean the actual provisions in the state constitutions are widely known or even appreciated. They were adopted *because* those rights were popular when the constitutions were drafted. The same seems to be true of Baby Ninths. Protecting rights is broadly popular among Americans, and the Baby Ninths (and similar clauses) reflect that. Unlike with cosmetology laws, it is not as though there is an interest group that stands to benefit from them that explain the laws' widespread adoption even though voters are largely ignorant. There is no "association for unenumerated rights" that has sponsored delegates or lobbied the sixty-six different conventions or similar gatherings where Baby Ninths have been adopted. Thus that Baby Ninths nevertheless were adopted over and over again shows us that across American history there has been a broad popularity for protecting rights beyond those enumerated in constitutions, even if the Baby Ninths themselves may not be all that well known.

Why Do "the People" Like Baby Ninths?

"The people" is a delicate construct in the first place, and it refers to all kinds of individuals in all kinds of locations, in all kinds of time periods, and of all kinds of ideological persuasions. It deserves to be used measuredly, and, due to its overuse, usually with scare quotes. "The people" are a varied bunch without a singular "will." Even so, why do so many different individual people, who undoubtedly have had different views on what rights exist or need protection, want Baby Ninths, or at least want unenumerated rights protected? This book does not provide the "right" answer. There probably are many different factors that explain their prevalence, only some of which we have discussed. But here is one theory that the author thinks makes sense.

A Baby Ninth seems to represent a kind of compromise. Constitutional drafters, and those ratifying a proposed constitution, do not know what rights the government may violate once the constitution is enacted. Of course they have a good guess at some, which is why many are often enumerated. But they know that legislators and executive officers are crafty men and women capable of all manner of mischief. Thus, for example, a conservative constitutional delegate who fears that future legislatures might confiscate property, and a left-liberal delegate who fears that those same legislatures might restrict family planning, are aligned in wanting broad protection of unenumerated rights. Each knows that future judges might find laws the delegates like to be unconstitutional. They might want to have the rights they support actually enshrined in the constitution but have other priorities and do not want a bill of rights that goes on and on and on. They both understand, as did James Madison, that it is futile to list all possible rights they might care about. And they are willing to trade the risk that laws they support might be struck down against the *greater* risk that rights they hold dear would be imperiled, and without judicial protection. Thus they compromise by inserting an "etcetera" clause that might not do everything they would like, and might get in the way of some laws they support, but hopefully will protect some of the rights they most value.

This would explain why so many delegates of so many different ideological backgrounds include Baby Ninths in so many states. Unenumerated rights, and judicial protection of unenumerated rights, unite us all. A story of coming together to broadly protect unenumerated rights is much more plausible than the opposite, that people of different ideological stripes are so afraid of judges striking down laws that they protect against judges using unenumerated rights to do so. The author is unaware of *any* provision in any American constitution that instructed or instructs judges not to find unenumerated rights. Some states have provisions limiting the interpretation of certain rights provisions. For example, California and Florida amended their constitutions to forbid their courts from construing some of their constitutions' protections of criminal defendants to be more protective than how the federal courts interpret the United States Constitution.[3] No state anywhere, however, has anything like a provision saying "unenumerated rights are dangerous, and the judiciary cannot declare them" or even "the judiciary should shy away from doing so." The absence of these provisions is the dog that did not bark. It would be perfectly unsurprising if delegates to a constitutional convention feared each other ideologically and compromised by explicitly denouncing unenumerated rights. Yet that has literally never happened. "The people" seem to err on the side of rights protection, not law protection.

This has implications beyond just state constitutions. Namely, the United States Constitution. We have discussed the modern debates about what the Ninth Amendment means and do not need to wade back into those matters. We have not discussed the modern debates on whether the Privileges or Immunities Clause or the Due Process Clause of the Fourteenth Amendment protects unenumerated rights against state governments. But we do not need to discuss those debates either (which often, are similar, in essence, to the Ninth Amendment debates) for present purposes. Instead it is simply important to note that the fact that so many various Americans supported the constitutional protection of unenumerated rights in their state constitutions tells us that the general understanding of our constitutional system has been, since at least 1819, that it is normal to protect unenumerated rights in a constitution. By 1866, when Congress proposed the Fourteenth Amendment, more than a dozen states had adopted Baby Ninths. To the Americans who elected that Congress, it was normal that constitutions protect rights beyond just those explicitly listed in the constitution itself. That they would do so in the Fourteenth Amendment would not be surprising at all. This, on its own, does not prove that the Fourteenth Amendment protects unenumerated rights. But it demonstrates that unenumerated rights were popular and that it was "mainstream" at the time to include them in a constitution.

What's Up with the Judges?

But despite all this "normalcy" the courts have not gone along with the unenumerated rights compromise. Instead, they have largely done exactly the opposite and mostly failed to meaningfully protect *any* rights with Baby Ninths, seemingly believing that "the people" enacted "anti-Baby Ninths" instead. Now, as detailed in chapter 4, some courts, on occasion, give Baby Ninths their due. These examples show that Baby Ninths can function according to their plain text, individuals can be protected, and the heavens do not fall. But most courts have not agreed. Courts do interpret Baby Ninths to protect individual rights, but generally apply a level of scrutiny to make them ineffective. Or they use them in shotgun form, along with other more prominent provisions arguably less suited to the task, such as due process clauses. And more often than not they simply do not mention Baby Ninths when discussing unenumerated rights, instead using those same less-suited provisions (and generally these days applying rational basis review). Very seldom have courts used Baby Ninths as the obvious central players in protecting unenumerated, individual rights that "the people" wanted Baby Ninths to protect. Literally no state's judiciary uses its Baby Ninth as a central character in constitutional drama.

If only one state had once adopted a Baby Ninth, and then its judiciary had failed to enforce its language, that failure could be chalked up to a misunderstanding or a local idiosyncrasy. But thirty-three times? There is something more going on here.

And the answer seems obvious. Judges often do not like the power constitutional drafters and the citizenry—the people who draft and adopt the foundational documents judges are supposed to enforce—place in their hands. The words of Iowa's Justice Cole are important to listen to here. As we saw in chapter 4, he read Justice Beck's straightforward reading of Iowa's Baby Ninth—that it in a sense creates an "unwritten constitution"—and shuddered. Rather than comply with Iowa's framers and interpret what "other" rights were retained by the people, he tossed the Baby Ninth, and those rights, aside.

This is already, of course, what the U.S. Supreme Court has done with the Ninth Amendment, essentially rendering it meaningless.[4] But apologists for not using the Ninth Amendment to enforce individual rights argue that it does not actually mean what it says. As we have seen, that simply does not work when it comes to Baby Ninths: even if you accept this view of the Ninth Amendment, Baby Ninths *do* mean what they say. Behind each Baby Ninth are the citizens who came together and purposely wanted to give judges the power to enforce unenumerated rights, whether as part of a compromise or for other reasons. And yet, for the most part, state judiciaries simply refuse to wield this constitutional power.

Why judges refuse to exercise this power is a political (and perhaps even psychological) inquiry, the full answer to which is beyond the author's reach. In fact, many readers will object and say "what do you mean? Judges illegitimately use their power all the time!" Those on the left will name cases such as *Lochner v. New York* or the gun rights case *Heller v. District of Columbia*. Those on the right will throw out the now-overturned *Roe v. Wade* and the case that constitutionalized same-sex marriage, *Obergefell v. Hodges*. Whether you think these cases are examples of judicial overreach or not, they are a tiny portion of when judges decide whether a law violates a constitution. Far more often judges side with the government, deferring to the "will of the people" over constitutional strictures.[5]

But whatever the reason, under the constitutions those judges have sworn to uphold they *should* wield this power the people have entrusted to them. Instead, they simply do not enforce the constitution because they do not like what it says. This is hardly constitutional of them, written or otherwise. Judges put in this position could learn from Justice Scalia when he was faced with the First Amendment and a statute criminalizing flag burning (and not, of course, when he was faced with the Ninth Amendment). Although he personally thought the flag-burning law was a good idea, he voted to find it unconstitutional because that was his reading of the right of freedom of speech.[6]

The same should be true of state judges who personally wish they were not entrusted with the same power to find laws unconstitutional that violate unenumerated rights but who are nevertheless also entrusted to protect enumerated rights. They may not want to protect unenumerated rights, but the Baby Ninth in their state's constitution requires them to do so. Ignoring that duty and ignoring their Baby Ninth is . . . unconstitutional.

Americans like their rights. And perhaps because we like our rights more than we like our government, we, time and again, have put Baby

Ninths in our constitutions to protect those rights, even though we do not spell all those rights out. In order for those protections to have full effect, however, it falls to judges to enforce them. There lies a disconnect between Americans' desire to have judges do just that, and judges' wish to obey. The promise of Baby Ninths will not be fulfilled until state judges engage with their own constitutions and enforce these "other" rights "retained by the people."

Baby Ninth Amendments
in State Constitutions

Alabama

1819: Art. I, § 30. This enumeration of certain rights shall not be construed to deny or disparage others retained by the people: and, to guard against any encroachments on the rights herein retained, or any transgression of any of the high powers herein delegated, we declare, that every thing in this article is excepted out of the general powers of government, and shall forever remain inviolate; and that all laws contrary thereto, or to the following provisions, shall be void.

1861: [Same as 1819.]

1865: Art. I, § 36. [Text same as 1819.]

1867: Art. I, § 38. That this enumeration of certain rights shall not impair or deny others retained by the people.

1875: Art. I, § 39. [Text same as 1867.]

1901: Art. I, § 36. That this enumeration of certain rights shall not impair or deny others retained by the people; and, to guard against any encroachments on the rights herein retained, we declare that everything in this Declaration of Rights is excepted out of the general powers of government, and shall forever remain inviolate.

Alaska

1959: Art. I, § 21. The enumeration of rights in this constitution shall not impair or deny others retained by the people.

Arizona

1912: Art. II, § 33. The enumeration in this Constitution of certain rights shall not be construed to deny others retained by the people.

Arkansas

1836: Art. II, § 24. This enumeration of rights shall not be construed to deny or disparage others retained by the people; and, to guard against any encroachments on the rights herein retained, or any transgression of any of the higher powers herein delegated, we declare that everything in this article is excepted out of the general powers of the government, and shall forever remain inviolate; and that all laws contrary thereto, or to the other provisions herein contained, shall be void.

1861: Art. II, § 24. This enumeration of rights shall not be construed to deny or disparage others retained by the people; and to guard against any encroachments on the rights herein retained, or any transgression of any of the higher powers herein delegated, we declare that everything in this article is excepted out of the general powers of the government, and shall forever remain inviolate, and that all laws contrary thereto, or to the other provisions herein contained shall be void.

1864: Art. II, § 24. This enumeration of rights shall not be construed to deny or disparage others retained by the people, and to guard against any encroachments on the rights herein retained, or any transgression of any of the higher powers herein delegated, we declare that everything in this article is excepted out of the general powers of the government, and shall forever remain inviolate; and that all laws contrary thereto, or to the other provisions herein contained, shall be void.

1868: None.

1874: Art. II, § 29. This enumeration of rights shall not be construed to deny or disparage others retained by the people; and to guard against any encroachments on the rights herein retained, or any transgression of any of the higher powers herein delegated, we declare that everything in this article is excepted out of the general powers of the government; and shall forever remain inviolate; and that all laws contrary thereto, or to the other provisions herein contained, shall be void.

California

1849: Art. I, § 21. This enumeration of rights shall not be construed to impair or deny others retained by the people.

1879: Art. I, § 23. [Same text as 1849.]
   Repealed in 1974 by Proposition 7, which generally reorganized much of the constitution.

1974: Proposition 7 also added a new Article I, § 24 which reads: This declaration of rights may not be construed to impair or deny others retained by the people.

Colorado

1876: Art. II, § 28. The enumeration in this constitution of certain rights shall not be construed to deny, impair or disparage others retained by the people.

Connecticut

None.

Delaware

None.

Florida

1868: Dec. of Rts., § 24. This enunciation of rights shall not be construed to impair or deny others retained by the people.

1887: [Same as 1868.]

1968: Art. I, § 1. The enunciation herein of certain rights shall not be construed to deny or impair others retained by the people.

Georgia

1861: Art. I, § 27. The enumeration of rights herein contained shall not be construed to deny to the people any inherent rights which they have hitherto enjoyed.

1865: Art. I, § 21. The enumeration of rights herein contained is a part of this constitution, but shall not be construed to deny to the people any inherent rights which they have hitherto enjoyed.

1868: None.

1877: Art. I, § v, ¶ II. The enumeration of rights herein contained as a part of this Constitution, shall not be construed to deny to the people any inherent rights which they may have hitherto enjoyed.

1945: Art. I, § v, ¶ II. The enumeration of rights herein contained as a part of this Constitution shall not be construed to deny to the people any inherent rights which they may have hitherto enjoyed.

1976: Art. I, § 1, ¶ XXV. Same text as 1945.

1983: Art. I, § 1, ¶ XXIX. Same text as 1945.

Hawaii

1959: Art. I, § 22. The enumeration of rights and privileges shall not be construed to impair or deny others retained by the people.

Idaho

1890: Art. I, § 21. This enumeration of rights shall not be construed to impair or deny other rights retained by the people.

Illinois

1970: Art. I, § 24. The enumeration in this Constitution of certain rights shall not be construed to deny or disparage others retained by the individual citizens of the State.

Indiana

None.

Iowa

1846: Art. I, § 24. This enumeration of rights shall not be construed to impair or deny others, retained by the people.

1857: Art. I, § 25. [Text same as 1846.]

Kansas

1861: Bill of Rights, § 20. This enumeration of rights shall not be construed to impair or deny others retained by the people; and all powers not herein delegated remain with the people.

Louisiana

1868: Tit. I, art. 14. The rights enumerated in this title shall not be construed to limit or abridge other rights of the people not herein expressed.

1879: Art. 13. This enumeration of rights shall not be construed to deny or impair other rights of the people not herein expressed.

1898: Bill of Rts., art. 15. [Same text as 1879.]

1913: [Same as 1898.]

1921: Art. I, § 15. [Same text as 1879.]

1974: Art. I, § 24. The enumeration in this constitution of certain rights shall not deny or disparage other rights retained by the individual citizens of the state.

Maine

1820: Art. I, § 24. The enumeration of certain rights shall not impair nor deny others retained by the people.

Maryland

1851: Dec. of Rts., art. 42. This enumeration of rights shall not be construed to impair or deny others retained by the people.

1864: [Same as 1851.]

1867: Dec. of Rts., art. 45. This enumeration of Rights shall not be construed to impair or deny others retained by the People.

Massachusetts

None.

Michigan

1963: Art. I, § 23. The enumeration in this constitution of certain rights shall not be construed to deny or disparage others retained by the people.

Minnesota

1858: Art. I, § 16. The enumeration of rights in this constitution shall not be construed to deny or impair others retained by and inherent in the people.

In 1974 the constitution was reorganized and this provision of Article I, Section 16 was slightly changed by dropping the words "be construed to." It now reads: The enumeration of rights in this constitution shall not deny or impair others retained by and inherent in the people.

Mississippi

1868: Art. I, § 32. The enumeration of rights in this constitution shall not be construed to deny or impair others retained by and inherent in the people.

1890: Art. 3, § 32. The enumeration of rights in this constitution shall not be construed to deny and impair others retained by, and inherent in, the people.

Missouri

(Adopted in 1875. Removed in 1945.)
Art. II, Sec. 32. The enumeration in this Constitution of certain rights shall not be construed to deny, impair or disparage others retained by the people.

Montana

1889: Art. II, § 34. The enumeration in this constitution of certain rights shall not be construed to deny, impair, or disparage others retained by the people.

1972: [Same as 1889.]

Nebraska

1867: Art. I, § 20. This enumeration of rights shall not be construed to impair or deny others retained by the people, and all powers not herein delegated remain with the people.

1875: Art. II, § 26. This enumeration of rights shall not be construed to impair or deny others, retained by the people, and all powers not herein delegated, remain with the people.

Nevada

1864: Art. 1, § 20. This enumeration of rights shall not be construed to impair or deny others retained by the people.

New Hampshire

None.

New Jersey

1844: Art. I, § 19. This enumeration of rights and privileges shall not be construed to impair or deny others retained by the people.

1947: Art. I, § 21. [Same text as 1844.]

New Mexico

1912: Art. II, § 23. The enumeration in this constitution of certain rights shall not be construed to deny, impair or disparage others retained by the people.

New York

None.

North Carolina

1868: Art., § 37. This enumeration of rights shall not be construed to impair or deny others retained by the people; and all powers, not herein delegated, remain with the people.

1971: Art. I, § 36. The enumeration of rights in this Article shall not be construed to impair or deny others retained by the people.

North Dakota

None.

Ohio

1851: Art. I, § 20. This enumeration of rights shall not be construed to impair or deny others retained by the people; and all powers, not herein delegated, remain with the people.

Oklahoma

1907: Art. II, § 33. The enumeration in this Constitution of certain rights shall not be construed to deny, impair, or disparage others retained by the people.

Oregon

1857: Art. I, § 33. This enumeration of rights, and privileges shall not be construed to impair or deny others retained by the people.

Pennsylvania

None.

Rhode Island

1843: Art. I, § 23. The enumeration of the foregoing rights shall not be Construed to impair or deny others retained by the people.

1986: Art. I, § 24. [Same text as 1843.]

South Carolina

(Adopted in 1868. Removed in 1895.)
Art. I, § 41. The enumeration of rights in this constitution shall not be construed to impair or deny others retained by the people, and all powers not herein delegated remain with the people.

South Dakota

None.

Tennessee

None.

Texas

None.

Utah

1896: Art. I, § 25. This enumeration of rights shall not be construed to impair or deny others retained by the people.

Vermont

None.

Virginia

1870: Art. I, § 21. The rights enumerated in this bill of rights shall not be construed to limit other rights of the people not therein expressed.

1902: Art. I, § 17. The rights enumerated in this Bill of Rights shall not be construed to limit other rights of the people not therein expressed.

1971: [Same as 1902.]

Washington

1889: Art. I, § 30. The enumeration in this Constitution of certain rights shall not be construed to deny others retained by the people.

West Virginia

None.

Wisconsin

None.

Wyoming

1890: Art. 1, § 36. The enumeration in this constitution, of certain rights shall not be construed to deny, impair, or disparage others retained by the people.

Notes

Introduction

1. For example, North Carolina protects people's "enjoyment of the fruits of their own labor." N.C. CONST., art. I § 1.

2. We shall leave aside a reason constitutional lawyers would quickly raise on why the Ninth Amendment would not help you in this case: It only applies to the federal government, not the states. The Supreme Court long ago ruled that the Bill of Rights does not, on its own, apply to the states, and has only "incorporated" rights in the Bill of Rights against the states selectively since the adoption of the Fourteenth Amendment in 1868, in the wake of the Civil War. Whether the Ninth Amendment would ever be "incorporated" against the states is a fun debate but irrelevant to our discussion here.

3. John C. Yoo, *Our Declaratory Ninth Amendment*, 42 EMORY L.J. 967, 968 (1993).

4. *Id.* at 968 n.4 (stating that Professor Yoo "adopted this term from the 'baby' Federal Trade Commission (FTC) acts, which state governments passed to mimic the FTC's governing statute").

5. NEV. CONST., art. I § 20.

6. 4 THE DEBATES IN THE SEVERAL STATE CONVENTIONS ON THE ADOPTION OF THE FEDERAL CONSTITUTION 167 (Jonathan Elliot, ed., 1836).

7. Troxel v. Granville, 530 U.S. 57 (2000) (rearing one's children); NAACP v. Alabama, 357 U.S. 449 (1958) (freedom of association); New State Ice Co. v. Liebmann, 285 U.S. 262 (1932) (earning a living); Griswold v. Connecticut, 381 U.S. 479 (1965) (using birth control); City of Shreveport v. Curry, 357 So. 2d 1078 (La. 1978) (protecting the hunting of frogs).

8. RAOUL BERGER, GOVERNMENT BY JUDICIARY (1977).

9. This phrase is taken from a statement made regarding the struggles between Blacks and organized labor in the early twentieth century: "[A] colored worker who is denied the protection and the benefits of organized labor because they will not take

161

him in, has only one place of redress in case his right of employment is assailed, and that is in our courts." *Limiting Scope of Injunctions in Labor Disputes: Hearings on S. 1482 Before a Subcomm. of the Senate Comm. on the Judiciary*, 70th Cong., 1st Sess. 610 (1928) (statement of Harry E. Davis, Member, Ohio House of Representatives), quoted in David E. Bernstein, *Roots of the 'Underclass': The Decline of Laissez-Faire Jurisprudence and the Rise of Racist Labor Legislation*, 43 AM. U.L. REV. 85, 85 (1993).

10. Order Granting Plaintiffs' Verified Motion for Preliminary Injunction, Diaz v. City of Fort Pierce, No. 2018-CA-2259 (Fla. Cir. Ct. Feb. 22, 2019), https://ij.org/wp -content/uploads/2018/12/Order-Grandting-MPI.pdf.

11. Meghan McRoberts, *Judge Denies City of Fort Pierce's Motion to Dismiss Complaint about Food Truck Restrictions*, WPTV, Jan. 3, 2019, https://www.wptv.com/news/region -st-lucie-county/fort-pierce/judge-denies-city-of-fort-pierces-motion-to-dismiss-compl aint-about-food-truck-restrictions.

12. *Id.*

13. *See* Order Granting Plaintiffs' Verified Motion, *supra*.

14. Meghan McRoberts, *City of Fort Pierce One Step Closer to Repealing Law That Limits Food Truck Locations*, WPTV, Oct. 8, 2019, https://www.wptv.com/news/region-st -lucie-county/fort-pierce/city-of-fort-pierce-one-step-closer-to-repealing-law-that-limi ts-food-truck-locations.

15. George F. Will, *Surely Chicago Has Bigger Things to Worry About Than a Cupcake Truck*, WASH. POST, Aug. 14, 2019, https://www.washingtonpost.com/opinions/sure ly-chicago-has-bigger-things-to-worry-about-than-a-cupcake-truck/2019/08/14/1bc6 d268-bde4-11e9-9b73-fd3c65ef8f9c_story.html.

16. Felicia Dechter, *Cupcakes Aid the Courageous in Fighting Cancer*, CHI. TRIB., Jul. 10, 2019, https://www.chicagotribune.com/suburbs/oak-park/ct-oak-cupcakes-fight -cancer-tl-0718-20190710-xarvljzvjndnte75vny62xktdy-story.html.

17. Will, *supra*.

18. LMP Services v. City of Chicago, 160 N.E.3d 822, 828 (Ill. 2019).

Chapter 1

1. ROBERT L. MADDEX, STATE CONSTITUTIONS OF THE UNITED STATES xiii (2006).

2. Andrew T. Bodoh, *The Road to "Due Process": Evolving Constitutional Language From 1776 to 1789*, 40 T. JEFFERSON L. REV. 103, 121 (2018).

3. NICHOLAS VINCENT, MAGNA CARTA: A VERY SHORT INTRODUCTION 102 (2012).

4. EDMUND S. MORGAN, INVENTING THE PEOPLE: THE RISE OF POPULAR SOVEREIGNTY IN ENGLAND AND AMERICA 114–17 (1988).

5. A HISTORY OF US: SOURCEBOOK AND INDEX 23 (2003) (text of English Bill of Rights).

6. 7 THE FEDERAL AND STATE CONSTITUTIONS, COLONIAL CHARTERS, AND OTHER ORGANIC LAWS OF THE STATES, TERRITORIES, AND COLONIES NOW OR HERETOFORE FORMING THE UNITED STATES OF AMERICA 3788 (Francis Newton Thorpe, ed., 1909) (hereinafter "FEDERAL AND STATE CONSTITUTIONS") (First Charter of Virginia).

7. ANDREW LINTOTT, THE CONSTITUTION OF THE ROMAN REPUBLIC 34 (1999). The founding generation was steeped in the history of ancient Greece and Rome. "Colonial American grammar schools, particularly those associated with the handful of universities, prescribed a vigorously classical education." DAVID J. BEDERMAN, THE

CLASSICAL FOUNDATIONS OF THE AMERICAN CONSTITUTION: PREVAILING WISDOM 4 (2008).

8. PAUL LENDVAI, THE HUNGARIANS: A THOUSAND YEARS OF VICTORY IN DEFEAT 47–48 (2003; trans. Ann Major).

9. DONALD S. LUTZ, *The Fundamental Orders of Connecticut* 24–35, in ROOTS OF THE REPUBLIC: AMERICAN FOUNDING DOCUMENTS INTERPRETED (Stephen L. Schechter, ed., 1990).

10. Indeed, only a handful of Magna Carta's original provisions survive under English law today. MORGAN, *supra* at 102.

11. DAVID SKILLEN BOGEN, PRIVILEGES AND IMMUNITIES: A REFERENCE GUIDE TO THE UNITED STATES CONSTITUTION 4 (2003).

12. *See, e.g.*, PA. CONST. of 1776, § 47 (detailing manner of amending the constitution), in 5 FEDERAL AND STATE CONSTITUTIONS 3092; MASS. CONST. of 1780, ch. VI art. X (same), in FEDERAL AND STATE CONSTITUTIONS 1911. This is not to say that early state constitutions *followed* this requirement in their own formation. The need for a constitutional convention evolved and solidified as an idea through the adoption of state constitutions in the years before 1787. *See* JACK RAKOVE, ORIGINAL MEANINGS 96–100 (1996).

13. Steven G. Calabresi and Sofia M. Vickery, *On Liberty and the Fourteenth Amendment: The Original Understanding of the Lockean Natural Rights Guarantees*, 93 TEX. L. REV. 1299, 1314–15 (2015).

14. 7 FEDERAL AND STATE CONSTITUTIONS 3813 (VA. CONST. of 1776, Dec. of Rights, § 1).

15. Calabresi and Vickery, *supra*, at 1317–18; Pauline Maier, *The Strange History of "All Men Are Created Equal,"* 56 WASH. & LEE L. REV. 873, 879 (1999) (detailing how Jefferson took Mason's language and adapted it to the needs for the Declaration of Independence). Although there is controversy on whether Jefferson relied upon Locke for the Declaration, *see e.g.*, CLAIRE RYDELL ARCENAS, AMERICA'S PHILOSOPHER: JOHN LOCKE IN AMERICAN INTELLECTUAL LIFE 50–51 (2022), it is much clearer in Mason's case that he directly used Locke and his Second Treatise, including Locke's actual phrasing. Calabresi and Vickery, *supra*, at 1316. *See also* JEFF BROADWATER, GEORGE MASON: FORGOTTEN FOUNDER 88 (2006) ("Mason's strictures on equality, the citizen's inalienable right to life and liberty—he added the pursuit of happiness—and his idea that magistrates were trustees of the people's rights came directly from John Locke.").

16. 7 FEDERAL AND STATE CONSTITUTIONS 3813–14 (VA. CONST. of 1776, Dec. of Rights).

17. *See generally* Calabresi and Vickery, *supra*.

18. Bodoh, *supra*, at 122–45. In fairness, the others each protected at least a handful of liberties anyway, even if not in a stand-alone article. 2 FEDERAL AND STATE CONSTITUTIONS 784–85 (GA. CONST. of 1777) (protecting against excessive fines and bail, and guaranteeing freedom of religion and of the press); 5 FEDERAL AND STATE CONSTITUTIONS 2597–98 (N.J. CONST. of 1776) (protecting freedom of religion for all Protestants); *id.* at 2635–37 (N.Y. CONST. of 1777) (protecting right to counsel, freedom of religion, and trial by jury, among other liberties); *id.* at 3257 (S.C. CONST. of 1778) (including several rights protections, including a law of the land clause).

19. RAKOVE, *supra*, at 316.

20. *Id.*

21. *Id.* at 288.

22. *See* Ryan C. Williams, *The Ninth Amendment as a Rule of Construction*, 111 COLUM. L. REV. 498, 510–11 (2011). The well-known history of the Bill of Rights' adoption is retold in many books and articles. *See, e.g.*, DANIEL FARBER, RETAINED BY THE PEOPLE: THE "SILENT" NINTH AMENDMENT AND THE CONSTITUTIONAL RIGHTS AMERICANS DON'T KNOW THEY HAVE 29–44 (2007); KURT T. LASH, THE LOST HISTORY OF THE NINTH AMENDMENT 13–38 (2009). The following gives just the necessary minimum of facts drawn from these and other sources.

23. *See* Edward Lee, *Freedom of the Press 2.0*, 42 GA. L. REV. 309, 331–32 (2014).

24. *See id.* at 332.

25. THE FEDERALIST No. 84, at 513–14 (Alexander Hamilton) (Clinton Rossiter, ed., 1961).

26. For example, Hamilton argued that a bill of rights makes more sense when the government has broad unenumerated powers than when they are limited, as in the U.S. Constitution. *See id.* at 513 ("But a minute detail of particular rights is certainly far less applicable to a Constitution like that under consideration, which is merely intended to regulate the general political interests of the nation, than to a constitution which has the regulation of every species of personal and private concerns."). *See also* Thomas B. McAffee, *The Original Meaning of the Ninth Amendment*, 90 COLUM. L. REV. 1215, 1230–31 (1990) (demonstrating supporters of ratifying the Constitution argued reserving rights in state constitutions was proper due to the state's broad powers, and contrasting that to the proposed federal government's limited powers).

27. Michael J. Zydney Mannheimer, *The Contingent Fourth Amendment*, 64 EMORY L.J. 1229, 1266–67 (2015).

28. *Id.* at 1267.

29. 1 ANNALS OF CONG. 759 (1789) (statement of Rep. Sedgwick).

30. FARBER, *supra*, at 39–40.

31. *See, e.g.*, Gonzales v. Raich, 545 U.S. 1 (2005) (holding Congress has power to prohibit possession of marijuana that has not been bought or sold).

32. *See* U.S. CONST., art. I, §§ 9–10 (including, *inter alia*, prohibitions on both Congress and states passing bills of attainder and ex post facto laws, and on states impairing the obligations of contracts).

33. *See* FARBER, *supra*, at 34.

34. *See, e.g.*, 1 THE DEBATES IN THE SEVERAL STATE CONVENTIONS ON THE ADOPTION OF THE FEDERAL CONSTITUTION 338, 334–35 (Jonathan Elliot, ed., 2d ed. 1901) (hereinafter "ELLIOT'S DEBATES") (New York and Rhode Island proposals, respectively)

35. A number of these examples are in Kurt T. Lash, *The Lost Original Meaning of the Ninth Amendment*, 83 TEX. L. REV. 331, 355–58 (2004) (citing examples from ratifying conventions of New York, North Carolina, Pennsylvania, and Virginia).

36. 3 ELLIOT'S DEBATES 661.

37. James Madison, *Speech to the House Explaining His Proposed Amendments and His Notes for the Amendment Speech*, in THE RIGHTS RETAINED BY THE PEOPLE: THE HISTORY AND MEANING OF THE NINTH AMENDMENT 51, 55–56 (Randy E. Barnett, ed., 1989).

38. Obviously to some, at least. For reasons not relevant to Baby Ninths, others have seen it as less influential. *See* Lash, *The Lost Original Meaning, supra*, at 426–27.

39. *See id.* at 368.

40. *See id.* at 369–70.

41. Randy E. Barnett, *The Ninth Amendment: It Means What It Says*, 85 TEX. L. REV. 1, 11–21 (2006).

42. In full disclosure and having noted this controversy here, the author states that he is among those who call themselves "original public meaning originalists," who hold that constitutional language (indeed, all legal written language, including statutory language) should be interpreted as it was understood by the public at the time the language was adopted. But the controversy is beside the point for present purposes. Although "original meaning" will become more relevant when we discuss the original meaning of Baby Ninth Amendments later in this book, for purposes of this discussion it does not matter whether the original meaning of the Ninth Amendment is *the* (or even *a*) proper mode of constitutional interpretation. All we care about is this: What did the Ninth Amendment actually mean when it was adopted? We care about this whether or not it is at all relevant to today's judges when they interpret the Ninth Amendment. We just want to know what the Ninth Amendment might have meant when it was adopted, because that will be helpful when we try and figure out what *Baby* Ninth Amendments meant when they were adopted.

43. Russell L. Caplan, *The History and Meaning of the Ninth Amendment*, 69 Va. L. Rev. 223, 227–28 (1983), *discussed in* Barnett, *The Ninth Amendment: It Means What It Says*, 11–12.

44. *See id.* (discussing McAffee, *The Original Meaning of the Ninth Amendment*).

45. *Id.* at 13–15.

46. Randy E. Barnett, *Who's Afraid of Unenumerated Rights?*, 9 J. Const. L. 1, 21 (2006).

47. Farber, *supra*, at 144–52.

48. Akhil Reed Amar, The Bill of Rights 120 (1998).

49. *See* Lash, *The Lost Original Meaning, supra*, 342 ("The retained rights of the Ninth Amendment also may have been understood as being subject to the collective action of the people on a state-by-state basis.").

50. Barnett, *Who's Afraid, supra*, at 17–21.

51. Michael W. McConnell, *Natural Rights and the Ninth Amendment: How Does Lockean Legal Theory Assist in Interpretation?*, 5 N.Y.U. J.L. & Liberty 1 (2010).

52. Laurence H. Tribe, *Contrasting Constitutional Visions: Of Real and Unreal Differences*, 22 Harv. C.R.-C.L. L. Rev. 95, 107 (1987).

53. Sanford Levinson, *Constitutional Rhetoric and the Ninth Amendment*, 64 Chi.-Kent L. Rev. 131, 134 (1988).

54. *Id.* at 158.

55. *Id.*

56. Griswold v. Connecticut, 381 U.S. 479, 484 (1965).

57. *Id.* at 488–94 (Goldberg, J., concurring).

58. *Id.* at 493.

59. Roe v. Wade, 410 U.S. 113 (1973), *overruled by* Dobbs v. Jackson Women's Health Org., 142 S. Ct. 2228 (2022); Troxell v. Granville, 530 U.S. 57 (2000); Lawrence v. Texas, 539 U.S. 558 (2003).

60. The Proceedings Relative to the Calling the Conventions of 1776 and 1790, the Minutes of the Convention that Formed the Present Constitution of Pennsylvania, Together with the Charter to William Penn, the Constitutions of 1776 and 1790, and a View of the Proceedings of the Convention of 1776 152–53 (Harrisburg, Pa., John Wiestling 1825) [hereinafter Pennsylvania Proceedings].

61. *Id.* at 163.

62. *Id.* This language was preceded by language in an earlier motion to appoint

the committee to draft the declaration of rights, which, in relevant part, said, "That that part of the constitutions . . . called A declaration of the rights of the inhabitants . . . of Pennsylvania requires alterations and amendments, in such manner as that the rights of the people, reserved and excepted out of the general powers of government, may be more accurately defined and secured . . ." *Id.* at 152.

63. Carroll C. Arnold, *Early Constitutional Rhetoric in Pennsylvania* 184, in AMERICAN RHETORIC: CONTEXT AND CRITICISM (Thomas W. Benson, ed., 1989).

64. It should be noted that there is a major omission from this discussion that a studied reader will notice. We do not here use the term "police power." This may seem odd, because today this term is nearly synonymous with the general powers of state governments. We do not because in the antebellum period "police power" did not catch on as a standard term of art until quite late, being infrequently used, at least in judicial opinions, until the 1850s. (This is demonstrated through a LEXIS search of "police power" in the state courts database.) Therefore, it is feared we may import some later understandings of state government power into this earlier period by using that term. Instead we here use the terms state constitutions from the period actually used, "general powers" or "high powers."

65. *See* Lash, *The Lost Original Meaning, supra,* at 370.

66. PENNSYLVANIA PROCEEDINGS, *supra,* at 303 (art. IX, § 1). We will see how other states did the same thing with a Baby Ninth.

67. Kenneth R. Bowling, *"A Tub to the Whale": The Adoption of the Bill of Rights,* in THE BILL OF RIGHTS AND THE STATES: THE COLONIAL AND REVOLUTIONARY ORIGINS OF AMERICAN LIBERTIES 57 (Patrick T. Conley and John P. Kaminski, eds., 1992).

68. ROBERT L. MADDEX, STATE CONSTITUTIONS OF THE UNITED STATES 335 (2006).

69. Lash, *The Lost Original Meaning, supra,* at 393.

70. The language in those constitutions were as follows:

Delaware: We declare, that every thing in this article is reserved out of the general powers of government hereinafter mentioned.
1 FEDERAL AND STATE CONSTITUTIONS 570 (DEL. CONST. of 1792, art. I).

Indiana: To guard against any encroachments on the rights herein retained, we declare, that every thing in this article, is excepted out of the general powers of Government, and shall forever remain inviolable.
2 FEDERAL AND STATE CONSTITUTIONS 1059 (IND. CONST. of 1816, art. I, § 24).

Kentucky: To guard against transgressions of the high powers which we have delegated, WE DECLARE, that every thing in this article is excepted out of the general powers of government, and shall forever remain inviolate; and that all laws contrary thereto, or contrary to this constitution, shall be void.
3 FEDERAL AND STATE CONSTITUTIONS 1276 (KY. CONST. of 1792, art. XII, § 28).

Mississippi: To guard against transgressions of the high powers herein delegated, we declare, that every thing in this article is excepted out of the general powers of government, and shall forever remain inviolate, and that all laws contrary thereto, or to the following provisions shall be void.
4 THE FEDERAL AND STATE CONSTITUTIONS 2035 (MISS. CONST. of 1817, art. I, conclusion).

Ohio: To guard against the transgressions of the high powers which we have delegated, we declare that all powers, not hereby delegated, remain with the people.

5 FEDERAL AND STATE CONSTITUTIONS 2912 (OHIO CONST. of 1802, art. VIII, § 28).

Tennessee: The declaration of rights hereto annexed, is declared to be a part of the constitution of this state, and shall never be violated on any pretence whatever. And to guard against transgressions of the high powers which we have delegated; We declare, that every thing in the bill of rights contained, and every other right not hereby delegated, is excepted out of the general powers of government, and shall for ever remain inviolate.

6 FEDERAL AND STATE CONSTITUTIONS 3421–22 (TENN. CONST. of 1796, art. X, § 4).

71. Illinois also had a Baby Tenth in a draft of its 1818 constitution during its convention, which for some reason was taken out before it was adopted. SOLON JUSTICE BUCK, ILLINOIS IN 1818 283–84 (1918).

72. 2 FEDERAL AND STATE CONSTITUTIONS 981 (ILL. CONST. of 1818, art. VIII, § 1); 3 FEDERAL AND STATE CONSTITUTIONS 1889 (MASS. CONST. OF 1780, Part the First, art. I); 4 FEDERAL AND STATE CONSTITUTIONS 2471 (N.H. CONST. of 1784, Part First, Bill of Rights, art. II); 5 FEDERAL AND STATE CONSTITUTIONS 2909 (OHIO CONST. of 1803, art. VIII, § 1); *id.* at 3099 (PA. CONST. of 1790, art. IX, § 1); 6 FEDERAL AND STATE CONSTITUTIONS 3762 (VT. CONST. of 1793, ch. I art. 1); 7 FEDERAL AND STATE CONSTITUTIONS 3813 (VA. CONST. of 1776, Dec. of Rights, § 1).

73. "If there is a holy grail in this field it is coming up with a story about judicial review that is simple enough and compelling enough to teach on the first day of Constitutional Law. In the old spoof on English history, *1066 and All That,* the authors point out that history isn't what happened, '[i]t is what you can remember.' So long as casebooks and constitutional law professors fall back on teaching that Marbury invents judicial review, it does not matter that much what scholars write." Mary Sarah Bilder, Response, *Expounding the Law,* 78 GEO. WASH. L. REV. 1129, 1143–44 (2010).

74. BERNARD SIEGAN, ECONOMIC LIBERTIES AND THE CONSTITUTION 12 (2d ed. 2006); A.E. DICK HOWARD, THE ROAD FROM RUNNYMEDE 119–20 (1968).

75. This was even more true in the colonies, where lawbooks were scarce. "Foremost among the titles to be found in private [American] libraries of the time were the works of Coke, the great expounder of Magna Carta, and similar books on English liberties." Howard, *supra,* at 118. *See also id.* at 119 ("[O]f all the books on either law or politics in these libraries the most common was Coke's *Institutes* (found in 27 of the 47 libraries).").

76. Siegan, *supra,* at 21–27.

77. See the discussion of the case in Siegan.

78. *See, e.g.,* Gary L. McDowell, *Coke, Corwin and the Constitution: The "Higher Law Background" Reconsidered,* 55 REV. OF POLS. 393 (1993).

79. *See id.*

80. EDGAR J. MCMANUS AND TARA HELFMAN, LIBERTY AND UNION: A CONSTITUTIONAL HISTORY OF THE UNITED STATES 20 (2014).

81. William Michael Treanor, *Judicial Review Before Marbury,* 58 STAN. L. REV. 455, 458 (2010).

82. *Id.* at 475 (describing the *Ten-Pound Act Cases*).

83. Calabresi and Vickery, *supra,* at 1329.

84. Suzanna Sherry, *Natural Law in the States*, 61 CINCINNATI L. REV. 171, 186 (1992).

85. HERBERT JAMES LEWIS, LOST CAPITALS OF ALABAMA 27–28 (2014).

86. *Id.* at 49.

87. *Id.*

88. PAUL M. PRUITT, TAMING ALABAMA 124 (2010).

89. *Id.*

90. JOURNAL OF THE CONVENTION OF THE ALABAMA TERRITORY 6, 13 (Huntsville, Ala., John Boardman, 1819).

91. *Compare* Malcom Cook McMillan, *The Original Draft of the Alabama Constitution of 1819*, ALABAMA LAWYER, vol. 20, no. 1 (Jan. 1959) (containing Clay's committee's draft), *with* 1 FEDERAL AND STATE CONSTITUTIONS, at 97–98 (ALA. CONST. of 1819, Dec. of Rights).

92. *Compare* 1 FEDERAL AND STATE CONSTITUTIONS, at 97–98 (ALA. CONST. of 1819, Dec. of Rights), *with* 4 FEDERAL AND STATE CONSTITUTIONS, at 2033–35 (MISS. CONST. of 1817, Dec. of Rights).

93. The author has found no records of the committee's work other than the draft constitution itself.

94. *See generally* JOURNAL OF THE CONVENTION OF THE ALABAMA TERRITORY, *supra*, at 21–36 (amending various provisions in the original draft, but not all).

95. *See id.* at 21 (amending only seven provisions out of the thirty in the Declaration of Rights).

96. 4 FEDERAL AND STATE CONSTITUTIONS, at 2035.

97. 1 FEDERAL AND STATE CONSTITUTIONS, at 98 (ALA. CONST. of 1819, art. I, § 30) (emphasis added).

98. *See supra* note 70.

99. ALA. CONST., art. I, § 36 ("That this enumeration of certain rights shall not impair or deny others retained by the people; and, to guard against any encroachments on the rights herein retained, we declare that everything in this Declaration of Rights is excepted out of the general powers of government, and shall forever remain inviolate.").

100. Ronald F. Banks, *The Maine Constitutional Convention of 1819*, in A HISTORY OF MAINE: A COLLECTION OF READINGS ON THE HISTORY OF MAINE, 1600–1976 179 (Ronald F. Banks, ed., 1976).

101. *Id.* at 153.

102. *Id.* at 181.

103. *Id.* at 181.

104. JOURNAL OF THE CONSTITUTIONAL CONVENTION OF THE DISTRICT OF MAINE (Augusta, Me., Fuller & Puller, 1856).

105. MARSHALL J. TINKLE, THE MAINE STATE CONSTITUTION: A REFERENCE GUIDE 67 (2d ed. 2013).

106. The First Congress in fact briefly considered substituting "impair" for "disparage." John C. Yoo, *Our Declaratory Ninth Amendment*, 42 EMORY L.J. 967, 979–80 (1993). Professor Yoo argues that the common use of "impair" in Baby Ninths demonstrates the drafters' assumption that the provisions protect unenumerated, pre-existing rights. *Id.* at 1009–10.

107. *See supra* note 70.

108. 6 FEDERAL AND STATE CONSTITUTIONS, at 3421–22 (TENN. CONST. of 1796, art. X, § IV) (emphasis added).

109. Wallace McClure, State Constitution-Making: With Especial Reference to Tennessee 452–53 (1916).

Chapter 2

1. *See generally* Democracy, Liberty, and Property: The State Constitutional Conventions of the 1820s (Merrill D. Peterson, ed., Liberty Fund, 2010).

2. 3 The Federal and State Constitutions, Colonial Charters, and Other Organic Laws of the States, Territories, and Colonies Now or Heretofore Forming the United States of America 1922 (Francis Newton Thorpe, ed., 1909) (hereinafter "Federal and State Constitutions") (amendments of 1820 convention to Massachusetts Constitution); 5 Federal and State Constitutions 2639–51 (N.Y. Const. of 1821); 7 Federal and State Constitutions 3819–3829 (Va. Const. of 1830).

3. 4 Federal and State Constitutions 2150–67 (Mo. Const. of 1820).

4. 1 Federal and State Constitutions 584, 582–600 (Del. Const. of 1831).

5. 4 Federal and State Constitutions 2049–68 (Miss. Const. of 1831).

6. 4 Federal and State Constitutions 1930–1943 (Mich. Const. of 1835).

7. Patrick T. Conley and Robert G. Flanders, The Rhode Island State Constitution: A Reference Guide 22 (2d ed. 2011).

8. *Id.* at 22.

9. Proposed Rhode Island Const. of 1824, art. VI, § 18, in Constitution of the State of Rhode-Island and Providence Plantations, as Adopted by the Convention, Assembled at Newport, June 21, 1824, 15 (Providence, R.H., Jones & Maxcy, 1824), http://babel.hathitrust.org/cgi/pt?id=mdp.35112105061842;view=1up;seq=27

10. 1 Federal and State Constitutions 268.

11. *Compare* 1 Federal and State Constitutions 97–98 (Ala. Const. of 1819, Decl. of Rights), *with* 1 Federal and State Constitutions 269–71 (Ark. Const. of 1836's Decl. of Rights).

12. *Id.*

13. 6 Federal and State Constitutions 3541–42 (Tex. Const. of 1836, Preamble to Decl. of Rights).

14. The provision stated, "This declaration of rights is declared to be a part of this constitution, and shall never be violated on any pretence whatever. And in order to guard against the transgression of the high powers which we have delegated, we declare that everything in this bill of rights contained, *and every other right not hereby delegated*, is reserved to the people." *Id.* (emphasis added).

15. The new Baby Tenth stated, "To guard against transgressions of the high powers herein delegated, we declare that everything in this bill of rights is excepted out of the general powers of government, and shall forever remain inviolate; and all laws contrary thereto, or to the following provisions, shall be void." 6 Federal and State Constitutions 3549 (Tex. Const. of 1845, art. I, § 21).

16. Although Florida drafted its first constitution in 1838, the constitution was not approved by Congress until 1845, when Florida was admitted to the Union. *See* 2 Federal and State Constitutions 662–64 (Enabling Act for Florida 1845, and Constitution of 1838).

17. Roy Raven, The Dorr War: Rebellion and the Fight for Reform in Rhode Island 16 (2010).

18. *Id.* at 19–20.

19. *Id.* at 33–34, 42.

20. *Id.* at 120.

21. 5 FEDERAL AND STATE CONSTITUTIONS 3224 (R.I. CONST. of 1842, art. I, § 23) (official, adopted constitution); CONSTITUTION OF THE STATE OF RHODE-ISLAND AND PROVIDENCE PLANTATIONS AS ADOPTED BY THE CONVENTION, ASSEMBLED AT PROVIDENCE, NOV. 1841 (Providence, R.I., Knowles & Vose, 1842) (proposed Rhode Island Constitution of 1841, art. I, § 21) ("official" proposed constitution, voted down); PROPOSED CONSTITUTION OF THE STATE OF RHODE-ISLAND AND PROVIDENCE PLANTATIONS, AS FINALLY ADOPTED BY THE PEOPLE'S CONVENTION, ASSEMBLED IN PROVIDENCE, ON THE 18TH DAY OF NOV. 1841, 2 (Providence, R.I., New Age Office 1841) ("People's Constitution" art. I, § 25).

22. JOURNAL OF THE PROCEEDINGS OF THE CONVENTION TO FORM A CONSTITUTION FOR THE GOVERNMENT OF THE STATE OF NEW JERSEY 15, 230 (Trenton, N.J., Franklin S. Mills, 1844).

23. 5 FEDERAL AND STATE CONSTITUTIONS 2594–98 (1909) (N.J. CONST. of 1776).

24. NEW JERSEY JOURNAL 236 (art. I, § 19).

25. JACK STARK, THE IOWA STATE CONSTITUTION 5 (1998).

26. *Id.*

27. *Id.* at 6.

28. *Id.; compare* PROPOSED CONSTITUTION OF THE STATE OF IOWA, ADOPTED IN CONVENTION, NOV. 1, 1844, http://publications.iowa.gov/13339/1/1844Constitutio nIA.pdf (art. I), *with* 2 FEDERAL AND STATE CONSTITUTIONS 1123–25 (IOWA CONST. of 1846, art. I).

29. The only difference being the 1846 version stuck a comma in after the word "others." *Compare* PROPOSED CONSTITUTION OF THE STATE OF IOWA, ADOPTED IN CONVENTION, NOV. 1, 1844, http://publications.iowa.gov/13339/1/1844ConstitutionIA .pdf (art. I, § 23), *with* 2 FEDERAL AND STATE CONSTITUTIONS 1123–25 (IOWA CONST., art. I, § 24).

30. 3 FEDERAL AND STATE CONSTITUTIONS 1392–1411.

31. 2 FEDERAL AND STATE CONSTITUTIONS 985 n.b, 985–1012 (ILL. CONST. of 1848; convention held in 1847); 7 FEDERAL AND STATE CONSTITUTIONS 4077–4099 (WIS. CONST. of 1848).

32. 1 FEDERAL AND STATE CONSTITUTIONS 391–92 (CAL. CONST. of 1849, art. I, § 21).

33. J. ROSS BROWN, REPORT OF THE DEBATES OF THE CONVENTION OF CALIFORNIA ON THE FORMATION OF THE STATE CONSTITUTION 31 (1850).

34. *Id.* at 50–51.

35. *Id.* at 50.

36. *Id.* at 51.

37. *Id.*

38. *Id.*

39. *Id.* at 52.

40. *Id.* at 53.

41. *Id.*

42. *Id.*

43. *Id.* at 53–54.

44. *Id.* at 54.

45. No roll call votes are given for these specific actions in the journal of the convention, so we do not know who voted for or against. *Id.* at 50–54.

46. 3 FEDERAL AND STATE CONSTITUTIONS 1712, 1716 (MD. CONST. of 1851, Decl. of Rights § 42).

47. 5 FEDERAL AND STATE CONSTITUTIONS 2913, 2915 (OHIO CONST. of 1851, art. I, § 20).

48. 2 FEDERAL AND STATE CONSTITUTIONS 1073–1093 (IND. CONST. of 1851).

49. 3 FEDERAL AND STATE CONSTITUTIONS 1292–1315 (KY. CONST. of 1850).

50. 4 FEDERAL AND STATE CONSTITUTIONS 1944–1974 (MICH. CONST. of 1850).

51. 7 FEDERAL AND STATE CONSTITUTIONS 3859–3852 (VA. CONST. of 1850).

52. OHIO REPORT OF THE DEBATES AND PROCEEDINGS OF THE CONVENTION FOR THE REVISION OF THE CONSTITUTION OF THE STATE OF OHIO 337 (Columbus, S. Medary 1850).

53. *Id.*

54. 5 FEDERAL AND STATE CONSTITUTIONS 2912 (OHIO CONST. of 1802, art. VIII, § 28).

55. A reading that this implication of "high powers" meant "general powers" of government—as other Baby Tenths had had—is almost compelled by a review of the rest of the 1802 constitution. The state government is not actually given many powers, at least explicitly. Apart from internal functions of government, such as electing legislators or how the courts are run, the power to provide for public education is about the only power the state of Ohio is given in the text of the constitution. There is no power, however general, that would cover, for example, making killing or stealing a crime, something at the core of the traditional function of government. The delegates obviously didn't think they needed to spell out such a power. This flies in the face of the notion that a state government only has the powers specifically delegated to it in its constitution.

56. The delegate was apparently working off of a prior draft of the language, before the amendment discussed above.

57. OHIO REPORT, *supra* at 337.

58. *Id.* at 444.

59. 5 FEDERAL AND STATE CONSTITUTIONS 2913–37 (OHIO CONST. of 1851). Curiously, there is also a provision stating that there shall be a Board of Public Works, and that the board's powers "shall be such as now are, or may be, prescribed by law." *Id.* at 2927 (art. VIII, § 13). This, therefore, allows the legislature to give the board whatever powers it sees fit, allowing quite a workaround of the Baby Tenth's requirement that powers be delegated in the constitution.

60. 1 DEBATES AND PROCEEDINGS OF THE MARYLAND REFORM CONSTITUTIONAL CONVENTION 225–26 (Annapolis, William M'Neir 1851).

61. MARYLAND CONST. DEC. OF RIGHTS, § 45.

62. 3 FEDERAL AND STATE CONSTITUTIONS 1411–29 (LA. CONST. of 1852).

63. FRANCIS H. HELLER, THE KANSAS STATE CONSTITUTION 5–12 (1992).

64. *Id.* at 6.

65. 2 FEDERAL AND STATE CONSTITUTIONS 1181 ("Topeka Constitution" of 1855, art. I, § 22).

66. The Ohio Constitution of 1851 was a prototype for the eventual Kansas Constitution of 1861. HELLER, *supra*, at 8.

67. HELLER, *supra*, at 6.

68. It read, "This enumeration of rights shall not be construed to deny or disparage others retained by the people; and to guard against any encroachments on the

rights herein retained, or any transgression of any of the higher power herein delegated, we declare that everything in this article is excepted out of the general powers of government, and shall forever remain inviolate, and that all laws contrary thereto, or to the other provisions herein contained, shall be void." 2 FEDERAL AND STATE CONSTITUTIONS 1217 ("Lecompton Constitution" of 1857, Bill of Rights, § 24).

69. HELLER, *supra*, at 6.

70. 2 FEDERAL AND STATE CONSTITUTIONS 1224 ("Leavenworth Constitution" of 1858, art. I, § 21).

71. HELLER, *supra*, at 12.

72. 2 FEDERAL AND STATE CONSTITUTIONS 1224 (KAN. CONST. of 1861, Bill of Rights, § 20).

73. 1 THE DEBATES OF THE CONSTITUTIONAL CONVENTION OF THE STATE OF IOWA ASSEMBLED AT IOWA CITY, MONDAY, JAN. 19, 1857 140 (Davenport, Iowa, Luse, Lane & Co. 1857).

74. JOURNAL OF THE CONSTITUTIONAL CONVENTION OF OREGON 104 (Salem, Or., W. H. Byers 1858) (Art. I, § 33).

75. MARY JANE MORRISON, THE MINNESOTA STATE CONSTITUTION 1 (2002).

76. *Id.*

77. *Id.*

78. DEBATES AND PROCEEDINGS OF THE CONSTITUTIONAL CONVENTION FOR THE TERRITORY OF MINNESOTA 112, 164 (T. F. Andrews, ed., 1858) [hereinafter REPUBLICAN CONVENTION].

79. THE DEBATES AND PROCEEDINGS OF THE MINNESOTA CONSTITUTIONAL CONVENTION 204, 348–49 (Francis H. Smith, ed., 1857) (hereinafter DEMOCRATIC CONVENTION) (demonstrating a Baby Ninth—section 20 of draft bill of rights—drafted in committee and approved without amendment or comment by the Committee of the Whole).

80. *Id.* at 20, 653 (drafted by the convention and then adopted as art. I, § 16 of the Minnesota Constitution of 1857).

81. *Id.* (drafted by the convention and then adopted as art. I, § 16 of the Minnesota Constitution of 1857).

82. Minnesota's proposed Baby Tenth was: "To guard against transgressions of the high powers which we have delegated, we declare everything in this article is excepted out of the general powers of government, and shall forever remain inviolate, and that all laws contrary thereto, or contrary to this Constitution shall be void." REPUBLICAN CONVENTION, 112.

83. *Id.*

84. *Id.*

85. Again, the prior day's debate was technically by the Committee of the Whole, while the second debate was by the convention itself to adopt the committee's recommendations. *Id.* at 152.

86. That, of course, is directly contradictory to the sentiments behind the Baby Tenths, which explicitly state "high powers" are being delegated that could transgress upon rights.

87. Troxel v. Granville, 530 U.S. 57, 91 (2000) (Scalia, J., dissenting).

88. 7 Port. 293 (Ala. 1838).

89. *Id.* at 359–60.

90. *Id.* at 360. Justice Goldthwaite also discussed other sections of the state bill of rights, as Calabresi and Vickery discuss. *See* Steven G. Calabresi and Sofia M. Vickery,

On Liberty and the Fourteenth Amendment: The Original Understanding of the Lockean Natural Rights Guarantees, 93 TEX. L. REV. 1299, 1412–13 (2015).

91. *In re Dorsey, supra*, at 375–77.

92. *Id.* at 377.

93. *Id.* at 378.

94. *Id.* at 387.

95. *Id.* at 407.

96. *Id.*

97. Ex parte Martin, 13 Ark. 198, 205–06 (Ark. 1853).

98. *Id.* at 206.

99. *Id.* at 207.

100. *Id.* at 207–11 (discussing Fletcher v. Peck, 10 U.S. 87, Gardner v. Village of Newburgh, 2 John Ch. 162 (N.Y. 1816), Crenshaw v. Slate River Co., 6 Rand 245 (Va. 1828), Bristol v. New Chester, 3 N.H. 524 (1826)).

101. Billings v. Hall, 7 Cal. 1, 6–7 (1857).

102. *Id.* at 16 (Burnett, J., concurring).

103. Calabresi and Vickery, *supra*, at 1419. Another case, *Miller v. State*, 3 Ohio St. 475, 485 (1854), considered and rejected a challenge under Ohio's Baby Ninth, as well as other provisions in the state bill of rights, to a liquor law. The law was upheld on the grounds that it merely regulated liquor sales and did not ban them. *Id.* at 486.

Chapter 3

1. GA. CONST. of 1861, art. I, § 27, http://vault.georgiaarchives.org/cdm/ref /collection/adhoc/id/374.

2. ALA. CONST. of 1861, art. I, § 30, http://www.archives.state.al.us/timeline /1861/alcon4.html. Alabama's combined Baby Ninth/Baby Tenth at the time read, "This enumeration of certain rights shall not be construed to deny or disparage others retained by the people: and to guard against any encroachments on the rights herein retained, or any transgression of any of the high powers herein delegated, we declare, that every thing in this article is excepted out of the general powers of government, and shall forever remain inviolate; and that all laws contrary thereto, or to the following provisions, shall be void." *Id.* This was unchanged from Alabama's former constitution. ALA. CONST. of 1819, art. I, § 30, in 1 THE FEDERAL AND STATE CONSTITUTIONS, COLONIAL CHARTERS, AND OTHER ORGANIC LAWS OF THE STATES, TERRITORIES, AND COLONIES NOW OR HERETOFORE FORMING THE UNITED STATES OF AMERICA 98 (Francis Newton Thorpe, ed., 1909) (hereinafter "FEDERAL AND STATE CONSTITUTIONS").

3. ARK. CONST. of 1861, art. II, § 24, http://ahc.digital-ar.org/cdm/ref/collec tion/p16790coll1/id/18. Arkansas's combined Baby Ninth/Baby Tenth at the time read, "This enumeration of rights shall not be construed to deny or disparage others retained by the people; and to guard against any encroachments on the rights herein retained, or any transgression of any of the higher powers herein delegated, we declare that everything in this article is excepted out of the general powers of the government, and shall forever remain inviolate, and that all laws contrary thereto, or to the other provisions herein contained shall be void." *Id.* This language was virtually unchanged from Arkansas's former constitution. ARK. CONST. of 1836, art. II, § 24, in 1 FEDERAL AND STATE CONSTITUTIONS 270–71.

4. FLA. CONST. of 1861, http://fall.fsulawrc.com/crc/conhist/1861con.html.

5. OFFICIAL JOURNAL OF THE PROCEEDINGS OF THE CONVENTION OF THE STATE OF LOUISIANA 295–330 (1861) (introducing the Louisiana Constitution as amended by State Convention of 1861).

6. S.C. CONST. of 1861, http://www.carolana.com/SC/Documents/SC_Constitution_1861.pdf.

7. TEX. CONST. of 1861, https://tarltonapps.law.utexas.edu/constitutions/texas1861/a1.

8. Florida and Texas also kept their Baby Tenths. *See* FLA. CONST. of 1861, art. I, § 27; TEX. CONST. of 1861, art. I, § 21.

9. *See, e.g.*, ARK. CONST. of 1864, art. V (abolishing slavery in Arkansas), in 1 FEDERAL AND STATE CONSTITUTIONS, 295–96.

10. W. VA. CONST. of 1863, in 7 FEDERAL AND STATE CONSTITUTIONS 4013–33.

11. MD. CONST. of 1864, Decl. of Rights, art. 44 ("This enumeration of rights shall not be construed to impair or deny others retained by the people."), in 3 FEDERAL AND STATE CONSTITUTIONS 1745.

12. MICHAEL W. BOWERS, THE NEVADA STATE CONSTITUTION 10–11 (G. Alan Tarr, ed., 2d ed. 2014).

13. NEV. CONST. of 1864, art. I, § 20, in 4 FEDERAL AND STATE CONSTITUTIONS 2404; REPORTS OF THE 1863 CONSTITUTIONAL CONVENTION OF THE TERRITORY OF NEVADA: AS WRITTEN FOR THE *TERRITORIAL ENTERPRISE* BY ANDREW J. MARSH & SAMUEL L. CLEMENS AND FOR THE *VIRGINIA DAILY UNION* BY AMOS BOWMAN 43 (William C. Miller et al., eds., Legislative Counsel Bureau, State of Nevada 1972) (reporting the introduction of the Baby Ninth language to the delegates at the 1863 constitutional convention). Yes, that is right, Samuel L. Clemens, aka Mark Twain, was a stenographer for the first convention. *Id.* at v.

14. MO. CONST. of 1865, in 4 FEDERAL AND STATE CONSTITUTIONS 2191–2219.

15. ARK. CONST. of 1864, art. II, § 24 ("This enumeration of rights shall not be construed to deny or disparage others retained by the people, and to guard against any encroachments on the rights herein retained, or any transgression of any of the higher powers herein delegated, we declare that everything in this article is excepted out of the general powers of the government, and shall forever remain inviolate; and that all laws contrary thereto, or to the other provisions herein contained, shall be void."), in 1 FEDERAL AND STATE CONSTITUTIONS 291.

16. LA. CONST. of 1864, in 3 FEDERAL AND STATE CONSTITUTIONS 1429–48.

17. ALA. CONST. of 1865, art. I, § 36 ("This enumeration of certain rights shall not be construed to deny or disparage others retained by the people; and to guard against any encroachment on the rights hereby retained, or any transgression of any of the high powers by this constitution delegated, we declare, that everything in this article is excepted out of the general powers of government, and shall forever remain inviolate, and that all laws contrary thereto, or to the following provisions, shall be void."), in 1 FEDERAL AND STATE CONSTITUTIONS 119.

18. FLA. CONST. of 1865, in 2 FEDERAL AND STATE CONSTITUTIONS 685–704. Florida did continue to have a Baby Tenth, which read, "That, to guard against transgressions upon the rights of the people, we declare that everything in this article is excepted out of the general powers of government, and shall forever remain inviolate; and all laws contrary thereto, or to the following provisions, shall be void." FLA. CONST. of 1865, art. I, § 26, in 2 FEDERAL AND STATE CONSTITUTIONS 687.

19. S.C. CONST. of 1865, in 6 FEDERAL AND STATE CONSTITUTIONS 3269–81.

20. GA. CONST. of 1865, art. I, § 21, in 2 FEDERAL AND STATE CONSTITUTIONS

811. The new language was: "The enumeration of rights herein contained is a part of this constitution, but shall not be construed to deny to the people any inherent rights which they have hitherto enjoyed." *Id.*

21. EDGAR J. MCMANUS AND TARA HELFMAN, 1 LIBERTY AND UNION: A CONSTITUTIONAL HISTORY OF THE UNITED STATES 310–11 (2014).

22. The one exception was Tennessee, which was rewarded for ratifying the Fourteenth Amendment. *Id.* at 310.

23. Although excepted from Congress's mandate, Tennessee adopted a new constitution in any case, in 1870. TENN. CONST. of 1870, in 6 FEDERAL AND STATE CONSTITUTIONS 3448–73.

24. *See* RICHARD L. HUME AND JERRY B. GOUGH, BLACKS, CARPETBAGGERS, AND SCALAWAGS: THE CONSTITUTIONAL CONVENTIONS OF RADICAL RECONSTRUCTION 1–2 (2008).

25. *Id.* at 11.

26. ALA. CONST. of 1867 art. I, § 38 ("That this enumeration of certain rights shall not impair or deny others retained by the people."), in 1 FEDERAL AND STATE CONSTITUTIONS 135.

27. ARK. CONST. of 1868, in 1 FEDERAL AND STATE CONSTITUTIONS 306–32.

28. FLA. CONST. of 1868, Declaration of Rights, § 24, https://www.floridamemo ry.com/items/show/189095?id=4 ("This enunciation of rights shall not be construed to impair or deny others retained by the people."). For whatever reason, Florida chose to use the word "enunciation" instead of "enumeration," and continues to this day. FLA. CONST., art. I, § 1.

The Thorpe compendium of constitutions seems to be in error as it does not include article I, section 24 in Florida's Constitution of 1868, which is included in the version cited here. *See* 2 FEDERAL AND STATE CONSTITUTIONS 706 (lacking section 24 in the Florida constitution of 1868's Declaration of Rights).

29. GA. CONST. of 1868, in 2 FEDERAL AND STATE CONSTITUTIONS 822–42.

30. LA. CONST. of 1868, tit. I, art. 14 ("The rights enumerated in this title shall not be construed to limit or abridge other rights of the people not herein expressed."), in 3 FEDERAL AND STATE CONSTITUTIONS 1450. At one point in the convention an alternative formulation for the Baby Ninth was proposed, but not adopted: "All rights not enumerated in this title, and not in conflict with its meaning and design, shall in no wise be infringed or abridged." OFFICIAL JOURNAL OF THE PROCEEDINGS OF THE CONVENTION, FOR FRAMING A CONSTITUTION FOR THE STATE OF LOUISIANA 127 (1867–1868).

31. N.C. CONST. of 1868, art. I, § 37 ("This enumeration of rights shall not be construed to impair or deny others retained by the people; and all powers, not herein delegated, remain with the people."), in 5 FEDERAL AND STATE CONSTITUTIONS 2803. As can be seen from the second clause, this is a combined Baby Ninth/Baby Tenth. *Id.*

32. S.C. CONST. of 1868, art. I, § 41 ("The enumeration of rights in this constitution shall not be construed to impair or deny others retained by the people, and all powers not herein delegated remain with the people."), in 6 FEDERAL AND STATE CONSTITUTIONS 3285. Interestingly, the convention first proposed a combined Baby Ninth/Baby Tenth, like Alabama's and Arkansas's original constitutions, but it was modified, without comment, in the final version. *See* PROCEEDINGS OF THE CONSTITUTIONAL CONVENTION OF SOUTH CAROLINA 86, 259, 357 (1868).

33. MISS. CONST. of 1868 art. I, § 32 ("The enumeration of rights in this constitution shall not be construed to deny or impair others retained by and inherent in

the people."), in 4 FEDERAL AND STATE CONSTITUTIONS 2071. Like South Carolina, Mississippi—which before had a Baby Tenth, but not a Baby Ninth—considered a dual Baby Ninth/Baby Tenth but removed the language before the text was made final. *See* JOURNAL OF THE PROCEEDINGS IN THE CONSTITUTIONAL CONVENTION OF THE STATE OF MISSISSIPPI 1868, at 349, 611 (1871).

34. VA. CONST. of 1870, art. I, § 21 ("The rights enumerated in this bill of rights shall not be construed to limit other rights of the people not therein expressed."), in 7 FEDERAL AND STATE CONSTITUTIONS 3875.

35. TEX. CONST. of 1868, in 6 FEDERAL AND STATE CONSTITUTIONS 3591–3619. Texas kept its Baby Tenth. TEX. CONST. of 1868, art. I, § 23, in 6 FEDERAL AND STATE CONSTITUTIONS 3593.

36. TENN. CONST. of 1870, in 6 FEDERAL AND STATE CONSTITUTIONS 3448–73. Tennessee kept its Baby Tenth. TENN. CONST. of 1870, art. XI, § 16, in 6 FEDERAL AND STATE CONSTITUTIONS 3469.

37. Arkansas and Georgia.

38. Florida, Louisiana, North Carolina, South Carolina, Mississippi, and Virginia.

39. Alabama.

40. Texas and Tennessee.

41. It is significant to note, however, as explained below, that both of these states re-adopted Baby Ninths in the next decade.

42. NEB. CONST. of 1866, art. I, § 20 ("This enumeration of rights shall not be construed to impair or deny others retained by the people, and all powers not herein delegated remain with the people."), in 4 FEDERAL AND STATE CONSTITUTIONS 2351.

43. MD. CONST., Decl. of Rights, art. 45 ("This enumeration of Rights shall not be construed to impair or deny others retained by the People."), in 3 FEDERAL AND STATE CONSTITUTIONS 1783.

44. Albert L. Sturm, *The Development of American State Constitutions*, 12 PUBLIUS 57, 58 tbl.1 (1982). By "this period" we mean 1870 to 1900, and we do not include Tennessee's 1870 constitution, as that was included in the Reconstruction discussion.

45. ILL. CONST. of 1870, in 2 FEDERAL AND STATE CONSTITUTIONS 1013–52.

46. W. VA. CONST. of 1872, in 7 FEDERAL AND STATE CONSTITUTIONS 4033–64.

47. PA. CONST. of 1873, in 5 FEDERAL AND STATE CONSTITUTIONS 3121–52. Pennsylvania kept its Baby Tenth. PA. CONST. of 1873, art. I, § 26 ("To guard against transgressions of the high powers which we have delegated, we declare that everything in this article is excepted out of the general powers of government and shall forever remain inviolate."), in 5 FEDERAL AND STATE CONSTITUTIONS 3123.

48. TEX. CONST. of 1876, in 6 FEDERAL AND STATE CONSTITUTIONS 3621–63. Texas kept its Baby Tenth. TEX. CONST. of 1876, art. I, § 29 ("To guard against transgressions of the high powers herein delegated, we declare that everything in this 'Bill of Rights' is excepted out of the general powers of government, and shall forever remain inviolate, and all laws contrary thereto, or to the following provisions, shall be void."), in 6 FEDERAL AND STATE CONSTITUTIONS 3623.

49. COLO. CONST. of 1876, art. II, § 28, in 1 FEDERAL AND STATE CONSTITUTIONS 478.

50. ALA. CONST. of 1875, art. I, § 39 ("That this enumeration of certain rights shall not impair or deny others retained by the people."), in 1 FEDERAL AND STATE CONSTITUTIONS 157.

51. NEB. CONST. of 1875, art. I, § 26 ("This enumeration of rights shall not be construed to impair or deny others retained by the people, and all powers not herein delegated remain with the people."), in 4 FEDERAL AND STATE CONSTITUTIONS 2363.

52. CAL. CONST. of 1879, art. I, § 23 ("This enumeration of rights shall not be construed to impair or deny others retained by the people."), in 1 FEDERAL AND STATE CONSTITUTIONS 415.

53. LA. CONST. of 1879, Bill of Rights, art. 13 ("This enumeration of rights shall not be construed to deny or impair other rights of the people not herein expressed.") in 3 FEDERAL AND STATE CONSTITUTIONS 1472.

54. ARK. CONST. of 1874, art. II, § 29, in 1 FEDERAL AND STATE CONSTITUTIONS 336. The provision was the same combined Baby Ninth/Baby Tenth from versions before Reconstruction.

55. MO. CONST. of 1875, art. II, § 32 ("The enumeration in this Constitution of certain rights shall not be construed to deny, impair or disparage others retained by the people."), in 4 FEDERAL AND STATE CONSTITUTIONS 2232.

56. GA. CONST. of 1877, art. I, § v, ¶ II ("The enumeration of rights herein contained as a part of this Constitution, shall not be construed to deny to the people any inherent rights which they may have hitherto enjoyed."), in 2 FEDERAL AND STATE CONSTITUTIONS 845.

57. HEATHER COX RICHARDSON, TO MAKE MEN FREE: A HISTORY OF THE REPUBLICAN PARTY 123–25 (2014).

58. *Id.* at 125.

59. IDAHO CONST. of 1889, art. I, § 21 ("This enumeration of rights shall not be construed to impair or deny other rights retained by the people."), in 2 FEDERAL AND STATE CONSTITUTIONS 920.

60. MONT. CONST. of 1889, art. III, § 30 ("The enumeration in this Constitution of certain rights, shall not be construed to deny, impair or disparage others retained by the people."), in 4 FEDERAL AND STATE CONSTITUTIONS 2304.

61. WASH. CONST. of 1889, art. I, § 30 ("The enumeration in this constitution of certain rights shall not be construed to deny others retained by the people."), in 7 FEDERAL AND STATE CONSTITUTIONS 3975.

62. WYO. CONST. of 1889, art. I, § 36 ("The enumeration of this Constitution of certain rights shall not be construed to deny, impair, or disparage others retained by the people."), in 7 FEDERAL AND STATE CONSTITUTIONS 4120.

63. N.D. CONST. of 1889, in 5 FEDERAL AND STATE CONSTITUTIONS 2854–96. North Dakota did adopt a Baby Tenth. N.D. CONST. of 1889, art. I, § 24 ("To guard against transgressions of the high powers which we have delegated, we declare that everything in this article is excepted out of the general powers of government and shall forever remain inviolate."), in 5 FEDERAL AND STATE CONSTITUTIONS 2856.

64. S.D. CONST. of 1889, in 6 FEDERAL AND STATE CONSTITUTIONS 3357–3408.

65. FLA. CONST. of 1885, Decl. of Rights, § 24 ("This enunciation of rights shall not be construed to impair or deny others retained by the people."), in 2 FEDERAL AND STATE CONSTITUTIONS 734.

66. MISS. CONST. of 1890, art. III, § 32 ("The enumeration of rights in this constitution shall not be construed to deny or impair others retained by, and inherent in, the people."), in 4 FEDERAL AND STATE CONSTITUTIONS 2093.

67. LA. CONST. of 1898, Bill of Rights, art. 15 ("This enumeration of rights shall not be construed to deny or impair other rights of the people not herein expressed."), in 3 FEDERAL AND STATE CONSTITUTIONS 1523.

68. UTAH CONST. of 1895, art. I, § 25 ("This enumeration of rights shall not be construed to impair or deny others retained by the people."), in 6 FEDERAL AND STATE CONSTITUTIONS 3704.

69. KY. CONST. of 1890, in 3 FEDERAL AND STATE CONSTITUTIONS 1316–58. Ken-

tucky's Baby Tenth read, "To guard against transgression of the high powers which we have delegated, we declare that every thing in this Bill of Rights is excepted out of the general powers of government, and shall forever remain inviolate; and all laws contrary thereto, or contrary to this Constitution, shall be void." Ky. CONST. of 1890, Bill of Rights, § 26, in 3 FEDERAL AND STATE CONSTITUTIONS 1318.

70. DEL. CONST. of 1897, in 1 FEDERAL AND STATE CONSTITUTIONS 600–36. Delaware's Baby Tenth reads, "We declare that every thing in this article is reserved out of the general powers of government hereinafter mentioned." DEL. CONST. of 1897, art. I (concluding sentence), in 1 FEDERAL AND STATE CONSTITUTIONS 602.

71. S.C. CONST. of 1895, in 6 FEDERAL AND STATE CONSTITUTIONS 3307–54.

72. JOURNAL OF THE CONSTITUTIONAL CONVENTION OF THE STATE OF SOUTH CAROLINA 137, 145, 275 (Columbia, S.C., Charles A. Calvo, Jr., 1895) (demonstrating two versions of a Baby Ninth/Baby Tenth were considered and one was included in a final report).

73. OKLA. CONST., art. II, § 33 ("The enumeration in this constitution of certain rights shall not be construed to deny, impair, or disparage others retained by the people."), in 7 FEDERAL AND STATE CONSTITUTIONS 4271, 4276.

74. ARIZ. CONST., art. II., § 33 ("The enumeration in this Constitution of certain rights shall not be construed to deny others retained by the people."), in THE STATE CONSTITUTIONS AND THE FEDERAL CONSTITUTION AND ORGANIC LAWS OF THE TERRITORIES AND OTHER COLONIAL DEPENDENCIES OF THE UNITED STATES OF AMERICA 57 (Charles Kettleborough, ed., 1918) [hereinafter THE STATE CONSTITUTIONS].

75. N.M. CONST., art. II., § 23 ("The enumeration in this constitution of certain rights shall not be construed to deny, impair, or disparage others retained by the people."), in THE STATE CONSTITUTIONS 939.

76. Luis R. Davila-Colon, *Equal Citizenship, Self-Determination, and the U.S. Statehood Process: A Constitutional and Historical Analysis*, 13 CASE W. RES. J. INT'L L. 315, 323 n.49 (1981).

77. ALA. CONST., art. I § 36 ("That this enumeration of certain rights shall not impair or deny others retained by the people; and, to guard against any encroachments on the rights herein retained, we declare that everything in this Declaration of Rights is excepted out of the general powers of government, and shall forever remain inviolate."), in 1 FEDERAL AND STATE CONSTITUTIONS 185.

78. VA. CONST. of 1902, art. I, § 17 ("The rights enumerated in this Bill of Rights shall not be construed to limit other rights of the people not therein expressed."), in 7 FEDERAL AND STATE CONSTITUTIONS 3906.

79. LA. CONST. of 1913, Bill of Rights, art. 15 ("This enumeration of rights shall not be construed to deny or impair other rights of the people not herein expressed."), in THE STATE CONSTITUTIONS 502.

80. MICH. CONST. of 1908, in THE STATE CONSTITUTIONS 685–709.

81. LA. CONST. of 1921, art. I, § 15 ("This enumeration of rights shall not be construed to deny or impair other rights of the people not herein expressed.").

82. Sturm, *supra*, 58 tbl.1.

83. *See id.* (detailing when each new state constitution before 1983 was adopted); Peter J. Smith and Robert W. Tuttle, *God and State Preambles*, 100 MARQ. L. REV. 757, 768 (2017) (stating the last new state constitution was Rhode Island's 1986 constitution).

84. Sturm, *supra*, 58 tbl.1, 71.

85. GA. CONST. of 1945, art. I, § V, ¶ II ("The enumeration of rights herein con-

tained as a part of this Constitution shall not be construed to deny to the people any inherent rights which they may have hitherto enjoyed."), http://georgiainfo.galileo .usg.edu/topics/government/related_article/constitutions/georgia-constitution-of -1945-as-ratified-without-subsequent-amendments.

86. Mo. CONST. The debate from that convention on dropping the Baby Ninth is interesting and is discussed below.

87. N.J. CONST., art. I, § 21 ("This enumeration of rights and privileges shall not be construed to impair or deny others retained by the people.").

88. ALASKA CONST., art. I, § 21 ("The enumeration of rights in this constitution shall not impair or deny others retained by the people.").

89. HAW. CONST., art. I, § 20 ("The enumeration of rights and privileges shall not be construed to impair or deny others retained by the people.").

90. MICH. CONST., art. I, § 23 ("The enumeration in this constitution of certain rights shall not be construed to deny or disparage others retained by the people.").

91. CONN. CONST.

92. FLA. CONST., art. I, § 1 ("All political power is inherent in the people. The enunciation herein of certain rights shall not be construed to deny or impair others retained by the people."). Intriguingly, this latest version of the Florida Constitution placed the Baby Ninth at the beginning of the state Declaration of Rights, along with the statement about political power being inherent in the people, instead of at the end.

93. PENN. CONST.; *id.* art. I, § 25.

94. ILL. CONST., art. I, § 24 ("The enumeration in this Constitution of certain rights shall not be construed to deny or disparage others retained by the individual citizens of the State.").

95. N.C. CONST., art. I, § 36 ("The enumeration of rights in this Article shall not be construed to impair or deny others retained by the people.").

96. VA. CONST., art. I, § 17 ("The rights enumerated in this Bill of Rights shall not be construed to limit other rights of the people not therein expressed.").

97. MONT. CONST., art. II, § 34 ("The enumeration in this constitution of certain rights shall not be construed to deny, impair, or disparage others retained by the people.").

98. LA. CONST., art. I, § 24 ("The enumeration in this constitution of certain rights shall not deny or disparage other rights retained by the individual citizens of the state.").

99. GA. CONST. of 1976, art. I, § 1, para. XXV ("The enumeration of rights herein contained as a part of this Constitution shall not be construed to deny to the people any inherent rights which they may have hitherto enjoyed."), http://georgiainfo.gal ileo.usg.edu/topics/government/related_article/constitutions/georgia-constitution -of-1976-as-ratified-without-subsequent-amendments.

100. GA. CONST., art. I, § 1, para. XXIX ("Enumeration of rights not denial of others. The enumeration of rights herein contained as a part of this Constitution shall not be construed to deny to the people any inherent rights which they may have hitherto enjoyed.").

101. R.I. CONST., art. I, § 24 ("The enumeration of the foregoing rights shall not be construed to impair or deny others retained by the people. The rights guaranteed by this Constitution are not dependent on those guaranteed by the Constitution of the United States."); Smith & Tuttle, *supra*, at 768 (stating Rhode Island's 1986 constitution is the nation's most recent).

102. California, Maryland, Minnesota, and Ohio.

103. The author should make clear that as an original public meaning originalist, he does not believe delegates' statements are dispositive of original meaning. The statements assist us, however, in understanding how the wider public understood the language the delegates selected. *See* Kurt T. Lash, *The Origins of the Privileges or Immunities Clause, Part II: John Bingham and the Second Draft of the Fourteenth Amendment,* 99 GEO. L.J. 329, 339 (2011) ("Original public meaning originalism does not dismiss the personal intentions of the framers of a given text (to the extent they can be determined), but considers such views as having weight only to the degree that they reflect or illuminate the likely public understanding of the text.").

104. 1 PROCEEDINGS OF THE CONSTITUTIONAL CONVENTION OF HAWAII OF 1950 304 (1960).

105. 6 MONTANA CONSTITUTIONAL CONVENTION, VERBATIM TRANSCRIPT MARCH 9, 1972 TO MARCH 16, 1972, at 1832 (1981).

106. Randy E. Barnett, *The Ninth Amendment: It Means What It Says,* 85 TEX. L. REV. 1, 1 (2006).

107. 4 DEBATES OF THE MISSOURI CONSTITUTIONAL CONVENTION OF 1875 309 (Isidor Loeb, Ph.D., LL.B. & Floyd C. Shoemaker, A.M. eds., 1938).

108. 1 REPORT OF THE PROCEEDINGS AND DEBATES OF THE CONSTITUTIONAL CONVENTION STATE OF VIRGINIA 105 (1906).

109. 7 DEBATES OF THE 1943–1944 CONSTITUTIONAL CONVENTION OF MISSOURI 1927 (1945).

110. *Id.*

111. *See, e.g., id.* at 1929 ("You haven't protected anything so that the provision is simply a shot gun provision without effect or meaning.").

112. 1 STATE OF NEW JERSEY CONSTITUTIONAL CONVENTION OF 1947 at 640 (1947). The reference to the militia and public schools is because the delegate was proposing a section protecting against discrimination within either institution. *Id.*; *see also* N.J CONST., art. I, § 5 ("No person shall be denied the enjoyment of any civil or military right, nor be discriminated against in the exercise of any civil or military right, nor be segregated in the militia or in the public schools, because of religious principles, race, color, ancestry or national origin."). Thus the "rights" referred to are rights against discrimination, not positive rights to a militia or public schools. *Id.*

113. *See* N.J CONST., art. I, § 5; 1 STATE OF NEW JERSEY CONSTITUTIONAL CONVENTION OF 1947 640.

114. 1 STATE OF NEW JERSEY CONSTITUTIONAL CONVENTION OF 1947 327–30.

115. As we will see later, Baby Ninths likely do not protect positive rights. On the Ninth Amendment itself scholars disagree. *Compare* Randy E. Barnett, *Who's Afraid of Unenumerated Rights?,* 9 U. PA. J. CONST. L. 1, 21 (2006) (Ninth Amendment does not protect positive rights), *with* DANIEL A. FARBER, RETAINED BY THE PEOPLE: THE "SILENT" NINTH AMENDMENT AND THE CONSTITUTIONAL RIGHTS AMERICANS DON'T KNOW THEY HAVE 146–53 (2007) (Ninth Amendment protects the right to an education).

116. However, it did include a Baby Tenth much earlier. *See* MICH. CONST. of 1908, art. II, § 1.

117. OFFICIAL RECORD, MICHIGAN CONSTITUTIONAL CONVENTION 470 (1962).

118. *Id.* at 569.

119. *Id.* at 470.

120. This was explicitly the case with Georgia's Baby Ninth.

121. 6 RECORD OF PROCEEDINGS, SIXTH ILLINOIS CONSTITUTIONAL CONVENTION OF 1969–1970 66 (1972).

122. 1 RECORD OF PROCEEDINGS, SIXTH ILLINOIS CONSTITUTIONAL CONVENTION OF 1969–1970 700 (1972).

123. 3 RECORD OF PROCEEDINGS, SIXTH ILLINOIS CONSTITUTIONAL CONVENTION OF 1969–1970 1613–14 (1972).

124. U.S. CONST. art. VI, cl. 2.

125. 3 RECORD OF PROCEEDINGS, SIXTH ILLINOIS CONSTITUTIONAL CONVENTION 1969–1970 1614.

126. Delegate Pechous also gave a brief discussion of a state case from Arkansas, *Wade v. Horner*. 3 RECORD OF PROCEEDINGS, SIXTH ILLINOIS CONSTITUTIONAL CONVENTION OF 1969–1970 1614 (1972). *Wade*, however, did not actually concern the Arkansas Baby Ninth, at least to any level of specificity. *Wade v. Horner*, 170 S.W. 1005, 1005–06 (Ark. 1914) (not naming or examining Arkansas's Baby Ninth). Instead, there the court upheld a Jim Crow liquor licensing scheme in the face of a challenge under unspecified sections of the state and federal constitutions. *Id.* at 1006. The charitable explanation for Delegate Pechous's invocation of the case is that he misidentified what constitutional provisions it concerned.

127. Griswold v. Connecticut, 381 U.S. 479, 491–93 (1965) (Goldberg, J., concurring).

128. 3 RECORD OF PROCEEDINGS, SIXTH ILLINOIS CONSTITUTIONAL CONVENTION OF 1969–1970 1614.

Chapter 4

1. *See, e.g.*, State ex rel. Burlington & M.R.R. Co. v. County of Wapello, 13 Iowa 388, 412 (1862).

2. This is based on searches in the Lexis electronic database for Illinois appellate courts from 1971 through the present. The search terms were "enumeration in this Constitution of certain rights" and "substantive due process."

3. State ex rel. Burlington & M.R.R. Co. v. County of Wapello, 13 Iowa 388 (1862).

4. *Id.* at 389–90.

5. *Id.* at 412.

6. *Id.*

7. *Id.*

8. 27 Iowa 28 (1869), *overruled by* Stewart v. Bd. of Supervisors, 30 Iowa 9 (1870), *and* Bonnifield v. Bidwell, 32 Iowa 149 (1871).

9. *Id.* at 42.

10. *Id.* at 73 (Beck, J., concurring).

11. *Id.*

12. *Id.* at 84–85 (Cole, J., dissenting) (citing People v. Mahony, 13 Mich. 481 (1865); People v. Gallagher, 4 Mich. 244 (1856)).

13. Troxel v. Granville, 530 U.S. 57, 91 (2000) (Scalia, J., dissenting) ("In my view, a right of parents to direct the upbringing of their children is . . . among the 'othe[r] [rights] retained by the people' which the Ninth Amendment says the Constitution's enumeration of rights 'shall not be construed to deny or disparage.' . . . however . . . the Constitution's refusal to 'deny or disparage' other rights is far removed from affirming any one of them, and even further removed from authorizing judges to

identify what they might be, and to enforce the judges' list against laws duly enacted by the people.").

14. Stewart v. Bd. of Supervisors, 30 Iowa 9, 10–12 (1870).

15. One might call what the court did here "proto-Thayerian." *See generally* James B. Thayer, *The Origin and Scope of the American Doctrine of Constitutional Law*, 7 HARV. L. REV. 129, 148–56 (1893).

16. *Stewart*, 30 Iowa at 9 (1870).

17. *Id.* at 17–19.

18. *Id.* at 18.

19. *Id.* at 17–18.

20. *Id.* at 17–19.

21. *Id.* at 44 (Beck, J., dissenting).

22. *Id.*

23. Atwood v. Vilsack, 725 N.W.2d 641, 652 (Iowa 2006).

24. *See, e.g.*, Santi v. Santi, 633 N.W.2d 312, 314 (Iowa 2001) (finding grandparent visitation statute unconstitutional under article I, sections 8 and 9 of the Iowa Constitution, and applying strict scrutiny analysis).

25. Coster v. Tide Water Co., 18 N.J. Eq. 54, 55–60 (Ch. 1866), *aff'd*, 18 N.J. Eq. 518 (1866).

26. *Id.* at 64.

27. Dennis v. Moses, 52 P. 333, 339 (Wash. 1898).

28. State v. Clark, 71 P. 20, 21, 23 (Wash. 1902).

29. *Id.* at 21.

30. 61 S.E. 61, 67 (N.C. 1908).

31. *Id.* at 63.

32. Roman Catholic Archbishop of Diocese of Or. v. Baker, 15 P.2d 391, 396 (Ore. 1932) (en banc).

33. *Id.*

34. 173 So. 266, 268 (Ala. 1937).

35. *Id.* (quoting Meyer v. Nebraska, 262 U.S. 390, 399 (1923)).

36. 14 N.W.2d 400 (Minn. 1944).

37. *Id.* at 402, 405–6.

38. *See, e.g.*, Zale-Las Vegas, Inc. v. Bulova Watch Co., 396 P.2d 683, 683–84 (Nev. 1964) (declaring fair trade law unconstitutional).

39. Nickola v. Township of Grand Blanc, 232 N.W.2d 604, 604, 610 (Mich. 1975) (striking down exclusion of mobile-home parks because rule denied low-cost shelter which "may be among the unenumerated rights" referenced by the Baby Ninth).

40. As the author has shown elsewhere, this is *not* more generally true about state constitutions, but courts have primarily used substantive due process for that work. *See* Anthony B. Sanders, *The "New Judicial Federalism" Before Its Time: A Comprehensive Review of Economic Substantive Due Process Under State Constitutional Law Since 1940 and the Reasons for Its Recent Decline*, 55 AM. U. L. REV. 457, 475–76 (2005).

41. *See, e.g.*, Troxel v. Granville, 530 U.S. 57, 77 (2000); Meyer v. Nebraska, 262 U.S. 390, 399 (1923).

42. *Troxel*, at 91 (Scalia, J., dissenting).

43. Espinoza v. Mont. Dep't of Revenue, 140 S. Ct. 2246, 2261 (2020).

44. Electors of Big Butte Area v. State Bd. of Educ., 308 P.2d 225, 231 (Idaho 1957).

45. *In re J. P.*, 648 P.2d 1364, 1372–73 (Utah 1982) (citing Baby Ninth and the Ninth Amendment in finding a constitutional right to rear one's own children).

46. T.R.F. v. Felan, 760 P.2d 906 (Utah Ct. App. 1988).

47. *In re Medworth*, 562 N.W.2d 522, 523–24 (Minn. Ct. App. 1997).

48. 556 So. 2d 545 (La. 1990).

49. *Id.* at 551.

50. *See* In the Interest of V.G., 834 S.E.2d 901, 911 n.12 (Ga. App. 2019) (Dillard, J., concurring) (invoking the Georgia Baby Ninth in discussing the right to raise one's child); Hewlett v. Hewlett, 825 S.E.2d 622, 627 n.21 (Ga. App. 2019) (Dillard, J., concurring) (invoking the Georgia Baby Ninth in discussing the right to raise one's child); Borgers v. Borgers, 820 S.E.2d 474, 480 n.5 (Ga. App. 2018) (Dillard, J., concurring) (invoking the Georgia Baby Ninth in discussing the right to raise one's child); In the Interest of R.B., 816 S.E.2d 706, 711 n.4 (Ga. App. 2018) (Dillard, J., concurring) (invoking the Georgia Baby Ninth in discussing the right to raise one's child); In the Interest of R.S.T., 812 S.E.2d 614, 626 (Ga. App. 2018) (Dillard, J., concurring) (invoking the Georgia Baby Ninth, and the Ninth Amendment, in recognizing the right to raise one's child).

51. Patten v. Ardis, 816 S.E.2d 633, 636 n.9 (Ga. 2018) (suggesting that Georgia's Baby Ninth may be the best clause to use in finding the right to raise one's child).

52. *In re Brown*, 478 So. 2d 1033, 1035–36, 1040 (Miss. 1985) ("This right of privacy, whether perceived as emanating from the common law or natural law, is given constitutional status by Article 3, § 32 of the Mississippi Constitution of 1890.").

53. Pro-Choice Miss. v. Fordice, 716 So. 2d 645, 654 (Miss. 1998) (en banc) (recognizing a right to obtain an abortion under the Baby Ninth, but concluding the challenged restrictions constitutional).

54. *Id.* at 653.

55. *Id.*

56. 142 S. Ct. 2228 (2022).

57. 410 U.S. 113 (1973), *overruled by Dobbs*, 142 S. Ct. at 2242.

58. 539 U.S. 558, 578 (2003) (invalidating law criminalizing homosexual sodomy).

59. Jegley v. Picado, 80 S.W.3d 332, 347, 350 (Ark. 2002).

60. Murphy v. Pocatello Sch. Dist. No. 25, 480 P.2d 878, 884 (Idaho 1971).

61. *In re White*, 158 Cal. Rptr. 562, 567 (Ct. App. 1979) (declaring area-specific probation restriction unconstitutional).

62. 1 ANNALS OF CONG. 759, 760 (1789) (Joseph Gales, ed., 1834) (statement of Rep. Sedgwick) (arguing that one can always name additional rights to those that might be enumerated).

63. 111 So. 850, 850 (Miss. 1927).

64. *Id.* at 851, 852, 853.

65. Sinclair v. State, 132 So. 581, 581–82 (Miss. 1932).

66. *Id.* at 591 (Griffith, J., concurring).

67. State v. Labato, 80 A.2d 617, 619–20 (N.J. 1951).

68. *Id.*

69. *Id.* at 622.

70. McCracken v. State, 518 P.2d 85, 91 (Alaska 1974).

71. *Id.*

72. *Id.*

73. Atwood v. Vilsack, 725 N.W.2d 641, 652 (Iowa 2006).

74. *See generally* Randy E. Barnett, *Scrutiny Land*, 106 MICH. L. REV. 1479 (2008).

75. St. Mary Anesthesia Assocs., Inc. v. Hosp. Serv. Dist. No. 2, 2001–2852 (La. App. 1 Cir. 12/20/02); 836 So. 2d 379, 382.

76. *Id.* at 386 n.9.

77. LA. CONST., art. I, § 24 ("The enumeration in this constitution of certain rights shall not deny or disparage other rights retained by the individual citizens of the state.").

78. *See, e.g.*, Williamson v. Lee Optical of Okla., Inc., 348 U.S. 483 (1955) (applying rational basis scrutiny to uphold a state statute under the Due Process Clause of the Fourteenth Amendment).

79. *In re Atkinson*, 291 N.W.2d 396, 398–99 (Minn. 1980) (en banc).

80. *Id.* at 400–401.

81. *See* 1568 Montgomery Highway, Inc. v. City of Hoover, 45 So. 3d 319, 343–44 (Ala. 2010) (reasonableness standard applied to challenge under Baby Ninth to sale of sexual devices); Atwood v. Vilsack, 725 N.W.2d 641, 651–52 (Iowa 2006) (reasonableness standard applied to right to bail in civil commitment proceedings); Otero v. Zouhar, 1984-NMCA-054, ¶ 43, 102 N.M. 493, 697 P.2d 493 (ruling that rights Baby Ninth protects are "subject to reasonable regulation"), *overruled on other grounds by* 1985-NMSC-021, 102 N.M. 482, 697 P.2d 482.

82. 233 P. 186, 187 (Okla. 1924).

83. *Id.*

84. *See id.* A similar collective rights opinion is State v. McCarroll, 70 So. 448, 455 (La. 1915), where the court boldly read the Baby Ninth out of the constitution by giving it a collectivist reading: "This article is meaningless, as the people of this state retain all rights the exercise of which is not prohibited by the Constitution of the state or of the United States."

85. 285 P. 92, 97 (Okla. 1930).

86. *Id.* at 93.

87. *Id.* at 96–97.

88. *Id.* at 97.

89. State *ex rel.* White v. Barker, 89 N.W. 204, 207 (Iowa 1902) (recognizing right in dicta in case concerning appointment of local officials). And, as we saw above, the Supreme Court of Iowa in the *Stewart* case found a right of the people to legislate at the state level.

90. State *ex rel.* Smyth v. Moores, 76 N.W. 175, 184–85 (Neb. 1898) (gubernatorial appointment of local board members found unconstitutional).

Chapter 5

1. The author has searched transcripts and journals of state constitutional conventions where no Baby Ninth was adopted and has not found any references to proposed but "failed" Baby Ninths, other than the Republican Convention in Minnesota (where the state eventually adopted a Baby Ninth anyway), the South Carolina convention of 1895, and the Missouri convention of 1945. Added to this could be the handful of other times (in addition to these South Carolina and Missouri examples) that a convention has not included a Baby Ninth in a new constitution when it was in the state's former constitution.

2. This channels Madison's draft of what then became the Ninth Amendment: "The exceptions here or elsewhere in the constitution, made in favor of particular rights, shall not be construed as to diminish the just importance of other rights retained by the people, or as to enlarge the powers delegated by the constitution; but either as actual limitations of such powers, or as inserted merely for greater caution."

James Madison, Speech in Congress Proposing Constitutional Amendments (June 8, 1789), in JAMES MADISON, WRITINGS 437, 443 (Jack N. Rakove, ed., 1999).

3. THE FEDERALIST No. 45, 292 (James Madison) (Clinton Rossiter, ed., 1961).

4. There is also one other view, propounded in the failed attempt to adopt a Baby Tenth in Minnesota, that the Baby Tenth itself protected unenumerated rights. This seems to have been rejected because the delegates believed the Baby Tenth did not in fact do this, and this was immediately followed by a more successful attempt to adopt a Baby Ninth instead.

5. As Randy Barnett has said, it is not necessarily contradictory to believe the Ninth Amendment protects *both* individual rights and some other kinds of rights, such as collective rights. Randy E. Barnett, *The Ninth Amendment: It Means What It Says*, 85 TEX. L. REV. 1, 3 (2006). As discussed below, however, it is hard to say the same thing about Baby Ninths.

6. 6 THE FEDERAL AND STATE CONSTITUTIONS, COLONIAL CHARTERS, AND OTHER ORGANIC LAWS OF THE STATES, TERRITORIES, AND COLONIES NOW OR HERETOFORE FORMING THE UNITED STATES OF AMERICA 3264 (Francis Newton Thorpe, ed., 1909) (S.C. CONST. of 1790, art. VIII § 2).

7. Such as in the Tenth Amendment: "The powers not delegated to the United States by the Constitution, nor prohibited by it to the States, are reserved to the States respectively, *or to the people.*" There is no "or to the cities" understanding of this language.

8. *See, e.g.*, Thomas v. Reid, 285 P. 92, 97 (Okla. 1930) (Baby Ninth Amendment protects the right of local self-government by majority rule).

9. Michael W. McConnell, *Natural Rights and the Ninth Amendment: How Does Lockean Legal Theory Assist in Interpretation?*, 5 N.Y.U. J.L. & LIBERTY 1 (2010).

10. *See* William Baude, *Is Originalism Our Law?*, 115 COLUM. L. REV. 2349, 2355 (2016) (describing various types of originalism that take into account precedent to a lesser extent than a common law judge would).

11. Heller v. District of Columbia, 554 U.S. 570, 614 (2008).

12. *See, e.g.*, *In re Dorsey*, 7 Port. 293 (Ala. 1838); Roman Catholic Archbishop of Diocese of Or. v. Baker, 15 P.2d 391, 396 (Ore. 1932); Thiede v. Town of Scandia Valley, 14 N.W.2d 400 (Minn. 1944); Pro-Choice Miss. v. Fordice, 716 So. 2d 645, 654 (Miss. 1998); Atwood v. Vilsack, 725 N.W.2d 641, 652 (Iowa 2006); 1568 Montgomery Highway, Inc. v. City of Hoover, 45 So. 3d 319, 343–44 (Ala. 2010).

13. *See, e.g.*, Nickola v. Township of Grand Blanc, 232 N.W.2d 604, 604, 610 (Mich. 1975); *In re Brown*, 478 So. 2d 1033, 1035–36, 1040 (Miss. 1985); *In re Medworth*, 562 N.W.2d 522, 523–24 (Minn. Ct. App. 1997).

14. MD. CONST., Decl. Rights § 4.

15. VT. CONST., ch. I, art. 18.

16. MONT. CONST., art. I, § 1.

17. N.H. CONST., part 1, art. 10.

18. N.J. CONST., art. I, § 2a.

19. MD. CONST., Decl. Rights § 6.

20. TENN. CONST., art. I, § 1.

21. VA. CONST., art. I, § 3.

22. N.J. CONST., art. I, § 19.

23. Professor Seidman makes an argument similar to this. *See* Louis Michael Seidman, *Our Unsettled Ninth Amendment: An Essay on Unenumerated Rights and the Impossibility of Textualism*, 98 CALIF. L. REV. 2129 (2010).

Chapter 6

1. OHIO CONST., art. I, § 20. Note that because it is not relevant to the current discussion, we have dropped the Baby Tenth language from the end of this provision.

2. VA. CONST., art. 1, § 17; GA. CONST., art 1, para. 29.

3. THOMAS HOBBES, LEVIATHAN 129–41 (Simon & Schuster 2008) (1651).

4. *See generally,* Eric R. Claeys, *The Private Society and the Liberal Public Good in John Locke's Thought,* 25 SOC. PHIL. & POL'Y 201 (2008); Alex Tuckness, *Locke's Political Philosophy,* in STANFORD ENCYCLOPEDIA OF PHILOSOPHY, https://plato.stanford.edu/entries/locke-political/ (Jan. 11, 2016); Howard I. Schwartz, *How Notions of Public Good Constrain Liberty In John Locke and the Early Liberty Tradition,* http://www.howardischwartz.com/uploads/LibertyIsNotFreedom.pdf (April 2007).

5. JOHN LOCKE, THE SECOND TREATISE in TWO TREATISES OF GOVERNMENT §§ 77–94 (1689).

6. For a general survey, see MARK HULLIUNG, THE SOCIAL CONTRACT IN AMERICA 25–35 (2007), discussing writers influential at the Founding including James Harrington, Samuel von Pufendorf, and Hugo Grotius, but especially Locke.

7. *See, e.g.,* Mark Niles, *Ninth Amendment Adjudication: An Alternative to Substantive Due Process Analysis of Personal Autonomy Rights,* 48 UCLA L.REV. 85, 117 (2000) ("The relevant statements of James Madison, essentially the sole author of the Ninth Amendment, make clear that the retained rights referred to in the provision are the same Lockean rights to self-determination that are retained by the people when they agree to the formation of civil government.").

8. At the time of the founding "retain" meant "to keep," "to depend on," "to belong to," "to continue" and most relevantly "not to lose," which was the definition Samuel Johnson attributed to the work of Locke. *See* SAMUEL JOHNSON, A DICTIONARY OF THE ENGLISH LANGUAGE (17th ed. 1783) (citing to "Locke" for the definition of "retain"), https://books.google.com/books?id=xxcTAAAAYAAJ&printsec=frontcover#v=onepage&q&f=false. A more contemporary dictionary defines "retain" as "(1) to keep possession of, (2) to continue to use practice, etc., (3) to continue to hold or have, (4) to keep in mind; remember, (5) to hold in place or position. WEBSTER'S ENCYCLOPEDIC UNABRIDGED DICTIONARY OF THE ENGLISH LANGUAGE 1223 (1989).

9. *See generally* CLAIRE RYDELL ARCENAS, AMERICA'S PHILOSOPHER: JOHN LOCKE IN AMERICAN INTELLECTUAL LIFE (2022) (especially chapter 2).

10. *See generally* RANDY E. BARNETT, RESTORING THE LOST CONSTITUTION: THE PRESUMPTION OF LIBERTY (2013).

11. *See e.g,* ALA. CONST., art. 7, § 1 ("The legislature shall by general law establish and maintain a system of public schools open to all children of the State, and may provide for other public educational institutions. Schools and institutions so established shall be free from sectarian control. No money shall be paid from public funds for the direct benefit of any religious or other private educational institution."); ARIZ. CONST., art. 11, § 1 ("The legislature shall enact such laws as shall provide for the establishment and maintenance of a general and uniform public school system, which system shall include: 1. Kindergarten schools. 2. Common schools. 3. High schools."); FLA. CONST., art. 9, § 1 ("The education of children is a fundamental value of the people of the State of Florida. It is, therefore, a paramount duty of the state to make adequate provision for the education of all children residing within its borders."); MICH. CONST., art. 8, § 2 ("The legislature shall maintain and support a system of free public elementary and secondary schools as defined by law."); N.Y.

Const., art. 11, § 1 ("The legislature shall provide for the maintenance and support of a system of free common schools, wherein all the children of this state may be educated."); Va. Const., art 8, § 1 ("The General Assembly shall provide for a system of free public elementary and secondary schools for all children of school age throughout the Commonwealth, and shall seek to ensure that an educational program of high quality is established and continually maintained.")

12. *See, generally* Gilbert v. Homar, 520 U.S. 924, 928–930 (1997); Cleveland Board of Education v. Loudermill, 470 U.S. 5325 (1985); Perry v. Sindermann, 480 U.S. 593 (1972).

13. *See generally* Randy Barnett, *Who's Afraid of Unenumerated Rights*, 9 U. Pa. J. Const. L. 1, 21–22 (2006); Michael McConnell, *Natural Rights and the Ninth Amendment: How Does Lockean Legal Theory Assist in Interpretation*, 5 N.Y.U J. L. & Liberty 1, 2–8 (2010)

14. Randy Barnett, *The Ninth Amendment Means What it Says*, 85 Tex. L. Rev. 1, 33–35 (2006); Michael McConnell, *The Ninth Amendment in Light of Text and History*, 2010 Cato Sup. Ct. Rev. 13, 15–17 (2010).

15. Lochlan F. Shelfer, *How the Constitution Shall Not Be Construed*, 2017 B.Y.U. L. Rev. 331 (2017).

16. *See e.g.* Const. of Belgium, Title 2, art. 23 & 24; Const. of Hungry, art. XI & XIX; Const. of Finland, ch. 2, § 16 & 19; Const. of Poland, arts. 67 & 70; Const. of South Africa, ch. 2, art. 26 & 27; Charter of Fundamental Rights of the European Union, art. 34.

17. John Dayton and Anne Dupre, *School Funding Litigation: Who's Winning the War?*, 57 Vand. L. Rev. 2351, 2353 (2004) (explaining "To date, the highest courts in thirty-six states have issued opinions on the merits of funding litigation suits, with nineteen courts upholding state funding systems and seventeen declaring the systems unconstitutional."). *See also* Jason R. Kopanke, Christine Kiracofe, and Spencer C. Weiler, *Can't Get No Satisfaction: An Examination of 65 Years of School Finance Litigation and State Aid for K-12 Public Education in States with High and Low Teacher Satisfaction Indicators*, 374 Ed. Law Rep. 1 (2020); Derek W. Black, *Educational Gerrymandering: Money, Motives, and Constitutional Rights*, 94 N.Y.U. L. Rev. 1385, 1389 (2019) (explaining "Ironically, the more plaintiffs win the more things seem to stay the same. States often quickly slip back into their bad habits or, even worse, never fully implement an effective remedy in the first instance.")

18. *See e.g.* Ala. Const., art. 1, § 21 & art. 7, § 1; Ariz. Const., art. 2, § 33 & art. 11, § 1.

19. 3 Record of Proceedings, Sixth Illinois Constitutional Convention of 1969–1970, 1613–14 (1972).

20. Debates and Proceedings of the Constitutional Convention for the Territory of Minnesota 152 (T. F. Andrews, ed., 1858).

21. *Ohio Constitutional Convention of 1802*, 51 Clev. St. L. Rev. 665, 667 (2004).

22. *See* William McAlpine, *The Origin of Public Education in Ohio*, 38 Ohio Hist. J. 409, 433 (1929).

23. Ohio Const. of 1802, art. VIII, § 27.

24. Ohio Const., art. XIII, § 2.

25. Randy E. Barnett, *In Defense of Constitutional Republicanism: A Reply to Criticisms of Our Republican Constitution*, 32 Const. Comm. 207, 214 (2017) ("Today, however, if legislators pay any attention to the Constitution at all—and they typically pay none—they merely debate whether or not the courts will uphold their acts.").

26. This is most well known because of *Kelo v. New London*, 545 U.S. 469 (2005). But the problem goes far beyond just that example. *See generally* ILYA SOMIN, KELO V. NEW LONDON AND THE LIMITS OF EMINENT DOMAIN (2015).

27. DANA BERLINER, OPENING THE FLOODGATES: EMINENT DOMAIN ABUSE IN THE POST-KELO WORLD (2006).

28. 198 U.S. 45 (1905).

29. *See generally* DAVID BERNSTEIN, REHABILITATING LOCHNER (2011).

30. 236 U.S. 1 (1915).

31. *See* Paula Abrams, *The Little Red Schoolhouse: Pierce, State Monopoly of Education and the Politics of Intolerance*, 20 CONST. COMM. 61, 67–70 (2003).

32. Meyer v. Nebraska, 262 U.S. 390 (1923).

33. In full disclosure, a number of the following examples are taken from cases litigated by the author's employer, the Institute for Justice.

34. Associated Press, *Hair Braider Says Utah Cosmetology Law Is Unfair*, Apr. 30, 2011.

35. Clayton v. Steinagel, 885 F. Supp. 2d 1212 (D. Utah 2012).

36. Associated Press, *supra*.

37. *Clayton*, 885 F. Supp. 2d at 1215.

38. Niang v. Carroll, 879 F.3d 870 (8th Cir. 2018).

39. Kevin C. Smith, *Unspooling the Furrowed Brow: How Eyebrow Threaders Will Protect Economic Freedom in Texas*, 48 TEX. TECH. L.R. 71, 90–91 (2016).

40. For example, the District of Columbia adopted regulations that require a college degree simply to look after children in a daycare. Sanchez v. Office of the State Superintendent of Educ., 995 F.3d 1121, 1123 (D.C. Cir. 2020). This kind of regulatory overreach threatens anyone who only has a high school education and wants to offer this basic human practice to needy families.

41. Dolphy v. City of Minneapolis, 2012 Minn. App. Unpub. LEXIS 1250 (city requiring tree trimming business to have a certified arborist on staff even if practitioner simply trims or cuts down trees).

42. Edward L. Glaeser, Joseph Gyourko, and Raven Saks, *Why Is Manhattan So Expensive? Regulation and the Rise in Housing Prices*, 48 J. L. & ECONS. 331, 366 (2005) (detailing how various land use regulations raise the cost of housing).

43. Scott Sexton, *Washington Law Firm Steps In to Help Small Homeless Shelter in North Wilkesboro*, WINSTON-SALEM J. (Oct. 12, 2020), https://journalnow.com/news/colum nists/washington-law-firm-steps-in-to-help-small-town-homeless-shelter-in-north-wilke sboro/article_14609db8-0caf-11eb-85eb-5faafaf487ac.html.

44. *Id.*

45. The shelter won on state law grounds and under the Fourteenth Amendment. The court applied the rational basis test but because the facts were so extreme it prevailed anyway. Catherine H. Barber Mem. Shelter, Inc. v. Town of N. Wilkesboro Bd. of Adjustment, 576 F. Supp. 3d 318, 343 (W.D.N.C. 2021).

46. Samantha J. Gross, *A Green Thumb Who Fought City Hall to Keep Her Vegetable Garden Has Died at 63*, MIAMI HERALD (Aug. 27, 2019), https://www.miamiherald .com/news/local/obituaries/article234401687.html.

47. Ricketts v. Village of Miami Shores, 232 So. 3d 1095, 1099–1100 (Fla. Ct. App. 2017).

Afterword

1. *See generally* BRYAN CAPLAN, THE MYTH OF THE RATIONAL VOTER: WHY DEMOC-RACIES CHOOSE BAD POLICIES (2008) (discussing the literature demonstrating the many reasons why voters are largely ignorant of the specifics of most policy).

2. These are broad statements that could turn into a book in its own right about the dynamics of constitutional convention politics versus legislative politics. For some backing *see, e.g.,* G. Alan Tarr, "Introduction," in STATE CONSTITUTIONS FOR THE TWENTY-FIRST CENTURY VOL. 1 7 (2006, Tarr & Williams, eds.) ("The delegates often cite the convention experience as among the most important in their lives, a chance to be statesmen rather than politicians."); Jeffrey S. Sutton, *What Does—and Does Not—Ail State Constitutional Law*, 59 U. KAN. L. REV. 687, 694–95 (2011); Peter J. Galie and Christopher Bopst, *Changing State Constitutions: Dual Constitutionalism and the Amending Process*, 1 HOFSTRA L. & POL'Y SYMP. 27, 35–41 (1996) (constitutional conventions are well suited for reforming states because they often escape political dynamics that stymie reform in legislatures).

3. *See* CAL. CONST., art. I, § 24 ("In criminal cases the rights of a defendant to equal protection of the laws, to due process of law, to the assistance of counsel, to be personally present with counsel, to a speedy and public trial, to compel the attendance of witnesses, to confront the witnesses against him or her, to be free from unreasonable searches and seizures, to privacy, to not be compelled to be a witness against himself or herself, to not be placed twice in jeopardy for the same offense, and to not suffer the imposition of cruel or unusual punishment, shall be construed by the courts of this State in a manner consistent with the Constitution of the United States. This Constitution shall not be construed by the courts to afford greater rights to criminal defendants than those afforded by the Constitution of the United States, nor shall it be construed to afford greater rights to minors in juvenile proceedings on criminal causes than those afforded by the Constitution of the United States."); FLA. CONST., art. I, § 12 ("This right [against unreasonable searches and seizures] shall be construed in conformity with the 4th Amendment to the United States Constitution, as interpreted by the United States Supreme Court. Articles or information obtained in violation of this right shall not be admissible in evidence if such articles or information would be inadmissible under decisions of the United States Supreme Court construing the 4th Amendment to the United States Constitution.").

4. *See* United Pub. Workers v. Mitchell, 330 U.S. 75, 95–96 (1947).

5. One study found that the United States Supreme Court finds laws of Congress unconstitutional less than 1 percent of the time. CLARK NEILY AND DICK M. CARPEN-TER II, GOVERNMENT UNCHECKED: THE FALSE PROBLEM OF "JUDICIAL ACTIVISM" AND THE NEED FOR JUDICIAL ENGAGEMENT 1 (2011).

6. *See* Saikrishna Bangalore Prakash, Response, *A Fool for the Original Constitution*, 130 HARV. L. REV. F. 24, 28–29 (2016) (recounting Justice Scalia's remarks on his view of his vote in Texas v. Johnson, 491 U.S. 397 (1989)).

Index

~~~~

abolition of slavery, 62

abortion, 27, 86, 146

Adams, John, 15, 37

adoption, 85

Adoption of B.G.S., In re, 85

Alabama: Baby Ninth Amendment,
9–10, 34–37, 43, 62, 63, 64, 65, 66,
101, 140, 149; Baby Tenth Amendment, 35–37, 43, 63, 97, 101; court
cases, 57–59, 82–83; influence of
constitution on other states, 42–43,
45, 47, 52, 53; right to education in,
186n11

Alaska: Baby Ninth Amendment, 66,
150; court cases, 87, 130

Aldrich (Minnesota delegate), 55, 56

Amar, Akhil, 24

antidiscrimination provisions, 69

Antifederalists, 20–21, 29

Arizona: Baby Ninth Amendment,
65–66, 150; right to education in,
186n11

Arkansas: Baby Ninth Amendment,
42–43, 62, 63, 64, 65, 150–51; Baby
Tenth Amendment, 63, 64, 173n3;
court cases, 59, 86; influence of constitution on other states, 45, 52, 53

arms, right to bear, 16, 89

attainder, bills of, 19, 20

Baby Ninth Amendments: "Baby Ninth"
term, 5; development of, early, 34–40;
development of, pre-Civil War, 41–60;
development of, Civil War to present,
61–73; examples of everyday protections, 1–6, 12–14, 113; increase in, 10,
43, 52–57, 61, 64, 66, 139–40; *vs.* Ninth
Amendment, 5–6; numbers of, 5, 6, 60,
61–62, 64, 66; objections to, 42, 47–48,
56–57, 68–69, 79–80, 94–95; overview
of, 5–14; placement of in state bills of
rights, 179n92; popularity of, 7, 11, 139–
45; as recourse for powerless, 2, 12–14,
133–37. *See also* court cases and Baby
Ninths; enforcement of Baby Ninths;
meaning of Baby Ninths; *specific states*

Baby Tenth Amendments: board work-
around, 171n59; court cases, 57–59;
development of, early, 27–30, 35–40;
development of, pre-Civil War, 42,
43, 45–46, 48–50, 53–55; development of, Civil War to present, 63, 66,
173n3, 174n8; and legislative capacity, 96; and meaning of Baby Ninths,
96–98; objections to, 42; in overview,
9, 15; popularity of, 141; and powers,
29, 48–50, 96–98, 172n86; and state
sovereignty, 28, 30, 91–92, 185n7. *See
also specific states*

bail, 16
bakeries, 133–34
Bangura-Clayton, Jestina Sunkarie. *See*
Clayton, Jestina
barbers, 82–83
Barnett, Randy, 22–24, 67, 119, 121,
185n5
Beck, Joseph M., 78–79, 80, 81, 145
Bibb, William Wyatt, 35
Billings (Minnesota delegate), 54–55
Billings v. Hall, 60
Bill of Rights: adoption of, 30; applica-
bility to states, 161n2; development
of, 19–22; enumerated rights in, 3–6;
opposition to, 6–7, 20, 94–95; ratification of, 22, 30; unenumerated rights
in, 4–6. *See also specific amendments*
Bill of Rights, English, 16, 17
bills/declarations of rights, state: Alabama, 35; Arkansas, 42–43; California, 45; collective rights in, 106–8;
Connecticut, 19; development of,
15–19, 28; Florida, 179n92; Iowa,
44, 45; Maine, 37–38; New Jersey, 44;
New York, 45; Pennsylvania, 28, 30;
placement of Baby Ninths in, 179n92;
popularity of, 19; Rhode Island, 19;
Vermont, 19; Virginia, 17–19
"Black and Tan" conventions, 63–64
blood transfusions, 85
Botts, C. T., 45, 46, 47
braiding, hair, 2, 134–35
Buford v. State, 87
*Burlington & M.R.R. Co. v. County of
Wapello, State ex rel.*, 77–78

Calabresi, Steven, 18
Calder v. Bull, 58
California: Baby Ninth Amendment,
45–48, 65, 96, 151; Baby Tenth
Amendment, 45–47, 96; court cases,
60; restrictions on criminal defen-
dants in, 144
Carroll, Tom, 2
Catherine H. Barber Homeless Shelter,
136
Cession, Treaty of, 87
Chase (Judge), 58
Chicago, food trucks in, 13–14

children: child care, 136; and grandparent visitation, 182n24; parental access
to, 84, 85; termination of parental
rights, 84; upbringing of, 27, 80, 83–
86. *See also* education and schools
cities: and collective rights, 90–91; lack
of sovereignty of, 25, 91–92, 101–2;
and local *vs.* state cases, 90–92
City of Mobile v. Rouse, 82
Civil War and Reconstruction, constitutions during, 62–64, 131
Clay, Clement Comer, 35
Clayton, Jestina, 2, 134–35
Clemens, Samuel L., 174n13
Coke, Edward, 31–33, 34, 58
Cole, Chester C., 79–80, 145
collective bargaining, 69, 96, 102, 107
collective rights: and collective bargaining, 69, 96, 102, 107; defined, 101;
model, 24, 47, 73, 76, 90–96, 101–2,
110, 185n5; in state bills of rights,
106–8
Collier (Judge), 58–59
Colorado and Baby Ninth Amendment,
65, 151
Commerce Clause, 20, 24
compensation, just, 59
Connecticut: constitutional development, 19, 66; contraception restrictions, 27, 72, 73; Fundamental
Orders, 16–17
Constitution, U.S. *See* U.S. Constitution
Constitutional Convention of 1787, 19
constitutional conventions: delegate
debates during, 66–73, 94–96, 124–
25; as events, 17, 41, 105, 128, 142,
144; right to, 101; state constitutional
development through, 17–18, 28–30,
34–38, 41–57, 61–71, 123–25; and
U.S. Constitution, 19, 21
constitutions, state. *See* state
constitutions
contraception, 27, 72, 73
contracts, 19, 59, 164n32
Coppage v. Kansas, 134
corruption of blood, 19
cosmetology, 2, 134–36, 141, 142
Coster v. Tide Water Co., 81–82
court cases and Baby Ninths: pre-Civil

War, 57–60; Civil War to 20th c., 75–82; 20th c. to present, 82–91; and collective rights model, 76, 80–81, 90–92, 105; and criminal procedure, 87–88, 129–30; and economic liberty, 81–83; and individual rights model, 57–60, 76, 81, 82, 85, 88, 105–6, 145–46; and judicial review development, 31–34; overview of, 75–77; and personal liberties, 76, 78–81, 83–86; and privacy rights, 85–86; and property rights, 76, 81–83; as recourse, 2, 12–14, 133–37; and scrutiny, 76, 81, 88–89, 113, 132–33, 145; shotgun/combination approach to, 76–77, 145
court cases and Baby Tenths, 57–59
COVID-19 pandemic, 2
criminal defendants, state restrictions on, 144
criminal procedure, 19, 87–88, 129–30
cruel and unusual punishment, 16

Declaration of Independence, 18
Declaration of Rights. See English Bill of Rights of 1689
declaration of rights, state. See bills/declarations of rights, state
Delaware: Baby Tenth Amendment, 30, 65; constitutional development, 30, 42, 65
delegation term, 28–29
Diaz, Benigno "Benny," 12–13, 14
diet restrictions, 1, 2, 3, 4
Dillard, Stephen, 85
disparage language, 38, 40, 44, 115
Dobbs v. Jackson Women's Health Organization, 86
Doctor Bonham's Case, 32–33, 34, 58
Dorr, Thomas, 44
Dorr Rebellion, 43–44
Dorsey, In re, 57–59
double jeopardy, 87, 129
Douglas, William O., 27
Due Process Clause of Fourteenth Amendment, 83, 84, 86, 144–45

economic liberty, 23–24, 81–83
education and schools: antidiscrimination provisions, 69; in everyday

examples of rights, 1, 2, 3–4; funding of, 123, 126; languages in, 134; restrictions on private, 2, 82, 84, 134; right to education as positive right, 120, 123, 125
eminent domain, 132–33
employee rights, 69, 96, 102, 107, 133–34
enforcement of Baby Ninths: assumption of enforceability, 34, 40, 93; and collective rights, 90–92, 94; vs. construing, 108–10; failure to as abdication of responsibility, 8; failure to as common, 6, 10, 73, 75, 77, 140, 141, 145–47; and individual rights, 94; judges' role in enforcing rights, 108–10; and level of scrutiny, 88–89, 132–33, 145; and positive rights, 123, 126; Scalia on, 57, 80; and unreasonableness, 81
English Bill of Rights of 1689, 16, 17
enumerated powers. See powers, enumerated
enumerated rights, 3–6
enunciation language, 175n28
Ex parte Martin, 59
Ex parte Sales, 90–91
ex post facto laws, 164n32
eyebrow threading, 136

Farber, Dan, 23–24
federalism model, 24, 102–3
Federalists, 20, 29, 94–95
Fifth Amendment, 132–33
First Amendment, 8, 132, 146
First Charter of Virginia, 16
flag burning, 146
Fletcher v. Peck, 59
Florida: Baby Ninth Amendment, 64, 65, 66, 151–52; Baby Tenth Amendment, 174n8; constitutional development, 43, 62, 63, 64, 65, 66, 144; court cases, 2, 12–13, 14, 134, 136–37; restrictions on criminal defendants in, 144; right to education in, 186n11
food and diet restrictions, 1, 2, 3, 4
food trucks, 12–14, 133–34
foreclosures, 82

Fort Pierce, FL, 12–13, 14, 134
Fourteenth Amendment, 83, 84, 86, 134, 135, 144–45, 188n45
Free Speech Clause of First Amendment, 8, 132
Fundamental Orders, 16–17

gardening, 2, 120, 136–37
general powers. *See* powers, general
Georgia: Baby Ninth Amendment, 62, 63, 65, 66, 115, 131–32, 152, 180n120; constitutional development, 62, 63, 64, 65, 66, 131–32, 163n18; court cases, 85
Goldberg, Arthur, 27
Goldthwaite (Judge), 58
government: right to alter or abolish, 24, 107; right to self-government, 91–92
grandparent visitation rights, 182n24
Griswold v. Connecticut, 27, 72, 73
gun rights, 16, 89, 146
Gwin, W. M., 45, 47

hair, 2, 86, 134–35
Hamilton, Alexander, 164n26
Hanson v. Vernon, 78–80
Hastings, L. W., 46–48
Hawaii and Baby Ninth Amendment, 66, 67, 152
Heller v. District of Columbia, 105, 146
high powers. *See* powers, high
Hobbes, Thomas, 115
homeless shelters, 136
home rule provisions, 102
homes and housing: eminent domain, 132–33; forcible removal from, 84; and positive rights, 120; right to establish a home, 84; zoning, 83, 136

Idaho: Baby Ninth Amendment, 65, 152; court cases, 84
Illinois: Baby Ninth Amendment, 61, 66, 71–73, 96, 106, 117–18, 124, 152–53; Baby Tenth Amendment, 167n71; constitutional development, 45, 65, 66, 71–73, 96, 124; court cases, 13–14, 77; floor debates, 67, 71–73, 96

immigrants, 134, 136
impair language, 38, 40, 44, 114–15
inalienable rights, 115–18. *See also* natural rights
incarceration, 120–21
income, right to, 120, 121, 123, 127
Indiana: Baby Tenth Amendment, 30, 36, 37; constitutional development, 30, 48; influence of constitution on other states, 36, 37
individual rights model: and Baby Tenths, 29, 97–98; and court cases, 57–60, 76, 81, 82, 85, 88, 105–6, 145–46; described, 23–24, 25; and libertarianism, 117–18; and meaning of Baby Ninths, 10, 25–26, 42, 44, 47–48, 57–60, 67, 71–73, 93–98, 104–6, 110–12, 140; and meaning of Ninth Amendment, 10, 23–24, 25–26; protected rights under, 113–24, 128, 132–37; unprotected rights under, 114
inherent rights language, 62, 115, 130
inheritance taxes, 82
In re Adoption of B.G.S., 85
In re Dorsey, 57–59
insanity defense, 87
interstate commerce regulation, 20, 24
Iowa: Baby Ninth Amendment, 44, 53, 153; court cases, 77–81, 87–88, 91, 145; influence of constitution on other states, 45, 47
Iredell, James, 7

Jefferson, Thomas, 18
Jenifer (Maryland delegate), 51
jeopardy, double, 87, 129
Jim Crow laws, 181n126
judges: attitudes before Civil War, 57–60; and criminal procedure, 87–88; and judicial restraint, 80; and judicial review, 31–34, 102; and rational basis, 88–89, 106, 113, 132, 135–37, 188n45; role in enforcing rights, 108–10; and scrutiny, 76, 81, 88–89, 113, 118–19, 132–33, 145; support for unenumerated rights, 7–8, 140. *See also* court cases and Baby Ninths; enforcement of Baby Ninths

judicial restraint, 80
judicial review, 31–34, 102
Judiciary Act of 1789, 87
jury, rights to trials by, 18, 121–22, 125

Kansas: Baby Ninth Amendment, 52–53, 153; Baby Tenth Amendment, 52
Kelo v. New London, 188n26
Kentucky: Baby Tenth Amendment, 30, 65; constitutional development, 48, 65
Kilgour (Maryland delegate), 51
King, William, 37

Law of the Land Clause, 59
Lawrence v. Texas, 27, 86
"Leavenworth Constitution" (Kansas), 52–53
"Lecompton Constitution" (Kansas), 52
legislative capacity, 46, 47, 96
legislature, as recourse, 2–3
Levinson, Sanford, 26
libertarianism, 117–18
liquor laws, 82, 87, 173n103, 181n126
"living constitutionalists," 22, 69–71
Lochner v. New York, 133–34, 146
Locke, John, 18–19, 24–25, 30, 115–17, 124, 127–30, 163n15. *See also* natural rights; social contract
Louisiana: Baby Ninth Amendment, 64, 65, 66, 153; constitutional development, 45, 62, 63, 64, 65, 66; court cases, 85, 88–89, 184n84
low-cost housing, 83

Madison, James, 7, 21–22, 96, 140, 143, 184n2, 186n7
Magna Carta, 16, 17, 83, 87
Maine and Baby Ninth Amendment, 37–38, 140, 154
Marbury v. Madison, 31, 33, 34
marijuana, 164n31
Marshall, John, 31, 33, 34
Martin, Ex parte, 59
Maryland: Baby Ninth Amendment, 48, 50–52, 63, 64, 94, 154; floor debates, 48, 50–52, 94; right of people to exercise political power, 106; right to change government, 107

Mason, George, 17–19, 30, 116
Massachusetts: constitutional development, 15, 42; influence of constitution on other states, 37, 38; natural rights and slavery, 34
McConnell, Michael, 22, 24–25, 39, 103–4, 121
meaning of Baby Ninths: and Baby Tenths, 96–98; and collective rights model, 24, 47, 73, 76, 90–96, 101–2, 110, 185n5; and delegate debates, 48–50, 66–73, 94–96, 124–25; and individual rights model, 10, 25–26, 42, 44, 47–48, 57–60, 67, 71–73, 93–98, 104–6, 110–12, 140; and "living constitutionalists," 69–71; and meaning of Ninth Amendment, 25, 98–105, 110–12; overview of, 5, 10, 93–94; "traditions" understanding, 129. *See also* court cases and Baby Ninths
meaning of Ninth Amendment: and individual rights, 10, 23–24, 25–26; and "living constitutionalists," 22; and meaning of Baby Ninths, 25, 98–105; nonoriginalist models of, 25–27, 110–12; originalist models of, 22–25, 99–105, 110–12; original meaning as term, 22–23, 98–99; overview of, 5, 9
Meyer v. Nebraska, 82–83, 134
Miami Shores, FL gardening ban, 2, 136–37
Michigan: Baby Ninth Amendment, 66, 69–71, 106, 154; constitutional development, 42, 48, 66, 69–71; court cases, 83; right to education, 186n11
militia, 50, 69
Miller v. State, 173n103
Minnesota: Baby Ninth Amendment, 53–57, 115, 124–25, 130, 154, 185n4; Baby Tenth Amendment, 54–55, 97, 185n4; court cases, 83, 84, 89
Mississippi: Baby Ninth Amendment, 64, 65, 115, 130, 131, 155; Baby Tenth Amendment, 30, 35–36, 176n33; constitutional development, 42, 64, 65, 184n1; court cases, 85–86, 87; influence of constitution on other states, 35–36, 54

Missouri: Baby Ninth Amendment, 65,
68–69, 94, 155; constitutional development, 42, 63, 65, 66, 68–69, 94,
184n1; court cases, 135
Mobile v. Rouse, City of, 82
monopolies, 32
Montana: Baby Ninth Amendment, 65,
66, 67, 155; right of people to exercise political power, 107
Morgan (Minnesota delegate), 54, 55
mortgage foreclosures, 82

natural rights: and Baby Tenths, 30;
court cases, 58, 59, 60, 76, 82, 87;
and double jeopardy, 87, 129; and
judicial review, 34; and Locke, 18–19,
24–25, 30, 34, 39, 117, 121, 127–30;
model of Ninth Amendment, 24–25,
103–4; "plus" concept, 39, 122, 128;
and retained rights concept, 115–18;
and slavery, 34
Nebraska: Baby Ninth Amendment, 64,
65, 155; court cases, 91
Necessary and Proper Clause of U.S.
Constitution, 20
negative rights, 24, 119–24, 132. *See also*
retained rights
Nevada and Baby Ninth Amendment, 5,
63, 155
New Hampshire: constitutional development, 15; right to change government, 107; Ten Pound Act, 33
New Jersey: Baby Ninth Amendment,
44, 66, 69, 94, 96, 102, 156; court
cases, 81–82, 87, 129; freedom of
religion, 163n18; influence of constitution on other states, 53; right to
change government, 107
New Mexico and Baby Ninth Amendment, 65–66, 156
New York: constitutional development,
42, 163n18; influence of constitution
on other states, 45
Ninth Amendment: *vs.* Baby Ninth
Amendments, 5–6; and collective
rights, 24, 101–2; development of,
5, 7, 19–22, 184n2; and enumerated
powers, 5, 9, 25; interpretations and
meaning of Baby Ninth Amendments,
98–105; language of, 4–5, 9, 115,
116, 117; and negative rights, 121;
and positive rights, 23–24, 119–23;
Scalia on limits of, 57, 80. *See also*
Baby Ninth Amendments; meaning of
Ninth Amendment
North (Minnesota delegate), 56–57
North Carolina: Baby Ninth Amendment, 64, 66, 156; court cases, 82,
136
North Dakota, constitutional development in, 65

oaths, 57–59
Obergefell v. Hodges, 146
occupational rights: barbers, 82–83; cosmetology licensing, 2, 134–36, 141,
142; in everyday examples of rights,
1, 2, 3–4; food trucks, 12–14, 133–34.
See also employee rights
Ohio: Baby Ninth Amendment, 48–50,
114–15, 125–27, 157; Baby Tenth
Amendment, 30, 48–50, 96; court
cases, 173n103; influence of constitution on other states, 52; positive laws
and rights in, 125–27; right to education, 125, 128
Oklahoma: Baby Ninth Amendment,
65–66, 157; court cases, 90–91
Oregon: Baby Ninth Amendment, 53,
157; court cases, 2, 82, 134
original meaning: and delegate statements, 180n103; and Ninth Amendment, 22–25, 99–105, 110–12; as
term, 22–23, 98–99
Ormond (Judge), 58
Otis, James, 33

parents, rights of, 27, 80, 83–86
Parke (Maryland delegate), 50–52
Pechous (Illinois delegate), 71–73, 96
Pekarik, Laura, 13–14
Pennsylvania: Baby Tenth Amendment,
28–30, 38, 66; Bill of Rights ratification, 30; constitutional development,
28–30, 43, 65, 66; influence of constitution on other states, 38
people, as term, 143
Perkins (Minnesota delegate), 54, 55

personal liberties and court cases, 76, 78–81, 83–86
petition, right of, 16
Petition of Right of 1628, 16
Pierce v. Society of Sisters, 2, 84, 85, 134
police, 115, 166n64
positive law, 125–30
positive rights: in Baby Ninths, 123–30; collective bargaining as, 69; defined, 114; and libertarianism, 23; and Ninth Amendment, 23–24, 25, 119–23
power: and levers of influence, 11–12; police power, 166n64; recourse for powerless, 2–3, 12–14, 133–37; right of people to exercise political, 106–7
powers, enumerated: enumerated *vs.* enunciation language, 175n28; and Federalists, 20, 29–30, 95; *vs.* general powers in Alabama constitution, 58–59; Ninth Amendment as about, 5, 9, 24, 25; and residual rights model, 100; of states, 25, 48–49, 103
powers, general: and Baby Tenths, 29–30, 38–39, 46, 49, 96–98, 100; and collective rights, 101; *vs.* enumerated powers in states, 58–59, 101; and Federalists, 20
powers, high: and Baby Tenths, 28, 29, 35, 36, 38, 49–50, 172n86; *vs.* general powers term, 171n55
powers, unenumerated: in delegate debates, 66–73; of the people, 9; powers *vs.* rights term in Ohio, 48; and residual rights model, 23, 100
price fixing, 82–83
privacy, right to, 85–86
Privileges or Immunities Clause of Fourteenth Amendment, 144
Pro-Choice Mississippi v. Fordice, 86
property rights, 76, 81–83, 116
Public Use Clause of Fifth Amendment, 132–33
punishment, cruel and unusual, 16

railway stock laws, 78–81
rational basis, 88–89, 106, 113, 132, 135–37, 188n45
Reconstruction, 63–64, 131

religious rights, 1, 3, 18, 53, 120, 163n18
representation, right to self-, 87, 130
residual rights model, 23, 100
restaurants, 12–14
retained rights: Baby Ninths and retained language, 5, 10, 36, 37, 38, 40, 71, 114–15, 118, 119, 123–25; concept, 10–11, 114–19, 121–30; Ninth Amendment and retained language, 9, 22, 24–25, 115, 116, 117, 121–22; Ninth Amendment and rights retained model, 24–25, 103–4; and positive law, 125–30; as reaffirmed rights, 127–28; retained term, 116, 117, 119, 122, 123–25; retained *vs.* inherent language, 62, 115, 130; and social contract theory, 115–17, 124, 127–30
retribution, right to, 115–16
Rhode Island: Baby Ninth Amendment, 42, 43–44, 66, 157; constitutional development, 19, 42, 43–44, 66
Ricketts, Hermine, 2, 136–37
rights: employee rights, 69, 96, 102, 107, 133–34; enumerated, 3–6; given up for government, 115–18, 124; gun rights, 16, 89, 146; inalienable rights, 115–18; negative rights, 24, 119–24, 132; of parents, 27, 80, 83–86; property rights, 76, 81–83, 116; and recourse for restricted liberties, 2–3, 12–14, 133–37; religious rights, 1, 3, 18, 53, 120, 163n18; same-sex rights, 27, 86, 146; and unenumerated powers, 9; voting rights, 44, 63. *See also* bills/declarations of rights, state; collective rights; individual rights model; natural rights; occupational rights; positive rights; retained rights; unenumerated rights
Roe v. Wade, 27, 86, 146

Sales, Ex parte, 90–91
same-sex rights, 27, 86, 146
Scalia, Antonin, 57, 80, 105, 146
Schley (Maryland delegate), 51
schools. *See* education and schools

scrutiny, 76, 81, 88–89, 113, 118–19,
132–33, 145
Secombe (Minnesota delegate), 55–56
self-determination, right to, 186n7
self-government, right to, 91–92
self-representation, right to, 87, 130
Semple, Robert, 46–47, 96
Seventh Amendment, 121–22
sex, restrictions on, 27, 86
Shelfer, Lochlan, 121–22
slavery, 34, 52–53, 62, 131–32
social contract, 115–17, 124, 127–30
Society of Sisters, 2, 84, 85, 134
sodomy, 86
South Carolina: Baby Ninth Amendment, 64, 157; constitutional development, 62, 63, 64, 100, 163n18, 184n1
South Dakota, constitutional development in, 65
sovereignty: individual, 102; popular,
30, 107; of states, 28, 30, 91–92, 101–
2, 185n7
stamp collecting, 1, 2, 3–4, 137
state constitutions: development of,
early, 15–19, 34–40; development,
antebellum period, 41–60; Civil
War and Reconstruction era, 62–64;
post-Civil War to present, 61–73;
development through constitutional
conventions, 17–18, 28–30, 34–38,
41–57, 61–71, 123–25; vs. federal, 3;
Federalists on bills of rights in, 20. See
also Baby Ninth Amendments; Baby
Tenth Amendments; bills/declara-
tions of rights, state
State ex rel. Burlington & M.R.R. Co. v.
County of Wapello, 77–78
state law rights model, 23, 99–100
State v. Williams, 82
Supremacy Clause of U.S. Constitution,
72

Taylor (Ohio delegate), 50
Tennessee: Baby Tenth Amendment, 30,
38–40; constitutional development,
38–40, 42, 64, 175nn22–23; proto-
Baby Ninth Amendment, 38–40, 42;
right to change government, 107
Ten Pound Act, 33

Tenth Amendment: development of,
21–22, 27–28; and federalism model
of Ninth Amendment, 24. See also
Baby Tenth Amendments
Texas: Baby Tenth Amendment, 43,
174n8; constitutional development,
43, 44–45, 62, 64, 65; Republic of
Texas, 43
Thiede v. Town of Scandia Valley, 83
Thomas v. Reid, 90–91
"Topeka Constitution" (Kansas), 52
"traditions" understanding, 129
transportation licensing, 90–91
travel, right to, 84, 86
Treaty of Cession, 87
tree trimming, 136
Tribe, Laurence, 26
Troxel v. Granville, 27, 80, 84
Twelve Tables of the Roman Republic,
16

unenumerated powers. See powers,
unenumerated
unenumerated rights: and Baby Tenths,
185n4; beneficiaries of, 11–12;
defined, 5–6; and First Amendment,
8; and Fourteenth Amendment,
144–45; in Ninth Amendment, 4–6;
popularity of, 11, 139–45
union rights, 69, 96, 102, 107, 133–34
U.S. Constitution: Constitutional Convention, 19; development of, 6–7,
19–22; and enumerated powers, 20;
Necessary and Proper Clause, 20; ratifying conventions, 21; vs. state constitutions, 3; Supremacy Clause, 72. See
also Bill of Rights; specific amendments
U.S. Supreme Court: Dobbs v. Jackson
Women's Health Organization, 86;
Griswold v. Connecticut, 27, 72, 73;
Heller v. District of Columbia, 105, 146;
and Ninth Amendment, 27, 145–46;
protection of unenumerated rights,
7–8; and same-sex rights, 27, 86; and
unconstitutional findings, 189n5
Utah: Baby Ninth Amendment, 65, 158;
court cases, 2, 84, 134–35

Vermont: constitutional development,